Through the Maelstrom

A History of the
Scottish National Party
1945-1967

Paula Somerville

Published by
Scots Independent (Newspapers) Ltd
51 Cowane St, Stirling FK8 1JW

I

ISBN 978-0-9572285-1-1

Cover photograph of the Gulf of Corryvreckan whirlpool by kind
permission of David Philip, Hebridean-Wild.co.uk

Typeset in Baskerville BT 9pt

Designed, printed and bound in Scotland by Celtic Connect Print
and Media Management, 24 Paton Street, Alloa FK10 2DY

Summary

The Scottish National Party was established in 1934 with the primary aim of achieving self-government for Scotland. From 1945 until the 1960s, the Party achieved few successes and existed on the periphery of Scottish politics. With few members, poor organisation, bitter infighting and operating within a two-party political system, the SNP made little impact on the political climate of Scotland. In the 1960s, however, the party's fortunes transformed as it dramatically increased its membership, it underwent significant organsational improvements and it began making electoral inroads into Scottish politics. In 1967, the SNP's candidate, Winnie Ewing, won a landmark by-election victory in the Labour stronghold of Hamilton. The SNP's breakthrough in this period has reshaped the political map of Scotland ever since.

This book examines the history of the SNP from the end of the Second World War until its breakthrough at the polls at Hamilton in 1967. It provides a comprehensive account of the SNP during this era, exploring the internal and external forces which have shaped the Party, and addresses the reasons why the SNP was able to transform from a fringe nationalist organisation in 1945 to become a mainstream political party by 1967.

Acknowledgements

I owe a note of gratitude to a number of people who have aided me in some way during the writing of this book. A thank you goes to Prof Richard Finlay who provided me with invaluable guidance when I undertook my thesis on this subject. I am also grateful to the late James Halliday for the assistance he gave me in sharing his first-hand accounts of the SNP and for encouraging me to publish this book. I would also like to thank Hamish McQueen for the invaluable narratives of the Party he shared with me as an activist in the post-war period. I would also like to express my gratitude to Dr Iain Hutchison for his assistance and the interest he has shown in this work.

A thank you also goes to my family and friends, in particular, Jamie Somerville-Liddle, Allan (Snr.), Mandy, Allan and Kerry Somerville, Mike Liddle, Bindy Bashir, Katie Dowling, Andrea Olukotun, Valerie Russell, and Amanda Stuart.

A final note of thanks goes to my late mum, Irene Somerville, who unfortunately did not get to see this research completed, and to whom this book is dedicated.

List of Abbreviations

ASNTU	Association of Scottish Nationalist Trade Unionists
CND	Campaign for Nuclear Disarmament
EEC	European Economic Community
GUSNA	Glasgow University Scottish Nationalist Association
ILP	Independent Labour Party
NALGO	National Association of Local Government Officers
NLS	National Library of Scotland
NPS	Nationalist Party of Scotland
PMG	Postmaster General
SNC	Scottish National Congress
SNP	Scottish National Party
SRA	Scottish Republican Army
SSP	Scottish Socialist Party

Contents

Contents

Foreword

In a bibliographic essay written over thirty years ago, the study of Scottish politics was likened to its teeth – most notable for its gaps. Another feature of the study of Scottish politics was the imbalance in the treatment of politics. One eminent political scientist frequently noted that more had been written on the Independent Labour Party than on the Conservatives despite the far greater impact the latter party had had on Scotland. A third weakness was that many accounts of Scottish politics and recent history were left uncontested while fierce battles of interpretation were on offer in other areas. This last weakness meant that the history of the national movement was dominated by a few highly partial accounts while arguments over Red Clydeside came to resemble medieval debates on how many angels could sit on the head of a pin.

The last three decades has seen a massive growth in our understanding of modern Scotland. The most refreshing aspect has been the growth in the number of different interpretations of Scottish politics and Scottish history. Myths have been challenged and busted. Gaps are being filled. We are learning that there can be no last word on many subjects.

Paula Somerville has made a major contribution in tackling each of these three deficiencies. This history of the Scottish National Party between 1945 and 1967 fills a massive gap in our knowledge. Her meticulous and careful analysis of contemporary records gives us a much better understanding of the internal politics of the SNP than has previously been on offer. It builds on Richard Finlay's *Independent and Free: Scottish Politics and the Origins of the SNP*, published in 1994. Without disputing the importance of 1967 as a key date in SNP, and indeed Scottish political, history, this work highlights the important developments that led up to the events in Hamilton in November that year.

The tendency to write-off the 1950s as a period of inactivity and failure by both many Nationalists and opponents is undermined by this study which highlights the important work that went on, against the odds, to build a movement and party capable of taking advantage in more propitious times. This was not a process of gradual advance but a chaotic period of experimentation and division with the SNP barely existing even as a fringe party. This was a pivotal period in twentieth century politics and one that has been paid insufficient attention from this perspective. Dr Somerville's book should make us all look at this period afresh.

Perhaps the most important contribution it makes is in challenging orthodoxies that remain very difficult to shift. Too many accounts of the national movement have relied too heavily on John MacCormick's *Flag in the Wind*, published in 1955. MacCormick was undoubtedly a charismatic and hugely talented campaigner whose dedication to the national movement cost him dear. This book does not deny MacCormick's importance but it sets it into a wider and more objective context. But most importantly, it confirms the sub-text of Jimmy Halliday's memoir that the SNP existed as a lively, if fractious, party long before most of those in the SNP today joined and even before 1967.

James Mitchell

Introduction

The Scottish National Party was formed in 1934 following the merger of the National Party of Scotland and the Scottish Party. Its overarching aim was to forge an independent Scotland free from the rule of Westminster by instituting a parliament in Edinburgh. From the year of its formation until the 1960s, the SNP was an inconsequential Party that existed on the margins of Scottish politics. It achieved little electoral progress against the backdrop of a prevalent two-party political system and a strong unionist tide and posed little, if any, threat to the political establishment. But in the 1960s, the fortunes of the Party changed dramatically as it moved from its fringe position to the political mainstream in just a few short years. Its breakthrough in this decade has changed the face of Scottish politics ever since.

The purpose of this book is to provide an in-depth analysis of the SNP during the period 1945-67 and assess why the Party was able to evolve from a small fringe organisation to a serious political force. The scope of this research will primarily focus on the internal history of the SNP. Although wider external forces are also important in explaining the rise of the Party, in order to give an exhaustive account of the Party's inner workings, such as its policy, organisation, strategy and factious elements, it will principally be concerned with intra-nationalist politics. This book will also bridge a gap which exists in the current literature on the SNP. Despite the large amount of research which has been conducted on the subject area of the SNP and Scottish nationalism, no comprehensive analysis of the Party, or indeed of any political party in Scotland, has yet been constructed in the post Second World War period. This book will fill this void by providing the first extensive internal history of the SNP during the era 1945-67.

Existing literature has been useful in setting the context for this study. Richard J. Finlay's *Independent and Free* provides a comprehensive study of the SNP from its pre-formation days until 1945. It is valuable in explaining the creation and early years of the SNP and has been useful in providing the pre-context of the Party for this study. Peter Lynch has also produced a worthwhile account of the SNP, from its origins until the first elections of the Scottish Parliament in 1999. Lynch examines the SNP's internal structures and some of its key figures as well as many of the struggles and successes which the Party has experienced over its long history. Jack Brand's *The National Movement in Scotland* is also helpful in its assessment of the growth of Scottish nationalism from after the First World War and puts forward class de-alignment and a growing interest in Scottish affairs as key factors in explaining the increasing support of the SNP. Brand also considers the effects which areas such as the economy, the political climate, youth culture and the press have had on the rise of nationalism and the SNP. Other works like *Scottish Nationalism* by H. J. Hanham, and *Strategies for Self-Government* by James Mitchell, present further useful examinations of the Party and mention significant issues such as breakaway factions and SNP policy. Hanham's analysis of the SNP includes an account of the formation of the Scottish Convention, the tactics it pursued and the figurehead behind it, John MacCormick. It also offers a critical assessment of the Party's 1946 policy statement and discusses some of the ideals behind it. Mitchell's study similarly looks at the Scottish Convention and other splinter groups that arose from the SNP such as the Nationalist Party of Scotland. It also reviews the SNP's first official policy programme as well as some later policies like European integration. Iain G. C. Hutchison's *Scottish Politics in the Twentieth Century* provides further analysis of the SNP and presents some helpful accounts of the Party's rise, for example, the perceived failure of the main parties to deliver social and economic benefits to Scotland. Hutchison also discusses the organisational decline of the major parties, which came at a time when the SNP's own organisational and propaganda efforts had markedly improved. Tom Devine's article 'The Challenge of Nationalism' in *Scotland and the Union* offers another beneficial assessment of the growth of the SNP. It addresses important issues like the changing nature of 'Britishness', the economy and the decline of the Tory Party in Scotland.

Other major works have also been useful in setting the background for this topic. Christopher Harvie's *Scotland and Nationalism*, for example, describes the economic scene in Scotland and provides an overview of Scottish politics from 1707 to the 1990s. Harvie's work covers key nationalist areas such as the Scottish Convention and the growth of the SNP in the 1960s. William Miller's *The End of British Politics* also offers an account of Scottish politics in the post-war period. It mainly focuses on voting behaviour and attitudes in the 1970s, but it also assesses issues like the Scottish economy, planning controls and the Scottish Office. J. G. Kellas's *The Scottish Political System* provides a more detailed discussion of the Scottish Office in his analysis of political institutions and government in Scotland. It includes a chapter on nationalism which charts the peaks and troughs of the national movement and looks at important factors like national consciousness. Arnold Kemp's *The Hollow Drum* presents a journalist description of Scotland since the end of the First World War. It looks at major Scottish political matters including the national movement in Scotland, and in keeping with its journalistic approach, it incorporates interviews with some key political figures. Tom Nairn's *The Break-Up of Britain* offers a more theoretical approach towards nationalism. It looks at Scottish and English nationalism and assesses the issue in a European context. It also addresses nationalism in Northern Ireland as well as Scottish and Welsh comparisons of the subject matter. Other writings such as Peter Clark's *Hope and Glory*, Kenneth Morgan's *The People's Peace* and Nick Toratsoo's *From Blitz to Blair*, provide a wider context of British politics in the post-war and twentieth century periods. These works and others have been helpful in providing background for this book.

Another reason for conducting this research is that much of the recent academic work addressing the subject area of Scottish nationalism has been carried out by political scientists rather than by historians. On the whole, political scientists have been at the forefront of research on the SNP and the national movement in Scotland whereas historians have contributed less on this topic and are therefore underrepresented in this field. From the list above, for example, only Devine, Finlay, Hanham, Harvie and Hutchison are historians who have written about Scottish nationalism in their research. Scholarly work carried out by political scientists can sometimes present theoretical structures and models which focus less on finer historical details.

Nairn, for example, places Scottish nationalism within a European model of nationalism in *The Break-Up of Britain*, and Brand uses Neil Smelser's theory on the rise of social movements as a framework in which to theorise the rise of the SNP in *The National Movement in Scotland*. While these works are important in adding to our understanding of Scottish nationalism, they vary from an historical approach which is primarily concerned with historical evidence and puts this at the core when explaining the past.[1] This study will go some way to redress the lack of research offered by historians by putting forward an historical perspective on the subject matter.

In much of the current literature on the SNP after 1945, the amount of Party archive material examined is also limited. Peter Lynch has delved into the archives of the SNP and of some SNP figures but beyond this little has been used by other writers. This book on the other hand has been constructed for the most part using this original source material. This includes the large archive of Robert McIntyre (principally Acc. 10090), who was Chairman of the SNP between the years 1947-1956; and the even larger archive of Roland Muirhead (Acc. 3721), who was one of the Party's founding fathers and President of the Party between 1936-1950. The smaller but significant archives of nationalist figures like Tom Gibson, Arthur Donaldson, Douglas Young, Wendy Wood, Archie Lamont and James Porteous have also been consulted as have the SNP's own archives deposited at the National Library of Scotland. Other primary source material includes the SNP's journal, the *Scots Independent*, newspaper articles and interviews with those who took part in SNP activities during the 1945-67 timeframe of this investigation. As mentioned above, secondary sources have also been useful in setting the wider context for this study.

In assessing the SNP's history, this book has been divided into six chapters and has been constructed chronologically in order to tell the SNP's story in the most comprehensible way. The chapters cover a particular timeline although Chapter Two somewhat transcends this to deal with the important subject area of the Scottish Convention, but it is still placed principally within a sequential framework in keeping with the overall structure of the book. Chapters One and Two primarily explore the SNP in the 1940s as it emerges from World War Two, as it undergoes important internal developments and as it becomes overshadowed by its breakaway faction, the Scottish Convention. Chapters Three and Four focus on the Party in the 1950s as it struggles to survive amidst a series of troubles including the establishment of new splinter groups, raging infighting and chronic electoral defeat. Finally, Chapters Five and Six survey the Party's turnaround in fortunes in the 1960s as it undergoes an organisational transformation and improves remarkably in the electoral field, culminating in its historic by-election victory at Hamilton in 1967.

1

Disillusionment and Development – 1945-50

Effects of War on the SNP

When World War Two ended in 1945, Scotland joined with the rest of Britain in the celebrations, welcoming home the war heroes and looked optimistically to the Brave New World and post-war reconstruction that was set to commence. The Scottish National Party emerged from war less hopeful about its future. It was just over a decade old and had struggled to eke out an existence for itself over that period amidst the slump of the thirties and the upheaval of war in the forties. Its position on the edge of Scottish politics meant that its impact on the political landscape had so far been minimal. By the end of war, it had less than 1,000 members enrolled,[1] it had little organisation in place and it was in debt.

War had been a double-edged sword for the Party. It had suffered from negative associations of nationalism as nationalism itself came to be cited as a major cause in the outbreak of war. Opponents of Scottish nationalism were keen to make this connection by portraying all nationalism, not just German nationalism, as damaging to future world peace and stability by promoting statements such as 'Nationalism Means War'.[2] One zealous opponent was Scottish Secretary of the Labour Party, John Taylor, who declared that the SNP's correct name should be the 'Scottish Nazi Party' as 'it had great similarities with the German Nazi Party and was growing in the same way and trying to develop on exactly the same lines as the Nazi Party began in Germany.'[3] This was a damaging statement that unsurprisingly outraged the SNP and which it strenuously denied, but its denials fell on deaf ears as rumour of the Nazis colluding with Scottish nationalists had already surfaced.

The rumour arose that Germany had given Scottish nationalists assistance in the hope that they would rise up against the British state at a time when it was vulnerable to attack and that British troops would have to be diverted to the home front. This rumour was fuelled by the German broadcast of Radio Caledonia which began operating from Germany in 1940 – though it claimed to broadcast from the South of Scotland - and ran for a two year period during the war until 1942. The Station campaigned for a Scottish Socialist Republic and was designed to hamper Britain's war effort by stirring up anti-English feeling.[4] The rumour was also spread when the authorities, fearing a similar situation to the Easter Rising in Ireland, raided a number of Scottish nationalists' homes. The simultaneous dawn raids included SNP President, Roland Muirhead, and future Chairmen, Arthur Donaldson and Douglas Young, who police suspected of subversive activities.[5] Donaldson was imprisoned following the raid under the Defence of the Realm Regulation 18b and joined fellow nationalist and inmate Duncan Graham who had been jailed the previous year under the same regulation. It was only after the intervention of Tom Johnston, as Secretary of State for Scotland, that Donaldson was released a few weeks later, though Graham's detention continued.[6] The following year Douglas Young also found himself incarcerated when he was sentenced to a 12-month term under the National Service (Armed Forces) Act, 1939. Young, who would soon become SNP Chairman, had refused to be conscripted into the British army. He argued that Britain did not have a right to conscript Scots as it contravened the 1707 Treaty of Union and that the so-called UK was 'a legal nonentity', an argument which the court and appeal court rejected.[7] Imprisonments such as these only fed the rumour that there was a Scottish national Nazi plot though it flew in the face of the evidence that the SNP had actually rallied behind Britain when war first broke out and it was set to do its bit for the British cause. For example, a month after the declaration of war in 1939, the SNP offered its premises for government use. It also published a manifesto which stated that it would play its part in the war effort and which outlined its staunch support for the freedom of small states.[8] Despite a lack of evidence of SNP involvement with Nazi Germany and the SNP's strenuous denials, not to mention its initial offers of help to the British cause, associations with Nazi Germany were still made. The speculation, the German broadcasts of Radio Caledonia and the imprisonment of some nationalists for hampering Britain's war effort did nothing to help the Party's image during the 1940s.[9]

War however did not spell complete disaster for the Party and it was in this era that it secured its first parliamentary victory. On 12 April 1945, Party Secretary, Robert McIntyre, won the Motherwell and Wishaw by-election seat by a slim majority of 617.[10] Robert McIntyre, son of manse preacher, John McIntyre, had lived his formative years in the constituency. He had joined the SNP in the late thirties and rose quickly through the ranks as Party Organiser then National Secretary within a few short years, and kept up his full-time career as a medical practitioner at the same time.[11] McIntyre's victory was largely the result of the wartime electoral truce that was in place at the time. Labour had held the seat during the war so the electoral truce deal was that no Tory candidate would oppose the sitting party; this worked vice versa where the Unionists held sway. The electoral truce, however, did not extend to smaller parties like the SNP which gave it the advantage of contesting seats where only one major party stood. It was in this climate in Motherwell and Wishaw in which many Tory supporters were unable to stomach a socialist candidate and voted in the first SNP Member of Parliament instead. For Labour, it was quite literally a Friday the 13th nightmare (being the day and date on which the result was announced) as the underdog swept the rug from under Labour's feet and took its seat in Parliament. Alex Anderson, the Labour candidate in the election, estimated that McIntyre owed his victory to at least 7,000 anti-Labour votes.[12] This was helped by a badly timed speech which Ernest Bevin had given shortly before the poll in which he signalled an end to the electoral truce and that 'the fight was on'.[13] This had provided the impetus for many Unionist supporters to dispense with electoral truce niceties and vote in McIntyre.

But the electoral truce itself does not explain the SNP's victory. There were other reasons why McIntyre came to find himself as the Party's first MP. McIntyre campaigned on issues other than nationalism, such as housing, and condemned the poor state of Scotland's housing stock which, he stated, stood at around 45,000 homes unfit for human habitation in 1938 and had only become worse since the war.[14] McIntyre also criticised the high unemployment rates and the number of people living in poverty in Scotland as compared to England, as well as the Government's actions over the aircraft industry at Prestwick.[15] Emigration and the 'drift down south' of Scots workers was also a major bone of contention in McIntyre's election rhetoric which seemed to strike a chord with voters. The practice by the Ministry of Land of conscripting young female workers in Scotland to work in areas of England which suffered from labour shortages came in for particularly harsh criticism and was capitalised on by the Party.[16] After his defeat, Anderson admitted that there was general apathy too amongst voters at the handling of Scottish affairs at Westminster.[17] According to the local press, McIntyre also attracted a variety of young voters from the working and middle classes as well as first time voters.[18] The unpredictable nature of the constituency, which was dubbed 'the rainbow constituency of Scotland' and 'as changeable as the fickle weather' by one Scottish daily national because it had only returned the same member for a second term once in more than 20 years, had also helped McIntyre's electoral chances.[19]

The SNP's experience of winning its first ever seat was accentuated by the fact that McIntyre was initially refused permission to take his seat in the House of Commons because he had not followed the tradition of the House by bringing sponsors to the table for his inauguration. This was an old tradition going back to 1688 in which two members of the House would introduce new members in order that no impostors were sworn in.[20] McIntyre took exception to this convention because it was a tradition of the old English Parliament which predated the 1707 Treaty of Union, and as the sole representative of his political Party, he did not want to be seen to identify with other parties. He was supported by George Buchanan, Labour MP for Glasgow Gorbals, who moved a motion to allow McIntyre to take his seat without sponsors on the grounds that the sponsor rule was 'outworn', and by Moelwyn Hughes, Labour MP for Carmarthen, who seconded the motion on the basis that the rule had no right to interfere with the returned will of the electorate. Churchill, however, intervened and urged the House not to 'shrink from upholding the ancient customs and traditions' which he claimed 'added to our dignity and to our power.' This clinched it and on a vote of 273 to 74, it was decided not to repeal the Standing Order which would allow a sponsorless McIntyre to be sworn in.[21] The next day, McIntyre, with his Labour sponsors, the Rev James Barr and Mr A. Sloan in tow, took his seat under protest as 'the only way in which [he could] represent the constituency of Motherwell.'[22] He did so on the understanding that he did not commit himself to his sponsors' party, in other words, the Labour Party. McIntyre's dramatic entry into the House of Commons was tremendous from an SNP perspective as it added to the blaze of publicity the Party had already received from winning the seat. It made front page news at home and even made the spread of some papers abroad. The fact that the House of Commons was crowded with MPs, diplomats, American and Soviet ambassadors, even a European princess, eagerly awaiting to hear Churchill's tribute to the late President Roosevelt on the day McIntyre was refused his seat, only boosted the drama and publicity the incident received at home and abroad.[23]

Beside the positive publicity the SNP received, the effect of McIntyre's victory was significant in several other ways. First, Scotland was back on the agenda. McIntyre's victory coerced Labour to take Scottish issues, and the Home Rule issue in particular, more seriously for fear of further nationalist inroads in the ensuing General Election. Scottish Labour in fact came to view a Scottish parliament as its second priority at the General Election, second only to ending war with Japan. Another effect of McIntyre's victory was that the SNP managed to win over some long-term voters in the constituency. With no Unionist candidate at the 1945 by-election, McIntyre attracted many Unionist voters and was able to retain some of their votes at the General Election that followed and beyond. According to one Unionist canvasser:

> Some of our people were so attached to Dr. McIntyre by his beating the Socialist and the stand he made in the House, that we simply couldn't get them to vote Unionist this time. They preferred to stick by the man they returned at the by-election.[24]

The General Election three months later on 26 July 1945 seemed to confirm this when McIntyre polled more votes than the Unionist candidate, obtaining 8,022 to the Unionist candidate, Major Hamilton's 6,197.[25] Nor was it just a proportion of Unionist votes that the SNP kept. Liberals too were won over by McIntyre's liberal national outlook. The Liberals had been championing the Home Rule cause for generations, and as no Liberal candidate stood at the Motherwell and Wishaw by-election, a significant number had backed McIntyre as the next best thing. Another positive effect of McIntyre's victory was that McIntyre now had the tools offered to MPs for obtaining information which could be used for the benefit of the Party. For example, McIntyre could obtain facts and figures far easier and far quicker from government departments through the medium of Parliamentary Questions. Information which he did obtain through this route included BBC statistics in relation to Scotland, which were subsequently used by the SNP for propaganda purposes.[26] Obtaining information in this way effectively amounted to free research for the Party and allowed it to acquire data that otherwise could have been difficult to obtain and without doing the usual leg work for it. In all, the experience of McIntyre's victory gave the Party a morale boost during what was otherwise an extremely difficult period. It gave the SNP a beacon of hope at a time when there was little else to be hopeful about. For one high-spirited SNP member, it was 'one of the greatest events since Bannockburn.'[27]

But it was short lived. At the General Election of 1945, the SNP put forward eight candidates to fight the nationalist cause, more than at any time in the past at a single General Election. The Party was still on a high following its experience in Motherwell three months earlier and was hoping for a repeat performance and more. In a mood of optimism it also appointed a full-time Organiser on 1 May 1945, and had hoped that the initial work of May Thomson, its new Organiser, coupled with the spin-off publicity from McIntyre's by-election triumph would see more of its candidates stroll to success. It was wrong. The Party returned no MPs on the day and polled just 30,595 votes, losing six of its eight deposits.[28] With war and the electoral truce now over, the SNP was brought down to earth with a thud as it was back to the cut and thrust of ordinary party politics and the SNP stood little chance. Included in the casualties was McIntyre, who had been dropped by the electorate for Labour's Alex Anderson who won by a landslide of 15,831 votes, the highest Labour vote ever won in the constituency.[29] Labour had learnt its lesson from its by-election defeat and stole the SNP's thunder as many of its candidates now vigorously backed the Scottish Home Rule cause and called for the establishment of a Scottish parliament and more interest in Scottish affairs. In Motherwell and Wishaw, Alex Anderson was particularly keen to note the new importance of Scotland and its affairs by stating in his General Election speech:

> Judging by the result, it seems that we in Lanarkshire at any rate are ready for a more vigorous Socialist policy in this country. And, secondly, it is perfectly obvious from the figures to-day that there is in Scotland a feeling of protest against the time allocated to Scottish affairs in the House of Commons and we must as Scottish Members, in future do our utmost to see that Scotland gets more control over its own affairs.[30]

This was a complete turnaround to his by-election brochure just months before, in which he slated nationalism:

> Nationalism in the past has been the cause of difference, dispute among peoples, it interposes barriers between the free flow of trade between nations; it makes impossible the planning of large scale international agreement and it weakens the age old struggle for social, economic and political freedom. In the light of present day development when the

world moves inevitably to internationalism it is retrograde and obstructive.[31]

Despite Labour's u-turn, a receptive Scottish public responded well to its stronger commitment to Scottish affairs and it swept the board with Labour members in all but one of the constituencies the SNP had fought.[32] Even some staunch Scottish nationalists who were determined to oust Tory power from Westminster and were heartened by Labour's nationalist rhetoric, decided to hedge their bets with Labour.

The inadequacy of SNP organisation at the General Election was glaring. It uncovered a deplorable lack of Party foot soldiers on the ground that were prepared to canvass and disseminate SNP propaganda as well as a lack of personnel suitable as election agents for the candidates. Also, unlike the Motherwell by-election where activists could be drafted from outwith the constituency, activists, who were already thin on the ground, had to be spread over eight constituencies and here the SNP's lack of organisation became obvious. Fighting the General Election at a cost of £3,000 had also exhausted the Party's financial reserves and diverted money away from other much needed areas of expenditure, like publications and the upkeep of Party Headquarters.[33] It must have also demoralised members who had given generously to the Party's General Election Fund only to see their money go down the proverbial drain with such a dismal outcome. It was a devastating state of affairs for the Party as it was now clear that McIntyre's by-election success had been a one-off event which had been won in unique circumstances and could not be replicated in peace time. The result disappointed and dismayed the SNP from the top down, and even some in the Party, like Muirhead, already sceptical about polling success, were left disillusioned with the result.[34]

The following month, opportunity presented itself for the Party to contest the Edinburgh East by-election. Despite the defeat suffered the previous month, Muirhead and Douglas Young supported a motion to contest the seat as all energy could be diverted into the constituency rather than spread thinly as had happened at the General Election and might just restore some hope in the party faithful if the Party received a respectable return. McIntyre and Donaldson, however, argued that the Party was not ready to contest so soon after the General Election, nor could it afford to, so the idea was subsequently turned down by the SNP Executive.[35] In February the following year, the Party passed up the opportunity to contest the Ayrshire South by-election but it did manage to front a candidate at Glasgow Cathcart. It had been less than a year since McIntyre's victory at Motherwell but the result could not have been more different. The SNP candidate lost his deposit in a three-sided race without any Liberal candidate. [36] Following Cathcart and with defeat still fresh in its mind, the SNP failed to put forward candidates for the Glasgow Bridgeton and Aberdeen South by-elections for reasons of lack of finance and poor organisation as had happened at the Edinburgh East by-election the year before. Party confidence was at a low ebb and only sunk deeper the more the Party shied away from one of the key reasons for which it was set up, to contest elections. It was time for action.

The Four-Year Programme

The National Council of the SNP put organisation squarely on the agenda when it called on the 1946 Annual Conference to instruct the Party 'To prepare and execute a four-year plan for the development and expansion of the Party organisation and for the establishment of new branches throughout Scotland.'[37] This, it was hoped, would prepare the Party to fight effectively at the next General Election with no repeat performance of 1945. The resolution sailed through the Annual Conference in May 1946 with a vote of 44 to nine and a Four-Year Programme Committee was soon established to frame the new Plan.[38] The Committee, which consisted of Bruce Watson, May Thomson, Arthur Donaldson, Tom Gibson, George Leslie and Robert McIntyre, reported in August 1946. It set its sights high by recommending that a minimum of 40 constituencies be contested at the next General Election. To achieve this, central organisation was to be given the responsibility of establishing at least one branch in each constituency, while area organisers and May Thomson as National Organiser, were to take on extra responsibilities to ensure that more branches and groups were established in order to achieve the 40 seat target by 1950.[39] Party propaganda was also to be disseminated to branches and the public at large to aid Party growth. It was agreed that securing a minimum of £300 for election expenses and having already selected the candidate and election agent would be prerequisites for contesting any parliamentary election.[40] By doing this, the Party believed:

> Parliamentary elections should be a demonstration of strength and not of weakness; that lost deposits had an adverse effect on public opinion and even on Party morale; and that for those reasons, unless in exceptional circumstances, elections should be fought only in constituencies where a fair measure of organisational and propaganda work had been continuously carried out well before the election.[41]

The Four-Year Plan, as it was dubbed, became the new organisation policy of the Party and crucially put the onus on branches to come up with candidates, secure the necessary deposits and still contribute towards the upkeep of Headquarters.

The SNP's first test of how successful or otherwise the Four-Year Plan would become came with the Kilmarnock by-election of December 1946. Kilmarnock presented an opportunity for the Party to claim back some self-esteem which had been lost at the last General Election and subsequent by-elections and rekindle SNP hope if it could only save its deposit and gain a respectable polling return. George Dott was chosen for the task as SNP candidate but almost immediately Dott's campaign got off to a bad start as not all office bearers supported him as being the appropriate choice. Muirhead in particular believed Dott was the wrong man for the job because he was not a native of the constituency and thought this would go against Dott. Muirhead believed George Bell Barker was more suited to be SNP candidate as he had local connections, including serving on the Ayrshire Planning Authority, he was already relatively well-known and he had undertaken propaganda work in the constituency.[42] Dott sought to counteract his lack of local roots by fighting his campaign on local issues, such as Prestwick. But other office-bearers like National Treasurer, Arthur Donaldson, believed it was a mistake to put up any candidate given the financial and organisational state of the Party. Donaldson called on the Party to put its precious few resources towards more effective means, as he saw it, by producing publications or organising meetings to widen branch membership, for example.[43] It was clear from the beginning that Dott had an uphill battle on his hands.

As it was, there had been little in the way of preparatory work done in the constituency as the SNP had not contested Kilmarnock in the 1945 General Election, and with finances so stretched following the General Election the previous year and Cathcart only a few months before, there were few resources to plough into the campaign. SNP publications and propaganda had also been curbed as a consequence of the financial constraints on the Party. Dott was also up against a strong Labour candidate by the name of Willie Ross. Ross was an up-and-coming local candidate fresh out of the army, who had pledged his support to some form of devolution for Scotland and would one day take the helm as Secretary of State for Scotland. To top it all, Dott lost vital campaigning time when he was involved in a car accident on the eve of polling. With a hand of cards like this, Dott stood little chance of turning the Party's electoral fortunes around. When polling day came, he obtained a poor eight per cent share of the vote which was not enough to save his deposit and was less than the SNP's poll at Cathcart. Dott was left quite literally crawling from the wreckage when the announcement of his vote was even lower than feared. He had not only realised, but had exceeded the worst fears of his critics.

Dott himself came in for much criticism for the result as he was accused of having a 'bureaucratic' and 'toe-the-line' attitude for not inviting individuals like John Macdonald, who had organised the constituency in the days of Alex MacEwen (the SNP's first Chairman), to speak on his election platform.[44] Critics of Dott's campaign also looked to the Welsh constituency of Aberdare, where a by-election had been held on the same day and where the Welsh nationalists had polled over 7,000 votes while the Tory candidate had lost his deposit. This result served to highlight the SNP's abysmal failings at the polls and sent out the signal that Welsh nationalism was a stronger force than Scottish nationalism.[45] But the fall-out from Kilmarnock for the SNP was not simply a defeat for George Dott or Scottish nationalism; it seemed to justify support for the government's programme of centralisation as Labour slightly increased its vote from 59.4 per cent to 59.7 per cent.[46] This was a good result for a sitting government whose vote generally tends to ebb at by-elections. It was a dismal start to the SNP's Four-Year-Plan.

Despite Kilmarnock, the SNP pressed ahead with its Plan and supported George Dott's wife, Mary Dott, as choice of candidature the following year when Edinburgh Branch put her forward for the Edinburgh East by-election. Edinburgh Branch, despite the SNP's recent past performance, decided to put its money on Mary Dott believing that the by-election gave it 'an unequalled opportunity to put across the SNP's policy and point of view to a thoroughly representative Scottish constituency.'[47] Mary Dott was one of the few women with a high profile in the Party. She was National Secretary and as such had good organisational skills, was kept abreast of Party issues and had extensive contact with branches throughout the country. Her credentials were good and it was hoped her candidature would also bring the house-wife appeal to the electorate. From the outset, Mary Dott's campaign had the edge over her husband's because she was standing in a constituency where the SNP had a long established branch and whose annual income topped £1,000.[48] But despite this and her house-wife appeal, Mary Dott's vote proved to be another disappointing blow to the Party when she polled a low of just five per cent. Like her husband, she too was blamed for being too narrow and for refusing help from individuals like Wendy Wood and Oliver Brown.[49] But her vote highlighted more than just individual failing, it reflected the failing of the whole Party.

The real test for the Four-Year Plan came with the General Election itself. The General Election of 1950 was judgement day on the Plan, which, four years previously, had been devised as the wonder plan to turn the Party's electoral fortunes around at the next General Election. But even before polling day, things did not look good for the SNP. Instead of fielding the 40 candidates it had set out to do in its Four-Year Plan, the SNP managed only three, which was five less than it had managed at the General Election of 1945. The results of the polls only made matters worse when all SNP candidates lost their deposits and obtained a measly 9,708 votes in total. Even McIntyre at Motherwell failed to save his deposit receiving only slightly over nine per cent of the vote, which was drastically less than the 26.7 per cent he had secured at the last General Election, not to mention his victory there the time before that.[50] What is more, McIntyre's nine per cent vote appears more pitiful when considering he had received hundreds of pounds in sponsorship from the British Medical Association (BMA) Medical Representation in Parliament Fund, which put his 1950 campaign at a distinct financial advantage over his previous campaigns.[51] It would also take the Party until 1970 before it would brave standing another candidate in the constituency again. Far from placing candidates in most Scottish seats, the SNP failed to do so for even half the number it had contested at the 1945 General Election, and with proportionally worse results. The Four-Year Plan had been an unequivocal failure.

A number of factors contributed to the failure of the Plan. One factor was that the Party was still blighted by poor organisation. The SNP had taken a stride forward in its organisation in May 1945 when it had hired May Thomson as full-time paid Organiser of the Party with the task of encouraging branch growth, organising events and generating income for the Party. But just as the Four-Year Plan was getting off the ground, Thomson resigned in protest of what she believed was the Party's scant recognition of organisation. Thomson was aggrieved at the lack of funds made available to her to adequately carry out her duties as National Organiser. In her Organiser's Report of 1947, she complained:

> Since May, 1946, I have received at least three different requests from the Treasurer to keep my expenses down as low as possible. When I state that the travelling expenses paid for me by the Party during the period from 3rd May, 1946, to 29th March, 1947, amount to £29:14:5 – an average of 12/7½ a week – it should be obvious that it is impossible to ask anyone to visit branches, arrange meetings in different parts of Scotland and do general organisational work on 12/7½ a week. In any other political party that sum would appear laughably small.[52]

Thomson's conclusion was that the Party was simply paying lip service to organisation and she felt that she had no alternative but to resign. This accusation did have more than a grain of truth to it considering Thomson had made inroads into organisation, which if harnessed, could have had a significant effect on the Party; but other areas of Party expenditure were prioritised instead, like subsidies to the Party's monthly journal, the *Scots Independent*. In her first year, Thomson by all accounts had successfully organised the Arbroath, Bannockburn and Wallace day celebrations with a marked increase in attendance, which turned the demonstrations for the first time in recent years into money-making rather than loss-making events.[53] At the 1946 Annual Conference, a 100 per cent increase in membership was also reported thanks in no small part to Thomson's efforts. This figure was repeated the following year with 600 or 700 new members believed to have joined just before Thomson's departure.[54] Thomson had also been a vital link between branch and HQ which had helped foster better communication and understanding between them. For the branches, she was a face and point of contact within the Executive of the Party to whom they could air their grievances and from whom she could receive feedback, and for the Executive she was a link to grass roots and what was happening on the ground. The lack of resources given to Thomson hampered the success of the Four-Year Plan and showed a lack of cohesion on the part of the SNP by adopting the Plan to encourage organisation and electoral performance yet significantly limiting the National Organiser's expenditure and ploughing it into other areas instead.

Thomson also endured something of a whispering campaign during her time as National Organiser from individuals who opposed her appointment. Douglas Young, perhaps the worst offender, had on several occasions called for her dismissal claiming that he had received reports from individuals who had complained of her rudeness and ineptitude. Young went so far as to threaten to stop speaking on behalf of the Party outside Kirkcaldy if her appointment was not terminated. Young believed Thomson's salary was a waste of Party funds which could be deployed to far better effect amongst other areas of Party expenditure:

> One can exaggerate the desirability of a paid National Organiser. In my view the funds could be more profitably spent in grants to our area organisers. Wherever I go branch members and office-bearers complain to me of the incompetence and sometimes of the bad behaviour of Miss T... I have already told the Council Miss T. has the effect on the Party of a wet blanket, and I will not labour that point.[55]

This, however, flew in the face of the evidence outlined above which suggested that Thomson had achieved results for the Party. But the National Council's unwillingness to put sufficient backing behind her, not to mention the backroom sniping against her, did hamper her efforts as National Organiser, and with it, stultified the Four-Year Plan's chance of success. It also showed the Party's strategy of adopting a Four-Year Plan on the one hand, but not sufficiently backing organisation on the other as incoherent. Furthermore it came at a time when the other parties were taking organisation much more seriously as politics became more professional in the post-war era.[56]

The Party's poor financial position was at the heart of its deficient organisation. The effect on the Party of contesting several seats at the General Election and two by-elections in 1945 was to liquidate its capital reserve of the previous year. With the appointment of a new National Organiser in 1945, the SNP also had the added expenditure of paying for the National Organiser's salary, which amounted to £378 in the first year.[57] Just as the Four-Year Plan began, the Party had only £17 in the bank, had rent outstanding, had yet to settle its stationery account and still owed the National Organiser's salary. The following year the Party sank deeper into the red with £200 resulting from the Kilmarnock by-election alone.[58] Citing its poor financial stance, the Party pointed to the heavy subsidies it gave to the Party's newspaper, the *Scots Independent*, which suffered poor sales and increased printing costs caused by a post-war shortage of paper which perhaps hit the SNP harder than the main political parties as a newer political party. It also noted the poor sales and high costs of other propaganda publications as well as the increased day-to-day office costs of expenses such as the telephone, stationery and electricity bills.[59] The Party was keen to notify

11

branches that outstanding affiliation fees were also a major drain on Headquarters finances, so much so that a resolution was passed at the Party's 1948 Annual Conference whereby branches would lose their status as a branch if they did not meet their financial obligations owed to HQ.[60] The extent of the crisis of SNP finances can be gleaned from the fact that the enforcement of this resolution was postponed due to so many branches still failing to meet their quotas.[61] Even for those branches that could afford their obligations, still came the letters to the Election Committee pleading poverty and their inability to gather the necessary funds to put up candidates in their constituencies in accordance with the Four-Year Plan.[62] The fact that financial responsibility for nominating and campaigning for SNP candidates, which was estimated around £600 an election, excluding candidate and helpers' personal expenses, also rested with the branches, put a tremendous strain on the rank and file who in some branches numbered only 15.[63] Some support was available via the SNP's General Election Fighting Fund, but in order to contest an election branches needed a bare minimum of £300 up front. This financial burden and the little hope of retaining deposits, never mind winning seats, meant that putting up candidates was simply beyond the reach of most branches and helps explain why the SNP contested only three General Election seats in 1950 and five by-election seats out of 16 between 1945 and 1950.

By 1950, the final year of the Four-Year Plan, the Party's finances had deteriorated to such an extent that the Party owed loans from its members amounting to £228 10s and its overdraft had reached £134 12s 6d. National Treasurer, Alex Aitken, referred to the situation as 'A financial crisis of unusual magnitude' in his Annual Report.[64] He believed the Party's finances were so dire that he devised a stringent spending plan and threatened to resign if the National Council did not implement it. Already living hand to mouth, the National Council refused to back Aitken's tough budget memorandum which would have significantly curbed Party activity and he subsequently resigned in January 1951, leaving one of the toughest posts in the Party vacant. As usual, SNP members came to the rescue with generous donations, loans and bequests which sustained the Party during its dark lean years. Roland Muirhead saved the Party on more than one occasion when in 1947 he gave the Party a loan in what was otherwise 'an almost income-less summer' and in 1949 when he generously loaned the Party £2,800 to enable it to purchase its HQ at 59 Elmbank Street in Glasgow.[65] Following Aitken's dismal report on Party finances, Muirhead converted his loan into a donation in September 1950.[66] The Hodge and Donald bequests brought to the Party £276 and a property value of £4,325 respectively before death duties and legal expenses, enabling it to pay off long-standing debts.[67] The Party was able to obtain some free services like having its books audited by chartered accountants sympathetic to the cause.[68] Contributions like these were vital in keeping the Party afloat as the Party lacked other sources to turn to for financial aid. Unlike the Unionists, it lacked finance from the corporate community which was reluctant to support any measure of

Home Rule in the belief that it would adversely affect the economy and hamper trading between Scotland and the UK. Nor did it have the Unions like Labour to turn to for financial support but instead had to rely on the generosity of its members whose financial contributions kept the Party from grinding to a halt during this period.

Also contributing to the failure of the Four-Year Plan was a lack of support from some office-bearers who would not rally behind the scheme. Arthur Donaldson, who was Treasurer when the Plan began, had initially supported the Programme and had even sat on the Four-Year Programme Committee, but following Kilmarnock he expressed doubt about the Plan and believed that the Party should concentrate its efforts on means other than contesting elections, like producing propaganda:

> The day for contesting elections because we are not doing anything else is past. I lost four days myself and spent quite a bit of money to take part at Kilmarnock. I felt that it was largely lost effort. It has kept me from attending two important Branch meetings, and it has had a bad effect on our prospects here and elsewhere.
>
> The cause of Scotland can no longer be well served by those forlorn hopes. They are wasteful of money, wasteful of effort and they are not productive of good results. This election will cost us £400 and with that amount of money we could have produced, at least, five good pamphlets and 100,000 good leaflets for national distribution, with far better results everywhere than even a good vote in Kilmarnock would have produced.[69]

Donaldson's view on contesting parliamentary elections intensified as the forties wore on. Writing in the SNP's internal newsletter at the end of 1948, he called on the Party to contest elections only in such normal circumstances where the constituency was prepared and offered a reasonable hope of success.[70] In reality this equated to the Party contesting no elections, as there was no constituency which was, as Donaldson described it, ripe and offered the Party a reasonable chance of success. This was ironic coming from a man who had sat on the Committee two years previously to devise the Four-Year Programme. Donaldson's view slightly mellowed when it came to contesting local elections as these presented a smaller and more affordable front on which to contest. He realised that the candidate was more important than the party at the local level and that the electorate would be more willing to vote in a smaller party or independent candidate. It would also get voters used to voting for the SNP. But even then Donaldson qualified this by urging that victory in municipal elections should be in the offing before SNP candidates stood.[71] Muirhead was another individual who did not commit to the Plan and believed that SNP efforts should look towards means other than elections. Muirhead had been a member of the Party since its inception and had a history with the Home Rule movement going back to the 1890s but was tiring of the parliamentary route which had so far yielded few results. Muirhead's strand of thought was now beginning to develop the need for a new organisation which would take Home Rule forward through extra-parliamentary means, such as civil disobedience. For Muirhead, contesting elections was worthwhile in so far as it would produce publicity for the Party but he saw it as secondary to the extra-parliamentary route. Douglas Young too shared the others' negativity towards the Party's electoral policy. He realised the Party's limitations and that its Four-Year Plan was overly ambitious. On repeated occasions he reiterated the Party's failure at the ballot box, that it did not have the funds, personnel nor the support to continue with its bold plan, and that the Four-Year Plan was effectively dead in the water. By 1948, Young refused to stand at Kirkcaldy where he had gained an impressive 41.3 per cent of the vote in 1944 during the electoral truce and 17 per cent in the General Election of 1945,[72] because he knew that the SNP would not reach its target of 40 candidates, which he believed was essential if the electorate was to take the Party seriously as a national Party.[73] Like Donaldson, he viewed having a weak parliamentary candidate as worse than having none at all and instead put forward his own ideas of alternative strategies that the Party could pursue. These ranged from undertaking a nation-wide referendum on the Home Rule issue, bombarding the press with pro-Home Rule propaganda, pushing the issue through external agencies like the UN and turning the Party into 'a non-Parliamentary association devoted to publicity from an academic separatist viewpoint.'[74] With such negativity towards the Plan coming from senior Party officials who sat on the National Council yet promoted other strategies, it was small wonder the Four-Year Plan failed to cut much ice with the ordinary Party members, who would be burdened with the high costs of putting up candidates, or the electorate it hoped to win over.

Another bearing on the SNP's failed Four-Year Plan and its dreadful electoral performance was the fact that the SNP was unwilling to act pragmatically at the polls and cut a deal with the Scottish Liberal Party which would have divided the constituencies between them. Some within the SNP had been calling for co-operation with the Liberals in order not to put candidates up in the same constituencies, because as both parties stood for Home Rule, albeit to varying degrees, it would only split the Home Rule vote. Young in particular was an advocate of this argument and pressed the National Council to enter into an electoral pact with the Scottish Liberal Party and Oliver Brown's small newly formed Scottish Socialist Party which also supported Home Rule. In a motion he wrote to the National Council in March 1947, he called on it to accept such a proposition:

> Accordingly, while re-asserting that the SNP must not compromise its aim or independence by freely entering into an electoral arrangement with another Party or other Parties for a specific object for a definite period, this Council agrees upon the desirability of avoiding, if possible,

electoral conflicts at the next general election with the SSP and SLP, and therefore resolves to enquire timeously into the practical possibilities of an electoral agreement with the SSP and/or the SLP to avoid competing candidatures at the next general election.[75]

Young realised that in the constituencies where the SNP stood but the Liberals did not, the SNP was largely trading on Liberal votes. He deduced that if both parties were to fight in the same constituency, the SNP would be the one to come away with the bloody nose. The electorate, he argued, would stick with the tried and tested formula of the Liberal Party, rather than some unfathomable SNP one. The Scottish Liberal Party was also streets ahead in terms of organisation which was led by Major Carson, and had a number of able speakers as well as the funds with which to contest.[76] But despite Young's reasoning, his motion was not passed by the National Council who preferred to safeguard the Party's independence than open up the sensitive subject of electoral agreements. A great opportunity, however, was passed by with the SNP's refusal to enter into such agreements. There was already goodwill in the air from the Scottish Socialist Party whose Secretary had written to the SNP's National Secretary to notify him that it would not oppose SNP candidates at municipal elections and sought the names of wards which the SNP intended to contest in order that it could then draw up its own plans to avoid the same seats.[77] The SNP chose to safeguard its independence though and not co-operate with the SSP or Liberals on the electoral front. But its refusal to enter into an electoral deal meant that it went head to head with the Liberals in some seats which only added to its electoral woes.

Political Party versus Interest Group

Despite the Party's glaring failure at the polls and in the general field of organisation, the Party did take a considerable leap forward when it adopted its first official policy statement in 1946. There had long been rumblings within SNP circles and further afield that the Party had no official policy, only a string of pamphlets, leaflets, articles and statements which had to be pieced together in order to gauge Party tendencies.[78] The main basis of SNP policy in the inter-war period had been a pamphlet entitled *Scottish Reconstruction* which listed only a brief number of points with little elaboration. It had been authored by the SNP's first Chairman, Sir Alex MacEwen, who wrote from a Liberal and Scottish Party standpoint, and by John MacCormick and Tom Gibson, who wrote from a National Party of Scotland viewpoint, giving it a somewhat Liberal-Socialist feel to it.[79] This was replaced in 1944 by McIntyre's pamphlet, *Some Principles for Scottish Reconstruction*, as the main policy source of the Party, which updated the original version and included some new policy additions like the Party's position on monopolies and light industry, but it still lacked detail and excluded many more important issues.[80] In an effort to silence its critics and develop the Party, the National Council put policy to the centre when it placed the issue on the 1946 Annual Conference agenda. At the Conference in Perth, the SNP took a significant step forward when it endorsed the setting up of a committee to formulate a comprehensive policy for the Party which would be placed before a special Party conference for approval. The National Council set the wheels in motion almost immediately and appointed committee members at its first meeting following the Conference. The Committee, which was to be headed by F. Cameron Yeaman, was given the remit of 'collating resolutions of past Conferences of the Party' and 'to consider further additions which are desirable'.[81] It was also given a tight timeframe in which to work with its draft submission due in by October that year.[82] With no time to spare, the Committee set to work in producing the Party's first comprehensive policy programme which would be like nothing the SNP had seen before.

The Committee soon delivered its policy statement to a two-day special SNP Conference held on 7 and 8 of December 1946, which endorsed a radical programme based around the themes of constitutional reform, planning controls and economic development. In the case of constitutional reform, Scotland would become a sovereign nation served by a democratically elected parliament, which would include more directly elected members than the ratio at Westminster to ensure a higher level of democratic representation. Local government would be given more powers wherever practically possible and institutions like the Convention of Royal Burghs and the Association of County Councils would be supported to champion local affairs. The judiciary would be overhauled and would practice exclusively within Scottish courts with the Court of Session in Edinburgh being the final Right of Appeal, as opposed to the House of Lords at the Palace of Westminster. In terms of planning, the system would be operated to ensure there was a more even spread of people and employment around the country and would maximise use of Scotland's natural resources. The administration in Scotland would also be designed so that central departments responsible for industry, education and the environment would work closely with one another while regional planning would gain permanent regional planning bodies. Finally on the economy, private and state monopolies would be broken up or become subject to stringent controls. Land reform would be introduced to limit the size of holdings and to tackle issues such as feudal law and access rights to the countryside, while minerals like coal would be controlled by the state. Agriculture, fishing and forestry would also be developed to encourage domestic production of food stocks and markets and to safeguard and support rural communities. Industry would be encouraged to diversify and develop new light industries and make fuller use of Scotland's natural resources while transport and communication networks and the trading and financial sectors would be strengthened to facilitate this. Economic activity would also be spread more evenly across Scotland to ensure a fairer distribution of wealth and income.[83]

The Party's new statement built on McIntyre's *Some Principles for Scottish Reconstruction* and past annual conference resolutions. It had also been influenced by constitutions and policy frameworks of other countries around the world from which its authors had gathered some of their ideas. It answered many of the questions which opponents had levelled at the Party in the past, such as whether the Party was socialist or free market capitalist, centralist or devolved, and what kind of a country might an independent Scotland become under the governance of the SNP?[84] It showed the Party to be leaning towards the left-of-centre of the political spectrum, as its socio-economic programme sought to redistribute wealth in order that no great inequalities would exist within Scotland. It showed the Party to be devolved rather than centralist, with its proposals to strengthen local government and target the rural economy which would silence some opponents who argued that SNP rule would simply exchange London for Edinburgh as the power-house of Scotland. It also showed the Party to be liberal democratic in nature as its programme leaned towards the individual rather than the state or business and with its emphasis placed on 'small man politics'. Hanham later criticised the Party for focusing on the 'small man' and not appealing to intellectuals whom he saw as more apt to lead the Party.[85] However, to do so would have conflicted with the SNP's ethos which was based on democratic principles where elitism had no place. In all, the SNP's new policy was a remarkable feat for a Party which had only just decided to formulate a policy strategy a few months earlier and was a far cry from the policy tinkering around the edges the Party had only ever attempted in the past in election brochures and *Scots Independent* articles. The Party could no longer be termed as simply an interest group that fought elections; it had now become a political party that had graduated to proper political party status. The SNP had revealed its colours and presented the electorate in Scotland with an alternative set of policies to those offered by the major parties.

But for all this, the SNP's policy had no great weight behind it. It had set out the political, the social and the economic vision of what the Party wanted Scotland to become but crucially forgot to include how it would achieve this. With the exception of the odd reference to 'fully developing Scotland's resources' and encouraging and more evenly spreading industries 'to secure the development of a more balanced industrial fabric', it failed to give an account of how its policies would be transformed into reality. It had left out the sums and critics remained sceptical of the Party's new policy claim. It also left out some important questions, like whether the Church of Scotland would remain the established church after independence was achieved, which possibly lost it support from this group of society. It also arrived at a time when consensus between the Labour and Unionist Parties was developing and policy issues like housing, the welfare state and the planned economy were placed high on their political agendas which were difficult to compete with. Also damaging, it caused upset amongst some SNP members themselves who believed that the Party should concentrate on its key objective of independence and not be side-tracked by the countless

17

socio-economic issues that would only lead to more squabbling and infighting within the Party. Even former SNP Chairmen were quick to criticise the Party's new policy plan, like Andrew Dewar Gibb, who leaned towards conservatism, and Douglas Young, who sided towards socialism, which highlighted in itself it was the Home Rule issue that united the Party not the socio-economic, and that any comprehensive policy statement was risky. In a letter to Tom Gibson, Young complained on the subject that:

> What the SNP is doing just now is to monger a mixture of Liberal and Socialist programmes, without the vote-gathering labels of either Liberal or Labour. By emphasising the so-called Policy, or programme, rather than the Aim, it is alienating far more people than it attracts, and is wholly failing to become a real National Party.[86]

However, the Party could not credibly compete at the polls with just one issue to its name, but required something far more elaborate to win over potential voters. In order to reach simply beyond interest group status it required a full policy plan with which it could mount plausible election campaigns. Certainly no serious electorate was likely to vote for a party where a blank cheque was required because it was unaware of what lay beyond the attainment of independence; rather a full policy statement was required. Most SNP members recognised this fact and, while there were rumblings from some quarters of the Party, most simply accepted the new policy statement with little fuss. The SNP's adoption of an official policy programme was an area of significant development for the Party in the 1940s, which though not a definitive list, was an important starting point from which to commence.

With its policy programme in place, the SNP now turned its attention to the equally important issue of dual membership within the Party. Dual membership was an old issue which had dogged the Party from its infancy but had never been properly resolved. Something of an attempt had been made in 1935 when John MacCormick put forward a resolution to restrict office-bearers from carrying out duties in English controlled political parties.[87] This was extended in 1943 to prohibit office-bearers from being members of other political parties and extended further in 1947 to include all National Council members, but still no comparative ban existed for ordinary members. Such a void gave way to multiple memberships which undermined the SNP as a political party in its own right and threatened its programme with the possibility of inputs and affiliations from other political parties. With the Party's new policy statement in place, it was also more important than ever to ban SNP members who affiliated to other parties. Such dual membership could lead to embarrassment for the SNP because, for example, pushing a left-of-centre policy programme was incompatible with having Tory members and would leave the electorate unconvinced of its intentions. By banning dual membership, the Party would close the door to outside influences and make itself less vulnerable to infiltration and possible take over. It would also stamp its authority as a political party independent in its own right.

With these issues in mind, the Party sought to lay the issue to rest in 1948 when it resolved to extend the ban to the whole of the Party faithful and laid the issue before the Party's governing body, the Annual Conference. The Conference was won over by the arguments advanced for prohibiting dual membership and duly accepted a wholesale ban for all members. Accordingly, the Party's constitution was amended to read 'Persons eligible for membership of the National Party shall be those who... are not members of any other Political Party.'[88] A new Committee was soon established to decide what would constitute a political party and, therefore, be prohibited under the terms and conditions of SNP membership. McIntyre, Mary Dott, Yeaman, Gibson and Muirhead all volunteered for committee duties and got to work writing up a list of banned organisations for SNP members.[89] They produced the following list: Labour, Unionist, Liberal, ILP, SSP, the Communist Party, the Scottish Resistance Committee, the Co-operative Party, Socialist Party of Great Britain; and the SNP's main competitor in terms of members, the Scottish Convention. Despite the number of ordinary SNP members that were likely to be affected by this, the National Council approved the Committee's list with the addendum that members of the above organisations were not permitted to address SNP public meetings without the Council's prior consent.[90] In order that new members would not be ignorant of the SNP's new constitution, the Party also approved plans for an additional sentence to be inserted into membership forms which stated that 'From this date, I will not be a member of any other political party.'[91] It was a momentous and brave step for the Party and its leadership who had finally found the courage to seize the contentious issue by the horns. But the repercussions soon followed.

A number of senior Party individuals were set against any attempt to remove dual membership status from ordinary members, Douglas Young being the most ardent opponent. Young, who had been an SNP member since 1938 and Party Chairman from 1942 to 1945, believed that the Party should remain as it had begun, that is to say 'organisationally independent of other political parties, while welcoming individual members of any or all of them for particular objectives, electoral and other.'[92] Young's view was that to be a truly national Party, the SNP needed a variety of members and candidates of any political persuasion and quoted point 89 from Walter Murray's *Home Rule for Scotland: The Case in 90 Points* handbook which stated: 'The demand for Scottish self-government is, therefore, not a party one, but a national one.'[93] Young, however, did accept the restriction rule on dual membership which applied to office-bearers, though even then he admitted this was only on practical grounds because he thought that parties needed all the spare time of their office-bearers that they could get.[94] Young's initial reaction to the Conference's ban on dual membership was one of caution. He took the view that as resolutions passed by Conference had been rescinded in the past, this resolution would simply become 'dead-lettered' too.

19

But when the SNP produced its list of organisations that were now 'off limits' to SNP members, the realisation hit home and he knew the ban on dual membership was here to stay. Young had been disgruntled with the SNP for a long time with its decisions over policy, the Four-Year Programme, suspensions of its members, but now it had overstepped the mark and there was only one course of action he felt he could take, resign.

Young's break-away from the Party was something of an acrimonious affair. Almost immediately he was lambasted by Party Secretary, Mary Dott, for informing the press of his intentions before the Party itself. It was an accusation which Young denied, claiming he had posted the letters together and that it was not his fault the Party was less efficient at dealing with its mail than the press was with theirs, and in any case he had verbally conveyed his intentions to Mary Dott before writing his resignation and he could not help it if she had missed the point.[95] Young also denied accusations levelled against him that he had been a member of the Labour Party when he had taken the SNP Chair in 1942. He admitted that he had been a member of the Labour Party until 1942, but he did not renew his membership after he was nominated by Archie Lamont for the job of SNP Chairman. He did, however, concede that his reason for not renewing was more to do with the wartime electoral truce Labour had hatched with the Tories at the time than out of any moral obligation to the SNP.[96] Young made attacks of his own, like referring to the SNP as the 'SNP Ltd' which had 'about as much use to the movement as a fifth wheel to a coach.'[97] Once out of the Party, Young sought new ventures and possibilities in which to do his bit for the national movement. He toyed with Niall McPherson's idea of a West European Federation Committee of Convention, which sought a Scottish parliament within a federal Europe, but it never really got off the ground. He also took an active part in the Scottish Convention's Covenant petition but then had a falling-out with them. Eventually he rejoined the Labour Party in 1950 after an eight-year absence and sought to influence its policy on constitutional reform as the best way forward to advance the Home Rule cause.[98]

Muirhead also opposed the SNP's dual membership ban. On a similar wavelength to Young, Muirhead thought that the SNP rank and file should be allowed to retain memberships of other political parties if they so desired, but that this should not extend to SNP officials. He was not adverse, however, to a dual membership ban if the Party faithful were members of British political parties, but stopped far short of organisations like the SSP and the Scottish Convention.[99] Muirhead's way of thinking was coming more and more round to the idea of a type of Scottish national congress, which he envisaged would encompass members of all parties with the aim of establishing a Scottish parliament through non-parliamentary means. Muirhead too was concerned with the direction the Party was heading in. Its Four-Year Plan had so far been a resounding disaster, he saw no real need for the Party to adopt a policy and he now looked upon the wholesale ban of dual membership as folly. All of which simply intensified Muirhead's outward focus on the need for some kind of Scottish national congress within the movement to concentrate on extra-parliamentary means.

The ban caused discontent for ordinary Party members themselves who were directly affected by its introduction. To many of them, the ban on dual membership was a restrictive clause which would only decrease Party membership, not increase it. For Scotland to obtain Home Rule, one member argued, 'The doors of the Scottish National Party must be wide open to all – and kept that way... all absurd restrictions and red tape... must be swept away.'[100] Those in the Party who were dual members now had the stark choice to make between the Liberals, the Unionists, Labour, or one of the other banned organisations. Abandoning the SNP may have been the first choice for some of them. For those who stayed, an attempt was made to have the ban repealed when a resolution was put forward at the next Annual Conference in 1949, but it lacked the support it needed to have the previous Conference ruling overturned and so the ban stayed.[101] Dual membership was a seedbed of discontent amongst the leadership and the rank and file of the Party which damaged it in the short-term at a time when Party morale and support were already at a low ebb. Nevertheless, it was an issue which had beleaguered the SNP for a long time and did have to be addressed at some point for the future stability of the Party. By ridding itself of those members who were also members of other political organisations which supported weaker types of self-rule, such as the Scottish Convention, the SNP was also left with a core membership which firmly supported its full independence line and was more ideologically in tune. By finally tackling the dual membership issue, the SNP took a significant stride forward in its development and in affirming its position as not merely an interest group but a conventional political party.

Dissent and Disorder

But conflict over dual membership was only the thin end of the wedge. Infighting was as much a pastime for the SNP in the 1940s as fighting the independence cause itself. In the winter of 1946, Robert Wilkie, editor of the *Scots Independent*, threw in the towel with the nationalist paper on the grounds that the National Council of the SNP no longer had confidence in him; a move which had come about because of his earlier suspension from Council meetings for defiance of the Chair and his subsequent refusal to apologise.[102] The following year he was expelled from the Party when he made statements to the press that were 'inimical to the interests of the Party' in relation to his decision to stand as an independent candidate at the Camlachie by-election. Wilkie had decided to stand at Camlachie despite an earlier National Council ruling that it should not be contested because of insufficient funds. His statements relating to his candidature which led to adverse headlines such as 'Scots Nationalist Dispute' and 'Nationalist Defies Ban' damaged the Party by portraying it as an unruly and splintered organisation.[103] Supporting Wilkie, however, was Douglas Young who believed that he had been victimised for his decision to stand as an independent nationalist candidate rather than for his damaging press statements. In January 1948, Young moved a motion of no confidence in Party Chairman, Robert McIntyre, over the matter. This failed by a vote of 24 to seven.[104] For Young, the National Council of the SNP had 'put the cause ten years back by its purging attitude', and he accused the Party of becoming 'a fusionless bunch of factionaries who cannot even agree among themselves.'[105] The Camlachie affair and the Party's general lack of progress also began to bring Young round to the view that the SNP should no longer remain a political party but should become a non-parliamentary propagandist group:

> What the 20 years work has done is to gather about 50 local branches talking about self-government and to circulate about 4000 copies of a monthly journal, with some leaflets and pamphlets. This is less than the old Home Rule Association did after its 1917 revival... I am considering whether the SNP would not help the movement at this stage by becoming a non-Parliamentary association devoted to publicity from an academic separatist's viewpoint whose members should, as in the Fabian Society, take their own ways of promoting practical political steps in the direction of separation and equality of rights for Scotland through whatever industrial or cultural or political organisation they individually feel right.[106]

But such an idea was swiftly dismissed by McIntyre who was quick to remind Young that a similar organisation already existed to a large extent in the shape of the Scottish Convention. Young went on to accuse the Party of being intolerant with its suspensions and expulsions of members at whim, as he saw it, and lamented the damage it wrought. It was an accusation that was unjustified as a shortcoming of the Party was that it was rather too tolerant by all too often revoking the suspensions of members like Wilkie and allowing them sufficient influence to undermine the Party. After the Wilkie-Camlachie affair, Young was no longer prepared to speak on the platform for the Party and it served to strengthen his resolve to quit the Party in the wake of the dual membership ban. As a consequence of Camlachie, Young's membership had simply become what he termed 'auld lang syne'.[107]

Archie Lamont was another prominent dissenter in the SNP whose antics also undermined the image of the Party. Lamont, who was a geologist based at Edinburgh University, sat on the SNP's National Council and wrote various publications and articles for the Party. *Scotland A Wealthy Country* was his most successful booklet which outlined a number of facts and statistics on Scotland's land and mineral wealth. In order to counteract the argument that Scotland could not afford self government, it set out to show that Scotland was a country rich in natural resources.[108] But Lamont's writings increasingly tended to verge on the scholarly side, which gave them less widespread appeal and became bogged down in detail, often reverting to his subject of choice, geology, which was not necessarily the first topic on Party members' and potential supporters' lips. Lamont's writings, as a consequence, became increasingly rejected from publications like the *Scots Independent*, which only influenced his notorious behaviour. His most notorious incident occurred at the Party's 1948 Annual Conference in Edinburgh when he rose in protest at the Conference's decision to close before a resolution on Scottish neutrality in future wars had been discussed. The Party could ill afford to debate on theoretical issues on future wars that may not even occur and when his protests were declined, Lamont refused to be seated and shouted to the panel 'we stand for Scotland's neutrality in war' then turned to McIntyre in the Chair and condemned him as 'a puppet of the English Government and a silly little bureaucrat.'[109] Lamont had to be physically ejected from the Conference by a half dozen or so delegates, with several blows being struck in the process. Just as McIntyre thought it was safe to resume and deliver his summing up speech, six foot three Lamont burst back into the hall with further insults and verbal abuse and had to be physically escorted again from the Conference.[110] It had been McIntyre's first Conference as Chairman and he had already suffered the indignity of having a glass of water thrown over him the previous day for his refusal to reinstate Wilkie's membership.[111] For McIntyre, it must have made the acrimonious 1942 Annual Conference, where half the delegates had walked out and formed the Scottish Convention, seem innocuous, and undermined what would otherwise have been an excellent conference. It had certainly been the largest SNP Annual Conference to date with its historic endorsements of the Party's new constitution that banned dual membership and its commitment to remain a political party after a national government of Scotland had been set up, both of which asserted its position on the party political stage, but these were overshadowed by the incidents that filled the press sheets the next day.[112] Even the placid Roland Muirhead felt the need to speak out against Lamont's behaviour and wrote to him after the event, penning what was essentially a lecture on his unacceptable behaviour:

> While agreeing that the Chairman might well have introduced the delegates to give an extra hour to deal with the remaining resolutions and I believe he might have done so had you not challenged him in the manner you did by your unreasoned outbursts and refusal to obey the Chair you lose support of many good members and so spoiled your appeal. I feel myself in a difficult position because while I realise all you have done for the S.N.P., on the other hand you have spoiled much of that work by the unreasonable way you have frequently acted. For Scotland's sake I wonder if it would not be possible for you to keep your remarks at meetings in line with the Standing Orders? As to the

23

newspaper reports of the Conference I do not agree with you. While no conscription was made prominent the Party as a Scottish National-ist body was made to look divided and irresponsible although the real fact is that the members of the Party are solid for independent self-gov-ernment for Scotland.[113]

It had not been the first time either that Lamont had been called to order but refused. In September 1946, he had been suspended from a National Council meeting fol-lowing his defiance of the Chair for being outspoken and refusing to leave the meet-ing.[114] A year later he was asked to leave another National Council meeting 'owing to...[his] persistent defiance of the Chair'.[115] Moreover, he had pulled a similar stunt at another SNP Conference with his outrageous behaviour as McIntyre recalls, 'when he threw a pile of books and pamphlets at the then chairman.'[116] Lamont had also supported Wilkie's candidature at Camlachie in defiance of the SNP's ruling not to contest the seat. Incidents like these only added to the negative press the SNP expe-rienced in the forties era which portrayed an image of a Party too engrossed in fight-ing itself than in fighting the nationalist cause. One small consolation following Lamont's 1948 outburst was that it resulted in his immediate expulsion and thereby removed one major agitator from the Party.

Christopher Grieve was another member who disrupted the Party in the forties. Grieve, a prominent poet who was better known under the pseudonym, Hugh Mac-Diarmid, was selected to stand as SNP candidate for Glasgow Kelvingrove in the Gen-eral Election of 1945. But Grieve was not the most pragmatic of politicians. In the run-up to the election, he made racist comments directed towards the English at a meeting in Cosmo Cinema in Glasgow. When confronted, his only excuse was that he had been careful to distinguish his own views from the Party's.[117] Grieve was also a communist who had openly stated that he was not a democrat but believed in the 'dic-tatorship of the proletariat', which was in conflict with the SNP's democratic consti-tution.[118] For the Party, this was a PR nightmare because it had a candidate standing in its name whose expressed views were at complete loggerheads to its own constitu-tion and policy. Austin Walker moved for Grieve's withdrawal as SNP candidate at a National Council meeting a month prior to the General Election, but this was defeated on the grounds that it was too late in the day to withdraw his candidature.[119] The de-cision not to withdraw Grieve's candidature and display to the outside world how se-rious it was about its respectability only served to undermine the Party and the fragile reputation upon which it sought to build.

As well as directing his abuse towards the English, Grieve also took pot shots at SNP colleagues, such as co-Party candidate, Arthur Donaldson, who had been selected for Dundee. Grieve referred to Donaldson as not fit to contest the constituency and claimed that Donaldson sought to 'hog' money raised in Dundee for himself.[120]

Grieve's accusations were flatly rejected by the National Council though it did not do Donaldson's cause much good as he polled the second lowest vote of the eight SNP candidates standing at the General Election, gaining only 4.6 per of the vote. Grieve himself was not far in front with just 4.9 per cent, though he did have the distinction of gaining 1314 votes, the date of Bannockburn - a situation which Wilkie similarly repeated three years later at Camlachie when he polled 1320 votes, the year of the Declaration of Arbroath, which showed if nothing else the Party's loose cannons were able to obtain votes of symbolic significance.[121] It was a relief to the Party when Grieve tendered his resignation at the end of July 1945 following a petty argument at a Council meeting that had arisen over the appointment of the SNP caretaker.[122] Grieve's departure enabled the SNP to conduct party business without his unhelpful and unwelcome comments which had only hampered the smooth running of the Party. Astoundingly, the following year, the SNP allowed Grieve to rejoin its ranks giving him sufficient opportunity once more to undermine its position. It was decisions such as these in the early days that scored the SNP own goals by allowing individuals like Grieve to re-enter its midst without properly assessing the damage they caused. Only after the Annual Conference of 1948 did the SNP begin to talk tough and put discipline before Party numbers. But in the meantime, the internal strife continued.

Wendy Wood also earned her place on the SNP's list of dissidents. Wood was an eccentric, middle-aged woman who had become a nationalist in her youth. She was a well-known nationalist both inside and outside the Party who delivered memorable oratory, but her line of thinking in terms of tactics did not match the SNP's. Wood, in like fashion to Muirhead, favoured extra-parliamentary means like tax evasion and promoting civil disobedience in order to disrupt the powers that be, though also like Muirhead, she was not averse to fighting elections either. Wood's rhetoric, which at times took on anti-English overtones, was also in conflict with the SNP's own image. Statements such as 'I saw a man on a bus brush his coat because an Englishman had passed. I said to him: 'Is that the way you feel?' 'Yes,' he said, 'damn their eyes'' were notorious from Wood.[123] Wood left the Party of her own accord in 1949 to the Party's delight, claiming she could do the cause more good as a freelancer than working within the SNP shackled by the National Council. She had also been disgruntled by the treatment she had received from members of the Council like Arthur Donaldson, Austin Walker and George Dott who, she claimed, acted uncivilly towards her.[124] Wood went off to form her own organisation, Scottish Patriots, where she could campaign unabated for a Scottish Parliament. Even after her departure from the SNP though, Wood still came to be associated with the Party and undermined its hopes of carving out a respectable image for itself.

Conclusion

The SNP in the 1940s failed to achieve much in the way of organisation, election results and internal unity. It failed to grapple with the important issue of building an effective organisation which could have expanded its membership and enabled it to mount more convincing election campaigns, whereas other parties had begun to address the important points of organisation and resources as politics took on a more professional appearance after the Second World War. Consequently, the SNP's troubles were largely self-inflicted and its internal conflict and infighting only added to its woes by displaying to the outside world a picture of a Party divided which simply existed on the margins of Scottish politics. But it would be wrong to write off this period as one of mere survival for the Party during which it simply fought to continue its existence, for the Party undertook two of its most important developments in this period – its adoption of an official policy and its ban on dual membership. The SNP's adoption of a new policy statement was a significant move forward for the Party as it set out its key policy areas in an official programme for the first time. However, it did have the misfortune of being presented at a time when Labour and the Unionists were beginning to show some policy consensus and had placed issues like the welfare state and the corporate economy high on the agenda with which it was difficult for the SNP's new policy statement to compete. The Party's ban on dual membership was also an important shift for the SNP as it strengthened party loyalties and settled the contentious issue once and for all. These moves were pivotal to the future development of the Party which underpinned its position as a proper political party leaving behind any notions of its existence as an all-party interest group. Although it would be many years before the SNP reaped the fruit of its new policy and dual membership ban, they were fundamental to its sustainable future as a serious political organisation.

2

The Rise and Fall of the Scottish Convention

Formation and Early Years of the Scottish Convention

The year 1942 was a year of reckoning for the Scottish National Party. The Party had begun the year with its failure to find the resources to contest the Edinburgh Central by-election followed hot on the heels by its inability to put up a candidate who would fly the SNP flag at the April Cathcart by-election. The closest it came to a candidate was rooting for an independent nationalist named William Whyte, who in the event came bottom of the poll. Moreover, the simmering issue of 'moderates' versus 'radicals' was yet to be resolved. Party Secretary, John MacCormick, was a moderate who favoured devolution over full independence and believed that the Party should take on a more conciliatory approach towards politics by linking up with other political parties and groups to form a united front in the battle for Home Rule. He wanted to see the Party become a blanket organisation for the national movement rather than a sectional political party that played to the Westminster tune.[1] Mac-Cormick also believed that co-operating with the war effort would score the Party some much needed points by removing its appearance as an extremist, separatist, party and portraying a more co-operative and respectable image. For other members of the Party and its leadership, however, conciliatory politics was off the agenda because it would undermine the very existence of the Party itself. The formation of the Scottish National Party in 1934 with the merger of the Scottish Party and National Party of Scotland was a clear endorsement then of the will to have an independent political party in Scotland that would champion Scotland's nationalist cause in the House of Commons and the 'radicals' of the Party were not about to give that up now to have the Party invaded or ruled by the influences of other political parties. Radicals also supported an independent Scotland that would not be tied in any way to Westminster. As for conscription, hardliners viewed the British army as an English army and, therefore, viewed the conscription of Scots into what they saw as a foreign army. When the Party met in May 1942 for its Annual Conference, the battle lines were drawn.

The Annual Conference of 1942 was a pivotal moment in the history of the SNP. The moderate camp, led by MacCormick, supported the continuation of William Power's leadership which they believed would enable the Party to support the conscription of Scots into a British Army and evolve the SNP into an umbrella organisation which would encapsulate the whole of the national movement. The fundamentalist camp supported the leadership of Douglas Young which they hoped would steer the Party on a radical course which would take a tough line against conscription and close the door to the co-operative politics that MacCormick preached. When the fundamentalists won the day by a marginal vote of 33 to 29 for Young's leadership, MacCormick was outraged. He responded by resigning his Secretary-ship and storming out of the Conference to the nearby Rutland Hotel with almost half the delegates who shared his moderate view following in tow. There, in haste, Mac-Cormick and his followers formed their own organisation known as the Scottish Union, which was soon changed to the more apt name of the Scottish Convention to conjure the spirit of co-operation and 'unity of democratic purpose.'[2] The newly formed and newly named Scottish Convention was to be the organisation that Mac-Cormick and other moderates had hoped the SNP would become. That is to say it would be non-partisan, inclusive, co-operative, and nationalist with a small 'n'.

The aim of MacCormick's Scottish Convention was two-fold. First, it sought to secure the establishment of a Scottish parliament which would have powers over domestic affairs, leaving defence, foreign, imperial and fiscal affairs to the UK Parliament; and second, it sought to provide ' a non-party medium for the discussion and advancement of all matters of Scottish interest.'[3] Like the National Government of its time, the Scottish Convention rejected confrontational politics and opted for a consensual approach instead based on cross-party agreement. It refuted the ballot box and believed the expression of consensus was all that was required to bring sufficient pressure to bear on the Government to introduce its objective of a Scottish parliament and was the fastest method in which to achieve it. It also viewed the question of Home Rule as one which was above normal party politics, whereas contesting elections would only lay the Convention open to the charge of 'splitting the vote' with the SNP which would harm both organisations and serve to undermine the whole national movement.[4] While stating its aims, the Convention was also keen to emphasise what it did not support, and a flag-waving, bagpipe and tartan type of Scottish nationalism with any extreme tendencies was not what it supported. It was strictly opposed to a republican self-governing Scotland, or a self-governing Scotland that had its own armed forces, or one that put up customs barriers at the border, or any other type of barrier for that matter that might disrupt the free flow of capital and trade between Scotland and the rest of the UK.[5] With its aim of establishing a Scottish parliament securely within the structure of the UK and its all-party no-party approach, it was rather much a re-run of the old Scottish Home Rule Association.

In the immediate years after the Convention was formed, few successes were recorded. As tempers cooled, many members who had left the Annual Conference and joined the Convention soon drifted back to the SNP, particularly so when it became apparent that new SNP leader, Douglas Young, was not the militant they first took him to be. On the contrary, Young was closer to the Convention's ideals in terms of all-Party support than he was to the hardliners of the SNP. Like MacCormick, he believed in cross-party support and welcomed members of other political parties into the SNP. As discussed in Chapter One, he would later resign from the Party when it voted to extend its ban on dual membership to ordinary party members at its 1948 Annual Conference. Young also supported non-parliamentary approaches to fighting the Home Rule cause in tandem with elections rather than relying exclusively on the parliamentary electoral route. It was his steadfast stance against the conscription of Scots into the British army that had attracted hardliners to him. It was this stance, which in 1942 earned him a prison term and secured him an aura of martyrdom, that had drawn the radical wing of the Party to him; that and a complete lack of choice in leadership candidates with the only other competitor being William Power, an elderly, uncharismatic and moderate contender. Many members who drifted back to the SNP still retained a link with the Convention. They were attracted by the more moderate approach of the new organisation but were unable to cut the apron strings and let go of the SNP whose strength and emotional appeal remained strong. It was in these first few years that the Convention struggled to carve out its support base.

Despite the slow start, the Convention's prospects became markedly brighter at the end of the war. It had used the war years to develop a branch network across Scotland. By the second half of 1945, the Convention boasted 3,691 members, which was approximately quadruple the SNP's own membership.[6] This figure increased to 4,773 members the following year despite the Convention being left without the services of a full-time organiser for almost a year.[7] In financial terms, the Convention's balance sheet went from a deficit of £265 in 1943, £469 in 1944, and £225 in 1945, to a surplus of £84 in 1946, partly due to an increase in affiliation numbers and funding initiatives in the form of raffles and bazaar schemes.[8] The Convention was also being noticed in the parliamentary arena. At its Annual General Meeting in 1946, the Convention reported that 33 Scottish MPs had pledged their support to its ideals, while many more signalled an interest and willingness to be 'kept informed'.[9] Also, the Convention sent a delegation consisting of William Power, William Gallagher, and the Rev. D. F. MacKenzie, to London to be interviewed by some Scottish MPs in response to their request that 'they might be given "ammunition" to fire in the House of Commons'. The Convention's deputation, which was met by both Unionist and Labour MPs, received a warm reception from both sides of the political divide, with Labour MPs purporting to put the Convention's plans before their Scottish Conference.[10] Although nothing concrete in the way of devolutionary guarantees arose from the deputation, it highlighted to Scotland's parliamentarians the nationalist stirrings and agitations that were occurring in Scotland at the time. When the Convention set about its next project of organising a Scottish National Assembly, it was then that the Convention really took off.

Scottish National Assembly

Organising a Scottish National Assembly was an idea the Convention had grappled with soon after its formation. Its main role was to encourage inclusive politics in a non-partisan environment for the advancement of devolution and the Convention thought that organising some kind of assembly representative of civic society in Scotland was the ideal vehicle in which to achieve its aim. In 1945, its policy was published which stated that it would convene a Scottish National Assembly when the time was right which would thrash out the details of a Home Rule constitution. Only through discussion and consensus, the Convention believed, would a self-governing Scotland be achieved.[11] The early work of the Convention had indeed already focused on approaching various targeted individuals and groups to seek consensus on self-government. During the war, for example, it had put the 'feelers' out on cross-body support by sending a memorandum on reform of government to civic organisations for comment to which it received various messages of support.[12] It also approached the Scottish Secretary, Tom Johnston, with its memorandum. Johnston gave it a hearing but was too wrapped up in the immediate goal of delivering an effective Scottish war-time administration to take the proposals seriously.[13] The Convention's manifesto, issued in January 1946, also sought to unite civic support for a Scottish parliament by cajoling public bodies to support resolutions calling for self-government and to forward them to the Prime Minister which it would co-ordinate.[14] By 1947, the Convention had built up sufficient steam and momentum to take forward its vision of a Scottish National Assembly.

The Convention sent invitations to attend the Assembly to all political parties and sectors of civic life in Scotland. When a large volume of responses came back agreeing to send delegates, MacCormick knew he was on to a winner. The Scottish National Assembly met in the Christian Institute in Glasgow on 22 March 1947, with the aim of:

> …demonstrating to the Government the serious concern which is generally felt in Scotland about the future prospects of Scottish trade and industry, and to examine the possibility of stating an agreed measure of reform in Scottish Government which the Assembly will place before the Government…[15]

To this effect, it placed three resolutions on its agenda, the first called on delegates to accept a strengthening of the Scottish Grand Committee which would transform it into a Scottish Legislative Committee by allowing it to carry forth legislation on Scottish domestic affairs. The second called for an Act of Parliament to give effect to the document, *Declaration on Scottish Affairs*, more commonly known as the Leonard Declaration after its Chair, William Leonard, which proposed the establishment of a

Scottish parliament with control over Scottish domestic affairs, leaving defence, foreign, imperial, fiscal and customs affairs to Westminster.[16] The third resolution called for a referendum on self-government on the basis of that proposed in the Leonard Declaration.[17] The Assembly was made up of representatives from political parties, local authorities, churches, trade unions, co-operative societies, chambers of commerce, and other public organisations within Scotland. But an important section of the national movement was missing, the SNP.

The SNP had been high on the Convention's invitation list, but the SNP voted to turn down the invitation at its National Council meeting in February 1947 on three grounds. First, all resolutions on the Scottish National Assembly agenda were too limited for the SNP to support. The most radical was a Scottish parliament within the framework of Westminster which would only have control over domestic affairs and this fell far short of the SNP's own brand of Home Rule. For SNP Chairman, Bruce Watson, the resolutions were simply too 'weak-kneed.'[18] The second ground on which the SNP declined was its claim that even the most advanced resolution the Assembly had to offer failed to meet the level of self-government demanded by the majority of public opinion in Scotland at that time. Even if majority opinion did not share its own all-out independence line, the SNP claimed that majority opinion in Scotland wanted more than the limited form of devolution the Convention proposed. The final ground it mooted was the Assembly's standing order which gave the Chair the power to decline amendments to be made to any of the agenda resolutions.[19] Such a rule could make it problematic for the SNP to introduce a more radical measure of Home Rule on the day, particularly as the Assembly Chairman was John MacCormick who only supported a limited form of self-government. The SNP recognised that if it did attend with these constraints, it would have to move for the rejection of all three resolutions and this could be misconstrued that it was rejecting the principle of Home Rule itself.[20] On a conciliatory note, the SNP did agree to allow its members to attend the Assembly if they so desired, though only on the strict proviso that they attended as individuals and in no way represented the Party.

Despite the SNP's rejection, the Scottish National Assembly of 1947 was even more representative than the historic General Assembly of 1638 and was described by *The Scotsman* as being 'perhaps the most widely representative [meeting] ever held to discuss Scottish affairs.'[21] Most of the speakers at the Assembly spoke of the need for Home Rule in terms of practicalities rather than romantic notions of nationalism as was so often identified with the earlier Home Rule period. For example, William Gallacher, acting on behalf of the Scottish Convention, called of the need for Scottish self-government in order to encourage Scottish industry at home and curb emigration, as well as to alleviate a congested House of Commons. J. G. Wilson of the Edinburgh Liberal Council believed that a Scottish parliament was necessary in order to combat the increasing centralisation of Scottish industry controlled from London;

while David Gibson, representing the Independent Labour Party, argued for Home Rule in terms of housing.[22] Douglas Young also spoke at the Assembly, speaking for himself rather than Party due to the SNP's stipulation not to be represented. Young was not a devolutionist as some commentators like Richard Finlay, James Mitchell and H. J. Hanham have labelled him.[23] He desired self-government like that of Canada's or New Zealand's though he believed powers should be introduced gradually over a period of years rather than as a single event.[24] But he opted for the weaker first resolution which only sought to strengthen the Scottish Grand Committee that would give some limited element of legislative devolution to the committees. Young's reason for doing so was that he believed the other two resolutions were too limited to meet Scotland's self-government demands, whereas the first resolution empowered the Grand Committee to appoint commissioners after a two-year period who could then put forth more radical self-government proposals.[25] Young's thinking was somewhat ill conceived as surely a Scottish parliament limited by the Houses of Parliament could also put forth plans for a more comprehensive Home Rule policy; either way the decision would still rest at Westminster. Logical or not, it was at least a step further than the SNP was prepared to go at the time which had opted for an 'all or nothing' constitutional approach.

The outcome of the Scottish National Assembly was a majority 216 to two votes for the adoption of the second resolution which called for the establishment of a Scottish parliament as set out in the Leonard Declaration.[26] The Assembly had a positive effect on the Home Rule movement generally and the Scottish Convention in particular as it demonstrated the appetite which existed for non-partisan nationalism from an overwhelming and varied body of opinion in Scotland. It also produced widespread, and on the whole positive, publicity for the Home Rule movement when it was reported extensively in the Scottish press and recorded by the BBC in Scotland, an extract being broadcast the evening the Assembly convened.[27]

A special committee was appointed to take forward the Assembly's ruling with the task of framing a new constitutional plan for Scotland that would build upon the scheme set out in the Leonard Declaration. This Committee, which was something of a microcosm of Scottish society as it was representative of Assembly delegates who in turn were representative of Scottish civic society, convened on 7 June 1947 and took just three months to deliver its proposals.[28] These proposals, which were later published in the document, *Blue Print for Scotland*, came in four schedules and were centred on a parliament in Scotland that would have sufficient competency to deal with Scottish domestic affairs. The first schedule listed all the matters that would be reserved to the UK, the second schedule listed all the matters that would be dealt with jointly by the UK and the Scottish Parliament, the third stated that all other areas not mentioned in the first or second schedules would fall to the Scottish Parliament, and the final schedule noted the financial relations that would exist between the two Parliaments. One striking element of the proposals was that they did not state the domestic areas that would become the competency of the Scottish Parliament, but stated the reserved matters instead, which left only defence, Commonwealth, foreign affairs, immigration, treason, currency, the Crown and UK electoral law to Westminster. The proposals were not dissimilar in nature to the devolution settlement that followed 50 years later in the shape of the 1998 Scotland Act, which also noted the reserved matters, not the devolved, putting room for expansion firmly in the Scottish parliamentarians' court. The proposals also attempted to answer what would later be termed the West Lothian Question by proposing to exclude Scottish MPs from taking part in parliamentary dealings solely relating to English or Welsh domestic matters.[29]

The Committee also justified why a parliament was important for Scotland. It mirrored the view of many speakers at the Scottish National Assembly by stating the practical rather than the emotional need for self-government. It declared that Scottish MPs were limited in initiating or passing policies designed specifically for Scotland because of the inadequacy of the Scottish Grand Committee which lacked the ability to propose legislation and only dealt with matters set out before it on behalf of Westminster, nor was it always representative of Scottish members. The Committee also warned that the Secretary of State for Scotland, who is appointed by the sitting Government, could vary from public opinion in Scotland and fail to represent the democratic mandate of the Scottish people (a fear that was realised during the 1979-1997 Conservative administrations when the Scottish electorate consistently voted for a Labour government). The Committee also cited the remote control argument, whereby Labour's nationalisation programme resulted in power transferring from Scottish to London control and underlined the implications of this policy on Scotland. The Committee also argued that the nature of governance in Scotland was having an adverse effect on Scotland's economic and social condition, which it claimed was evident by Scotland's high emigration rate. As with many speakers at the Scottish National Assembly, it also asserted that the existing political apparatus was overburdened and complained that legislation was often drawn up for English Law with Scotland simply inserted as an addendum, put in brackets and tagged on the end.[30] There was nothing new in any of the arguments the Committee had put forward, they had all been cited at one time or another by various pro-Home Rulers and Home Rule organisations, but what was important about the Committee's proposals was that they were delivered by a unified voice with most of Scottish civic society agreeing both cause and cure of Scottish governance.

Now that the Home Rule condition and prescription had been decided, the next stop for the National Assembly Committee was to turn its proposals into reality. In an effort to do just that, the Committee contacted the Prime Minister, Clement Attlee, to arrange a deputation so it could present its new constitutional plan for Scotland before him. Attlee had expressed his support for Home Rule in the past but now in office his support for the cause had dried up. He quickly made his excuses and offered the services of Secretary of State for Scotland, Arthur Woodburn, instead. Woodburn was a poor substitute who did not back the Home Rule idea but believed Scotland's salvation lay with socialism not nationalism. Despite Attlee's rebuttal and Woodburn's ideology, the Committee decided to meet with Woodburn anyway - it had nothing to lose. On 9 January 1948, and with MacCormick commander-in-chief of the delegation, the Committee formally placed its proposals for a new Scottish constitution before the Government, but almost from the start Woodburn was dismissive. Despite the proposals being overwhelmingly accepted by the representative Scottish National Assembly, Woodburn proceeded to tell the MacCormick-led Committee:

> The proposals have obviously been carefully prepared and they are certainly the most complete and the most reasonable outline of a scheme for legislative devolution that I have seen. But I have yet to be convinced that there is any widespread demand in Scotland for such a measure. We have many more urgent things to tackle, such as the present food crisis, and I cannot promise that the Government will be able to give serious consideration to your demands. I have, however, made certain recommendations with regard to Scottish affairs which have met with the approval of my colleagues. I cannot disclose them now but they will be the subject of a White Paper which I shall present to Parliament within the next few weeks.[31]

Woodburn's comments flew in the face of the evidence that the Committee and several polls carried out over the years had highlighted, that is to say that there was widespread demand in Scotland for a legislative measure of Home Rule. When the Government's White Paper on Scottish affairs was presented a few weeks later as promised, it proved another let down for nationalists. It sought to increase slightly the time given to Scottish matters in Parliament and to marginally improve the procedure of the Scottish Grand Committee.[32] It also proposed to launch a Scottish Economic Conference, headed by the Scottish Secretary, and to keep the running of government and the nationalised industries under reappraisal for opportunities to expand administrative devolution.[33] But these measures fell far short of nationalists' expectations and the Committee had come away from the meeting with nothing except a lip-service measure of administrative reform, and a deeper-seated resolve to turn its proposals into reality.

The Covenant

Woodburn's rebuttal of the Committee's proposals led to a second Scottish National Assembly being convened on 20 March 1948. The second Assembly was originally convened to report the outcome of the Committee's meeting with Woodburn,[34] but following the government's unsatisfactory response and its inadequate White Paper on Scottish affairs, it was required to formulate a new strategy forward. The second Assembly endorsed the Committee's proposals on self-government and concluded that a nation-wide campaign such as a plebiscite or petition was needed to demonstrate the widespread support that existed amongst voters for a Scottish parliament.[35] Assembly officials were confident that such a campaign would produce the outcome they wanted. Indeed, results from a study by the Psychology Department of the University of Edinburgh had only just been published which showed that 75.2 per cent of its sample agreed that Scots should run their own affairs while only 17.8 per cent disagreed.[36] Moreover, the independent non-party Plebiscite Society had recently conducted a plebiscite in the north-east town of Kirriemuir, which asked the local electorate if they were in favour of a Scottish parliament. The results gave tremendous weight to the Home Rule camp with 2,310 of the 2,648 cross-section of the electorate returning their ballots and 92.3 per cent of them supported a Scottish parliament, with 23.3 per cent of that figure favouring outright independence as advocated by the SNP.[37] These statistics reinforced the National Assembly's view that overwhelming opinion was on their side and that if a nation-wide campaign was held in the form of a plebiscite, it was unlikely to lose. The Government, however, probably coming to the same conclusion, refused to concede an official plebiscite, which prompted the Scottish Convention and the Assembly Committee to meet at Aberfoyle in April 1949. There, the attendees decided to take matters into their own hands and agreed to launch a Scottish Covenant scheme which they hoped would demonstrate beyond all reasonable doubt the widespread desire felt in Scotland for a Scottish parliament.[38] Surely then Woodburn and the Labour government would have no conceivable argument against not implementing self-government?

A Scottish Covenant was soon drafted which demanded a Scottish parliament within the framework of the UK as endorsed by the Scottish National Assembly. The Covenant was essentially a petition whose sponsors sought signatures to support its demand, but it was more than just a petition because it pledged its signatories to do all in their power to secure Home Rule for Scotland in language somewhat akin to the seventeenth century Covenanters:

> We, the people of Scotland who subscribe this Engagement, declare our belief that reform in the constitution of our country is necessary to secure good government in accordance with our Scottish traditions and to promote the spiritual and economic welfare of our nation.
>
> We affirm that the desire for such reform is both deep and widespread throughout the whole community, transcending all political differences and sectional interests, and we undertake to continue united

in purpose for its achievement.

With that end in view we solemnly enter into this Covenant whereby we pledge ourselves, in all loyalty to the Crown and within the framework of the United Kingdom, to do everything in our power to secure for Scotland a Parliament with adequate legislative authority in Scottish affairs.[39]

The Covenant was not a new idea, similar documents had been drafted in the past by other Home Rule bodies. The National Party of Scotland, for example, drew up a National Covenant in 1930 not too dissimilar in tone which also commanded its signatories 'to do everything in... [their] power to restore the independent National status of Scotland.'[40] The authors of the latest Covenant, however, highlighted their more moderate stance by underpinning their loyalty to the Crown and their desire to remain within the UK parliamentary structure. Yet there was also a feeling of radicalism in the air about the document too, which was devised as a pledge and not just a petition, and its authors believed that if enough people committed themselves to it, then a Scottish parliament would be in the offing.

The Covenant was launched at the third Scottish National Assembly on 29 October 1949 at the Church of Scotland's Assembly Hall, which gave grandeur to the occasion. The Duke of Montrose was first in line to sign the Covenant, followed by MacCormick. The SNP's Chairman, McIntyre, was also present that day and declared: 'We need not discuss to-day the form of self-government, for, as Parnell said, no man can set bounds to the march of a nation', though he stopped short of actually signing the Covenant highlighting that there was no actual turnaround in SNP policy.[41] Despite McIntyre's refusal to sign, the Covenant's first day was a runaway success. By the end of the first week, at least 50,000 signatures were pledged to the Covenant, by six months, the figure had broken the million barrier, and by 1951, it had passed the two million mark. [42] It seemed everyone wanted to get in on the act and jump on the Covenant bandwagon, which was available to sign in a variety of public places, including post offices, shops, restaurants, public houses, community centres, churches, as well as college and university campuses, to name but a few.

Support also came from the most unlikely sources. The Covenant drew on a strong band of Unionist supporters who were attracted to its devolution demand as a countermeasure to the Labour Government's national planning programme. For those rank and file Unionists, a devolved Britain was more palatable than a socialist Britain and they duly signed the Covenant to counteract Labour's socialist policies and also as an act of protest against them. Students were a more obvious group who supported the Covenant and it did the circuit around the university campuses, particularly at Glasgow University which had a strong history of student nationalism and whose students voted in MacCormick as their Lord Rector half way into the Covenant campaign. With support coming from far and wide, a National Covenant Committee made up of Convention and Assembly Committee members was formed to co-ordinate the campaign and canvass more signatures. However, the Covenant proved to be something of a spontaneous event with signatories distributing and gathering batches of Covenant sheets themselves, which were soon cascaded again by new signatories. By the time it closed to new signatories in 1951, over two-fifths of the overall Scottish population had signed the Covenant; a staggering two-thirds of the voting population;[43] and more than the number of Scots who had voted in the then present Labour Government, which had won by a landslide. It was an extraordinary endorsement for the Home Rule camp and, crucially, provided the Convention and the Assembly Committee with the evidence they needed to show St Andrew's House the popular support felt in Scotland for a firm measure of Home Rule.

Some opponents of Home Rule argued that the number of Covenant signatures over-represented those who had actually signed it. Certainly it is true that a number of bogus signatures appear on Covenant's long list including cartoon characters, dead celebrities and duplicates (Chris Grieve's wife is said to have signed the Covenant five times).[44] However, not all signatures went towards the count either. Its sponsors claimed to have gathered two million signatures which is the figure most often quoted in text books,[45] but given the unorganised and spontaneous nature of the campaign, it would be logical to surmise that not all the sheets with signatures were collected in or counted centrally. The exact number of people who appended themselves to the Covenant is therefore uncertain, but it was a remarkable affair nevertheless.[46]

At a fourth Assembly Meeting, the decision was taken to appoint commissioners who would once again present the Assembly Committee's self-government proposals before the Government and Opposition, but now with overwhelming evidence to hand. As was becoming customary though, the Prime Minister was too busy to meet with the delegation and referred them to the Scottish Secretary, Hector McNeil (Arthur Woodburn's replacement), instead. Churchill did the same for the opposition by referring them to his deputy in Scotland, James Stuart.[47] Far from receiving backing for their proposals, the Commissioners' only concessions from these meetings were an indication from McNeil that a Committee of Inquiry could be appointed to look into the financial links between England and Scotland, whilst the Unionists set about drafting a pamphlet entitled *Scottish Control of Scottish Affairs*, which proposed to set up a Royal Commission on Scottish affairs.[48] Now that the Covenant manoeuvre had clearly failed, the Assembly Committee moved onto its next tactic, which was to press Parliament for a national referendum by means of a questionnaire; the response from the Government was unequivocal:

The questionnaire has been, I am sure, read with interest by all of us but in the view of my colleagues and myself the issues involved are complicated and cannot be dealt with by simple question and answer of the kind contained in the questionnaire, or by a plebiscite, I should add too that it is our view that constitutional change in this country is considered and settled by the normal process of Parliamentary democracy.[49]

The Unionists replied in similar vein emphasising that the ballot box was the tool to use if certain groups wished to achieve a Scottish parliament. MacCormick, disappointed with the substitute officials the Government and Opposition had offered, never mind their replies, had already set sail to the USA and Canada to raise support and press interest over there for the campaign, a trip that would prove even less fruitful.

Failure of the Scottish Convention

The Scottish Convention had been hugely successful in grabbing the headlines and gaining widespread support. It had organised some of the most representative assemblies of Scottish society and had helped mount the largest petition ever raised in Scotland. It spurred on investigations by both Government and Opposition which would later take the shape of the Catto Committee and the Balfour Commission. But in terms of fundamentals, the Convention ultimately failed. Its primary aim was to attain a Scottish parliament with adequate controls over Scottish domestic matters and this it failed to achieve. Given the weight of support the Convention and the Covenant campaign experienced, the question begs why did it fail?

One critical factor was the Convention's refusal to play the parliamentary card and contest elections. As the signatures mounted, the Convention and the Assembly Committee thought that no political party or government could possibly turn down their demand for a sub-parliament in the face of such overwhelming evidence and that the necessary negotiations and legislation would pass through Westminster: 'In the face of such proof no political Party and no Government in London has any right to refuse our demand and we believe that the demand, after suitable negotiation, will be conceded.'[50] But the problem with this view was that government under the parliamentary system did have every right to turn down their demands, and when it did, the Convention was left with no stick to fight with and the voters with no party to protest to, except the SNP, whose fully fledged independence line few were prepared to cross. The writing should have been on the wall for the Convention in 1947 when the Prime Minister was not even prepared to pay lip-service to the National Assembly Committee by accepting its delegation so it could present him with its self-government plans. Instead it had to make do with the Scottish Secretary who described its proposals as 'reasonable' then politely showed the Committee the door. After this experience, rather than channelling its energies into a Scottish Covenant only to have the Prime Minister and the Scottish Secretary spurn it again, perhaps it would have been more fruitful if the Convention had prepared to mount an election campaign, or at least had a contingency electoral plan in place in the event that the Government would say 'no' to its Covenant method. Certainly there was a danger that the Convention might lose support if it conducted its own parliamentary campaign due to its cross party make-up as dual members would inevitably be torn between the two. But by not conducting its own electoral campaign, those who had signed the Covenant were not given the opportunity to register their pledge at the ballot box. Even in the small number of constituencies where the SNP fielded candidates, its independence pill was too bitter for most to swallow. Furthermore, the plebiscite conducted in Kirriemuir had already shown a disproportionate amount of voters favoured a Scottish parliament, which was backed by various other surveys and opinion polls undertaken by Edinburgh University and others on the subject. In this respect, the Convention's Covenant scheme simply duplicated the evidence that was already there and wielded no additional threat to the Government if it refused to back it. The Convention's complete lack of foresight on this point was further highlighted when it backed a plebiscite in Scotstoun in November 1950; predictably this too showed a majority in favour of a Scottish parliament, albeit not quite on the scale as Kirriemuir.[51] Conducting such a plebiscite not only duplicated what had already been shown, but it was also expensive at a cost of around £600,[52] and highlighted to the Government that the Convention could simply be ignored because of its lack of political strategy. The Convention failed to realise that the numbers that became attached to the Covenant and unofficial plebiscites were no substitute for the ballot box and until petition signatures and plebiscite numbers were transformed into ballot numbers, the government could go on, and did, ignoring the Home Rule cause. It was the Convention's lack of realisation of this and its refusal to change tack and take up the ballot weapon that proved its fundamental weakness.

Another factor that undermined the Convention was that while it played to the pressure group tune and rebuffed the electoral route, it also embroiled itself in a wide range of political issues other than Home Rule. For example, the Convention held a special meeting to discuss the Education (Scotland) Bill in 1945 at which, after considerable opposing views as can only be expected with a cross-party group, it settled on the position that no rate-aided schools should be fee-paying.[53] On housing, a resolution at the Convention's 1946 Annual Conference called for the Government to increase the distribution of building material to Scotland, to develop a separate housing development programme and to reform the rating system within Scotland;[54] while on transport, the Convention lobbied Scottish MPs and issued a statement to the press on the state of Scotland's railway system.[55] These policies were devised to address some of the here and now issues facing Scotland rather than delaying them until a Scottish parliament had been implemented. However, pursuing such a strategy was incompatible with the Convention's all-party no-party approach because it embroiled the Convention in day-to-day party issues while at the same time its all-party no-party line allegedly shunned party politics. For members who were also members of other political parties, there was also the risk of affiliation to organisations with contradictory policies. The Convention's strategy left the organisation rather indefinable as not quite a political party but more than just an interest group. If the Convention had concentrated on the nationalist question leaving the everyday issues to the political parties, it could have focused its energy and drive onto its key issue of Home Rule and may have obtained better results. Or, on the other hand, it could have chosen full political party status and gone down the ballot route, albeit at a cost of some supporters who were members of other parties. The Convention's hotchpotch of a strategy, however, gave it the worst of both worlds by distributing its focus and energy across a diverse range of areas and by removing the electoral weapon which might have made its policies effective.

MacCormick himself did the Convention no favours when he stood as a parliamentary candidate in Paisley which evoked suspicions of an anti-Labour conspiracy. The Labour Party had initially jumped on the Convention bandwagon and was supportive of it in its formative years as a cross-party pressure group. The Convention's ideology as a group that would not succumb to the cut and thrust of party politics sat well with many Scottish Labour members who could show their leanings to the Home Rule cause without fear of supporting an organisation that was in direct competition to their own Party. The fact that the Convention stole the SNP's thunder, if indeed the SNP had any thunder in that era, only added to the Convention's appeal. But following the death of Earl Baldwin and the subsequent succession of Oliver Baldwin to the House of Lords, MacCormick went forward as a Liberal candidate for the constituency. Soon, however, his candidature became perceived as a front to undermine the Labour Party. This perception took root when some members of the Scottish Convention, who were also prominent members of the Paisley Unionist Association, sought to convince their local Unionist colleagues not to put forward a Tory candidate but to rally round MacCormick instead. Letters were sent to the editor of the local press encouraging those who opposed centralisation to rally behind MacCormick and before long a meeting was held between the local Tory and Liberal Associations at which MacCormick delivered a forthright speech urging agreement on the devolution question:

> We believe that the distinctive national traditions and characteristics of Scotland are of great value to the United Kingdom and to the world, and that they constitute a priceless heritage of the Scottish people. If the process of centralising the economic control of Scotland in Whitehall is allowed to continue that heritage will be lost and our national ex-

istence endangered. We therefore consider that a measure of devolution in the government of Scotland is a matter of urgency.

We recognise that there are differing opinions as to the extent to which such a measure is immediately practicable, but we urge that all parties in Scotland should seek to reach agreement on this question and that it should not be made an issue in party politics.[56]

MacCormick's statement was cleverly constructed so as not to scare away the Unionists with the 'devolution' word by playing adversary to Labour's centralising policies and by leaving open to debate the level of devolution sought, yet it also struck a chord with the local Liberals whose Party supported a Home Rule policy. The statement was unanimously adopted and hailed as a 'joint-declaration' between the two Associations.

But MacCormick's Paisley candidature was harmful to the Scottish Convention as it smacked of an anti-Labour plot that had been hatched to ensure no socialist candidate won at Paisley. It meant that MacCormick was standing in direct competition to a Labour candidate while at the same time he was a prominent leader of a non-partisan organisation which avoided party politics and ballot box tactics. Such a manoeuvre led Labour to view the Convention as something of an anti-Labour agent and it became reluctant to endorse its campaigns or proposals. Also, with Tory heavyweights like Walter Elliot, Peter Thorneycroft and Lady Tweedsmuir supporting MacCormick together with Liberal support, Labour could be forgiven for feeling somewhat 'ganged up' on.[57] As well as evoking suspicions from Labour quarters, MacCormick's stunt also lost the Convention the support of a band of Liberal Convention members who were upset at the suggestion of a Tory-Liberal pact. Indeed, Liberal leaders Sir Archibald Sinclair and Lady Glen-Coats publicly condemned the Tory-Liberal 'coalition' at Paisley and attempted to distance their Party from the Unionists by advising Liberal voters not to vote for MacCormick.[58] It was an incredible situation for the Scottish Liberals to be in, to have on the one hand its Paisley Association making a pact with the local Tories, but on the other hand having its top brass actively dissociating itself from the pact and its candidate. Lady Glen-Coats, who was Vice-Chairwoman of the Convention, also took the step of resigning from the Convention's National Committee a few months later over the Paisley affair, leaving it without the services of one its key leaders.[59] MacCormick's by-election tactic had thus proved damaging. Not only had he lost the faith of the Labour Party and some within the Liberal Party, but he also lost the seat to Labour by 6,545 votes.[60]

MacCormick's transatlantic voyage also played a role in the Convention's decline. MacCormick had set sail to North America on 24 June 1950 in the wake of Attlee and Churchill's decision not to meet personally with the Assembly Committee's Commissioners. His main objective was to dispel notions of the Covenant being an irresponsible and unrepresentative body, which was a view that sometimes appeared in the foreign press. He also sought to obtain support from Scots living in North America and raise Scotland's Home Rule profile abroad. For MacCormick, looking beyond Britain's shores for help in implementing the Covenant scheme was the next natural step as domestic extra-parliamentary measures had so far failed. In an article in the *Glasgow Evening News* he explained: 'The trip is timed to coincide with the decision that, since we were turned down by the Tories and Socialists, we shall go into politics for ourselves – even possibly on an international scale.'[61] MacCormick, accompanied by fellow Covenant officials, William Graham, John J. Campbell and Robert Turpie, visited New York, Washington, Chicago and Toronto. In Washington they met with senators who listened sympathetically to their campaign for a level of autonomy for Scotland not too dissimilar to that enjoyed by every state within the USA. In Chicago they visited the home of Colonel R. R. McCormick, editor of the *Chicago Tribune* and a well-known republican, who laid on a press conference for them. In Toronto they were received by the city's Mayor and Town Council and MacCormick was invited to speak at the North America Annual Convention of Scottish Clan Societies, which was attended by hundreds of delegates.[62] Their visit was successful in dispelling some myths about the Covenant and in raising Scotland's Home Rule profile abroad, but, on the whole, the trip was negative for the Convention and the Covenant campaign, not least because it caused acrimony amongst its own ranks. Scottish nationalist Eric Linklater for one, strongly criticised MacCormick's decision to go transatlantic and demanded that his signature be removed from the Covenant which, he believed, had now become 'a weapon loaded with American dollars.'[63] Others followed suit. MacCormick was also criticised for seeking the help of Colonel McCormick who was labelled a foe of Britain and who had frequently voiced his distaste of England. In the left-wing weekly journal, *Forward*, he was described as an 'isolationist, hater of Britain and friend of Franco, and by any standards one of the world's most reactionary public figures.'[64] Seeking the support of such a controversial individual also led to damaging claims in the British press that MacCormick was simply replicating the actions of De Valera in stirring up trouble for the English.[65] Although MacCormick's North American journey dispelled some untruths about the Covenant movement abroad, it also damaged it at home and ultimately did more harm than good.

Another factor running against the Convention was that it was missing the support of an important section of the national movement – the SNP. The SNP was uncooperative towards the Convention mainly because it was unwilling to water down its policies to a limited form of legislative devolution which the Convention advocated. The official line was that the Convention was off limits due to its watered-down version of self-government. For SNP officialdom, only an independent Scotland without the constraints of Westminster and secured through electoral mandate would do and it was not prepared to compromise its ideals for something that fell far short of this. To do so and support the Convention would mean undermining the whole basis of the Party and it might just as well as have ceased back in 1942 and flown under the non-partisan Convention banner, or voted in moderate William Power and become the Convention in everything but name. One of the reasons for the Party's survival, if not success, was its fundamental commitment to an independent Scottish state and it was this, its grand design, which set it aside from other parties. Even when the SNP did appear to become more co-operative by accepting an invitation to send delegates to the second Scottish National Assembly in March 1948, it was not done so for co-operative reasons. It was only in order to expose the 'weakness' of the Assembly's proposals and highlight independence as the only viable alternative that SNP delegates attended rather than any sudden conversion to co-operative politics.[66] It was that and also perhaps a feeling of being left somewhat out in the cold after witnessing the level of support received for the first Assembly and now wanting a slice of the action. The SNP's unwillingness to support the Convention and its attendance at the Scottish National Assembly in subsequent years only as a means to undermine it meant that the Convention did not receive a full spectrum of support from the national movement.

As well as not receiving the support of SNP officialdom, many individual Scottish nationalists, members and non-members of the SNP. were also unsupportive of the Convention. One critic was Muirhead, who despite supporting the idea of co-operative and cross-party politics, refused to sign the Covenant because he perceived its devolution demand to be a 'half loaf'.[67] Muirhead was also sceptical of the Convention's tactics and believed that sending signed Covenant sheets to Westminster would not be enough to secure a Scottish parliament. Somewhat prophetically, he predicted: '...my belief is that after the Covenant has been sent down to the House of Commons it will be received with a great show of interest and that it will then be stored away and little more heard of it.'[68] Other Scottish nationalists, including Major Hume Sleigh and Chris Grieve, refused to sign the Covenant on the basis that its demand for a Scottish parliament with limited powers was too weak and ineffectual for them to put their names to. Some nationalists were also unsupportive of the Convention because of MacCormick's leadership style. Douglas Young, for example, repeatedly criticised MacCormick on an array of issues, ranging from his Paisley candidature and North American tour, to MacCormick not deploying chartered accountants to authenticate Covenant signatures. In a letter to Muirhead, Young complained that: 'the strongest argument yet offered against self-government is the incompetence and irresponsibility of the executive of the Covenant movement.'[69] There was also the suspicion amongst some nationalists that the Scottish Convention served only as a springboard for MacCormick to acquire power where the ballot box had previously failed him. By the time of the Covenant, for example, MacCormick had unsuccessfully thrown his hat five times in the parliamentary ring. MacCormick's first parliamentary contest was as a National Party candidate, then as a Liberal, then as an Independent with Conservative and Liberal backing. Given his failed cross-party parliamentary attempts, MacCormick was quickly exhausting his options of obtaining a power base or voice for his type of Scottish nationalism. According to the *Observer*: 'This severe experience greatly influenced him. It led to his adoption of the Covenant method, and his great reluctance to be drawn into a further contest at the polls against the existing political parties.'[70] This rather harsh view of MacCormick though is perhaps unjustified for, if MacCormick's main goal was simply personal power, he could have obtained it long ago by standing again for one of the main parties. Nevertheless, mud sticks and for fellow Scottish nationalists, the question over MacCormick's new Convention strategy as a means to gain power for himself was not an attractive thought and may have made some nationalists reluctant to back the Convention.

The Scottish Convention and the Labour Government

As mentioned above, Labour had come to look upon the Convention suspiciously following MacCormick's Paisley candidature. But it is important to note that Labour's change in direction towards the Convention and Scottish nationalism also came from wider concerns. Labour had traditionally been a Party of Home Rule. Its Scottish founding fathers, Keir Hardie and Robert Cunningham-Graham, amongst others, were exponents of the self-government cause who supported a separate parliament in Edinburgh. In June 1918, the Party officially committed itself to the principle of Home Rule when it endorsed a resolution for legislative and administrative devolution for Scotland[71] - a commitment which it reasserted in 1928 at its British Party Conference. The Scottish Council of the Labour Party was equally keen to show its commitment to self-government and reaffirmed its pledge in June 1941. Many individual Scottish Labour candidates also carried the Home Rule torch at the 1945 General Election campaign and positioned it as second priority on their agendas behind only the defeat of Japan.[72]

When the Labour Government was elected to office in 1945, however, Home Rule conflicted with its nationalisation programme and it began to backtrack on its earlier promise of Scottish self-government. Staying supportive of the Convention would have put a great deal pressure on the Labour Government to act upon its Party's earlier Home Rule pledges and it was a move it was not prepared to make at that time. It faced the huge task of post-war reconstruction and it could ill afford to back the Home Rule horse, which in any case was running against its own Clause Four (nationalisation) programme. Socialism was the number one priority of the Party after all and its key objective was to bring a new socialist dawn to Britain where national planning played a central role, whereas nationalism would simply detract from this goal. The Labour Government also knew that most Scots, despite supporting some element of Home Rule, prioritised the economy more and it could effectively ignore the Home Rule question so long as it was delivering on the economic front. The Labour Government also thought that the introduction of its economic and social policies would go a long way in tackling Scotland's socio-economic problems which in large part gave rise to the demand for Home Rule in the first place.[73]

Attlee illustrated the change in Labour Home Rule policy when, as Prime Minister, he warned of the dangers of Scottish nationalism as a threat to world peace and stability, whereas not long before taking office, he championed the merits of a Scottish parliament and gave his personal promise to its implementation.[74] The appointment of staunch anti-devolutionist, Arthur Woodburn, as Scotland's new Secretary of State in 1947, was another indicator of Labour's change of heart towards Home Rule and the Convention. Like many Labour men, Woodburn had once been a supporter of Home Rule in his younger idealistic days believing that self-government could lead the way to socialism for the Scots. But with sight of a socialist government at Westminster, there was no longer a need for a separate Scottish government and Woodburn became an ardent believer that any kind of Scottish parliament would simply become a stumbling block to a socialist national planning utopia. His strong views on the subject sometimes clouded his judgement. On one occasion he attempted to link MacCormick and the Convention to terrorism when he made a speech in the House of Commons on 16 November 1949, taking out of turn an innocent statement MacCormick had made which made reference to the word 'bomb.'[75] Woodburn's over-the-top statement to the House of Commons and his failure to tackle nationalism eventually led to his dismissal as Scottish Secretary in February 1950. Labour's change in Home Rule policy was highlighted again when Hector McNeil, another anti-devolutionist, though a somewhat more level-headed Labourite, took over as Woodburn's successor.[76]

Impact of the Scottish Convention on the SNP

One important aspect of the Convention in this period was its short and long term impact on the SNP. In the short term, the Convention proved damaging to the SNP because it took resources and supporters away from the Party while emphasising that a moderate form of Home Rule was what the majority of Scots wanted, not full-blown independence as the SNP advocated. The Convention also stole the limelight, obtaining more publicity than the SNP could muster and instigated the largest petition ever mounted in Scotland. It dwarfed the SNP and basked in the political mainstream while contrasting the SNP as an insignificant rump on the fringes of Scottish politics.

But in the long term, paradoxically, the Convention proved beneficial to the SNP.

The departure of MacCormick and other moderate SNP members who joined the Convention left the SNP stronger and more united in its commitment to a fully independent Scotland as radicals consequently made up the majority of the membership. Also, when the Convention failed to deliver its key objective of a Scottish parliament and fell into obscurity in the fifties, the SNP's strategy was vindicated. The failure of the Convention demonstrated to the SNP's party faithful and the wider nationalist community that there was no short-cut to success, only a long slog using the existing apparatus of the parliamentary system. It justified the SNP's decision in 1942 to remain a political party and underlined the weakness of interest group strategies. It also left those who had been members of the Party, but had left to join the Convention, effectively 'homeless' when the Convention dwindled away. Many simply returned to the fold of the SNP which they viewed as the best viable option for self-government. For nationalists who could not swallow the independence pill it was either banishment to the political wilderness or to one of the small nationalist splinters that had surfaced in the fifties (both effectively amounted to the same thing). The significance of the Convention's effect on the SNP was that it enabled the SNP's membership to form a stronger ideological attachment to the central issue of full independence. It also focused the nationalist movement back into the parliamentary framework through the failure of non-parliamentary means and left the SNP as the principal bearer of the nationalist cause. Some new members were also introduced to the SNP through the vehicle of the Convention. The Convention also brought Home Rule into the public eye which had a publicity spin-off effect for nationalism generally which benefited the SNP.

Conclusion

The Scottish Convention was an important chapter in the history of the SNP and the Scottish national movement. Its interest group tactics and 'all-party no-party' approach were significant in securing support and publicity for the Convention and for the wider nationalist cause. Its ability to promote public pressure was immense and unrivalled by any other section of the national movement in Scotland. But its failure to convince the major parties to support its Home Rule policy only justified the SNP's position that pressure group tactics were not enough in themselves and that no amount of signatures or support could replace votes. Its failure to devise an electoral strategy and the ineptitude of its leadership only demonstrated to the nationalist community and to the SNP in particular, that an electoral mandate with strong leadership was crucial in the battle for self-rule. The Convention was a gimmick organisation in many respects that captured the imagination and support of the public with its various strategies and tactics. But when the novelty wore off, the Convention's failure to alter its approach and devise an electoral strategy ensured its hope for a Scottish parliament remained elusive. The SNP in the meantime took a back seat, solidified its commitment to its key separatist aim and concentrated on defining its long-term plan for a sustainable future, ensuring that when the fire went out of the Convention, it was itself that cashed in the nationalist vote. The SNP's slow and deliberate parliamentary policy had ensured its survival and would eventually lead to its growth. It may have taken the passing of a decade, but the hardliners of the SNP had won the 1942 argument.

3

Preservation and Perseverance – 1950-54

The Scottish National Congress

When the fifties arrived, the fortunes of the SNP were at an all-time low. The Party's organisation was disjointed in some areas while non-existent in others, evident by the disastrous results of its 1950 election campaign. Its central membership had more than halved, analysis of its General Election campaign had found the Party to be lacking 'cohesion and purpose at all levels' and its Four-Year Plan lay in tatters.[1] Financially the Party was struggling to make ends meet. The sharp decline in the SNP's central membership had had an obvious detrimental effect on Party revenue as had the General Election campaign which had eaten into Party funds, while the *Scots Independent* was still proving to be a money pit. Internally the Party was at war, fractious with internal strife as members fought more amongst themselves, it seemed, than they did for the Party cause. The Party had also been overtaken and eclipsed by its breakaway faction, the Scottish Convention, and now existed within its shadow. It was against this backdrop that Roland Muirhead, one of the SNP's chief protagonists, its past President and a frequent benefactor, went off to form his own nationalist organisation known as the Scottish National Congress.

Muirhead was the SNP's oldest office-bearer. Born in Lochwinnoch in 1868, he trained as a tanner at his family's business in Bridge of Weir. After completing his apprenticeship, he left Scotland for South America aged 19, travelling from Uruguay to the Argentine Republic. Muirhead observed the progress which these self-governing countries had made, particularly the small republic of Uruguay, and surmised that if Scotland could control her own affairs, then she too would progress further than under the rule of Westminster. He returned to Scotland in 1891 with a strong sense of nationalism and became heavily involved in the national movement through his membership of the Scottish Home Rule Association (SHRA) and the Independent Labour Party (ILP). Muirhead left the ILP and became the first Chairman of the SNP's forerunner, the National Party of Scotland (NPS), when it was formed in 1928 following the merger of the SHRA and other Home Rule organisations. Initially, he endorsed the electoral policy of the NPS and the SNP. Indeed, he stood himself as a candidate at three General Elections between 1928 and 1935, all without success. But as the thirties and forties wore on, Muirhead came to regard the SNP's electoral policy as a failure which had yielded few votes for the Party and he became convinced that a new strategy was needed. He argued that even if the Party did obtain a majority of Scottish seats in the House of Commons, which was a far stretch of the imagination, England's 512 MPs could easily ride roughshod over Scotland's 71.[2] Muirhead became increasingly influenced by the policy of Gandhi and the Indian National Congress which had fought and secured self-government for India through civil disobedience. He believed that the SNP should adopt a similar approach by pursuing tactics such as encouraging boycotting and tax evasion.[3] By doing so, he believed the road to self-determination would be shorter and more direct. Muirhead repeatedly pressed the SNP to redirect its efforts away from the electoral route to these less conventional means. But despite gaining the support of his local Lochwinnoch Branch, which placed such a proposal before the Party's 1949 Annual Conference, Muirhead's idea was ignored by the SNP Executive and was turned down overwhelmingly by the 1949 Conference. The Party was struggling to project a respectable image for itself as it strove to become a contender to the main political parties. Encouraging civil disobedience may have worked for India, but Scotland was a world apart and it would have blown the SNP's attempts at respectability out of the water. Unable to convince the Party to change tack, Muirhead took the decision with a heavy heart to form his own nationalist organisation.

On 28 January 1950, plans for Muirhead's new organisation were set in train when around 100 nationalists met to discuss the approaching General Election. The main purpose of the meeting was to find ways to boost the nationalist vote at the Election. Many called for independent nationalist candidates to stand in order to supplement the SNP's scant number of three. However, despite Chris Grieve being chosen for the job in Kelvingrove, Muirhead's idea won the day when he convinced the majority of attendees round to his idea of creating a body that would fight for nationalism by ways other than parliamentary means. After gaining support from the floor of the meeting, a Committee of 10 was appointed to take forward Muirhead's proposal which was instructed to meet once the results of the Election had been announced.[4] After the results were declared, the small Committee, presided over by Muirhead, met on 11 March 1950 to thrash out the details of the new nationalist body, from which the Scottish National Congress was born.

The Scottish National Congress (SNC) was formally established the following month and its office-bearers elected at a public meeting in Glasgow. Muirhead took the Chair while Harry Gardiner served as Vice-Chairman, Kenneth MacLaren took on the role of Secretary, R. G. MacMillan became Treasurer and Gordon Murray, Organiser.[5] The SNC soon took on the appearance of a left-wing organisation due to the left-wing tendencies of its members as individuals like Muirhead brought a strong sense of social justice and anti-conscription views to its ranks. The aim of the SNC was the same as the SNP, that is to say it demanded an independent Scotland with full control over all domestic and foreign affairs. Its way of achieving its objective was totally different.

Inspired by the Indian model, the SNC's key policy was the promotion of civil disobedience in order to make the Scots so troublesome to the Government in London that it would no longer want to govern them. It sought to promote nationalism not through propagandist means like other nationalist organisations, but through practical means, and to assist it in its fight, the SNC hoped to recruit trade workers such as carpenters and engineers who could provide practical support in the civil disobedience war.[6] Though with few takers, the SNC was happy to welcome anyone willing to come on board. The SNC also saw the value of contesting parliamentary seats which would generate publicity for the movement, and, if elected, its MPs could stir up trouble for the Government from within the House of Commons. However, this was secondary to the extra-parliamentary route which lay at the heart of its policy. The policy of the SNC soon attracted ardent left-wingers like Oliver Brown, Archie Lamont and Mary Ramsay to its ranks. Brown even allowed his small Scottish Socialist Party to be swallowed up by the SNC, which cemented its radical left-wing position.[7]

The civil disobedience tactics that the SNC and its members deployed were varied and colourful. One tactic it used was to encourage Scots to boycott English goods and to opt for Scottish-made goods instead in an effort to hinder trade between the two countries and make the Union less profitable to England. To help the consumer, the SNC produced a list of products made in Scotland. The SNC also called on food exports from Scotland to England to be stopped and named and 'shamed' shareholders who sold Scottish companies to English concerns.[8] Another tactic it turned to was to encourage its members to stamp bank notes with the slogan 'Scottish Self Government is Overdue'. The SNC ordered rubber stamps to be made with this slogan which it then made available to its members. By doing so, its propaganda entered general circulation at a fraction of conventional propaganda publishing costs. In a shrewd move, it paid bills it owed to local press and advertisement firms with such notes. It had the desired effect and the *Edinburgh Evening Dispatch* ran an article on the SNC after receiving such a note.[9] There were legal issues to this tactic though, as the Bank Act of 1928 protected Bank of England notes against defacing. However, Scottish bank notes were not covered by the Bank Act and the SNC encouraged as many Scottish notes as possible to be stamped with its slogan. Though in reality most in possession of a rubber stamp marked all notes that passed through their hands including the Bank of England's, but simply did not openly admit to the illegal ones.[10] Sticking to slogans, the SNC also encouraged voters to spoil their papers in constituencies where no Scottish nationalist candidate stood with the phrase 'Freedom for Scotland.' In the SNC's view - 'a vote given to any English-controlled party is a vote in favour of the misgovernment of Scotland by the English.'[11] The SNC was also keen to get its view across to the Government and the main parties directly and actively encouraged the heckling of Government ministers and politicians at public rallies and events. Literature was produced for would-be-hecklers including a list of possible heckle lines, such as: 'Are you in favour of the establishment of a National

Parliament in Scotland?' and 'Will you at all times put Scottish interests ahead of your Party's policies even if it may mean your expulsion from your Party?'.[12] The strategy of refusing to pay tax was also adopted by the SNC and sparked some publicity when ex-SNP veteran, Wendy Wood, was imprisoned for refusing to pay National Insurance contributions. Wood wanted to bring attention to the harsh conditions at Duke Street Prison as well as raise the nationalist cause and was given the option of a £15 fine or 60 days imprisonment.[13] She refused to pay the fine and was duly incarcerated at Duke Street Prison. The case attracted publicity in the local press and consequently gave the Home Rule lobbyists a louder voice. It also occurred around the time of the 1951 General Election when the Labour Government could least do with nationalist distractions. However, there was the small consolation for the Government that it got Wood off the streets for at least part of the campaigning period.

Another main policy feature of the SNC was its opposition to conscription. The SNC had more than its fair share of left-wing pacifists like Archie Lamont and Chris Grieve in its midst who strenuously opposed the National Service Act of 1948 which allowed for young men to be conscripted into the army during peacetime. Various pamphlets and booklets published by the SNC were devoted to the topic. In one booklet, Scots Awake!! Say "No"! to Conscription, the SNC argued: 'Many free minded Scots agree with the late Keir Hardie that Conscription is the badge of the slave, and that, as it is wrong in principle, it is evil irrespective of who imposes it or by whom it is received.'[14] A large part of SNC activists' time was spent staging protests and demonstrations outside army recruiting offices attempting to persuade young men to disobey their calling cards by refusing to join up. On a few occasions it worked and the SNC offered the young men legal support in their subsequent battle with the authorities. Chris Grieve's son, Michael, was one such young man who refused service then received support from the SNC, though he was later jailed for his stance.[15] The SNC also appeared to oppose instruments of war generally, such as its campaign against proposals to establish a South Uist missile scheme and its opposition to controversial plans to turn farmlands over to the military.[16] For an outsider looking in on the organisation, they could be forgiven for thinking the SNC was more an anti-war body than a nationalist one. It certainly took on the appearance of an early-day version of the Campaign for Nuclear Disarmament (CND).

The impact which the arrival of the SNC had on the SNP was mixed. Initially the SNC had an adverse effect on the Party as it projected an even more fractured image of the nationalist movement. When the SNC was established, there were several small nationalist bodies already operating in Scotland as well as the main nationalist organisations, the SNP and the Scottish Convention. Groups such as the Scottish Patriots, directed by Wendy Wood, United Scotland, led by Mary Ramsay, the Scottish Socialist Party, headed by Oliver Brown, and the Scottish National Freedom League, run by Scots living outside Scotland in other parts of the UK, all shared the common goal of a Scottish parliament.[17] They were small in number, little more than one-man and one-woman bands in some instances, and were insignificant in power or influence. Muirhead hoped the establishment of his new organisation would help coordinate the activities of these nationalist organisations. He believed the greatest weakness nationalists faced was the number of organisations that existed which advocated nationalism but were unwilling to co-operate with each other.[18] However, he failed to see the irony of establishing another organisation which simply added to the numbers and portrayed an even more splintered image of a movement that was unable to exist under the one roof.

As well as fracturing the movement further, the SNC's arrival also lost the SNP precious resources as many SNC members were also SNP members and now diverted their time and money to their new organisation. Losing some of Muirhead's attention and resources was a particularly large blow to the Party as Muirhead was one of the SNP's wealthiest members who had bestowed generous loans and donations upon the Party on various occasions to see it through its most difficult times. His time devoted to the Party was just as impressive as he had spent a great deal of effort fighting the SNP's corner in the correspondence sheets of the press and through his contacts with influential figures. Although he still continued to do this for the Party and remained a member of its National Council after the SNC had been established, he did so far less often once the SNC was up and running. Muirhead's directorship of Scottish Secretariat also led to the SNC being favoured over the SNP. Scottish Secretariat was a publishing organisation devoted to nationalist literature. It also doubled as a reception point and was often the first port of call for people seeking to become involved in the national movement. Muirhead had directed nationalist enthusiasts towards the SNP in his Secretariat capacity in the past, but once the SNC was set up he encouraged them to join the SNC instead and provided them with SNC literature rather than the SNP's.[19] On one occasion he even stopped a cheque from going to the SNP in favour of the SNC.[20] Promoting the SNC was also made easier because it shared its premises with Scottish Secretariat at 28 Elmbank Crescent, Glasgow. The SNC also enjoyed a close relationship with other nationalist organisations like United Scotland, the Scottish Socialist Party and the Scottish Patriots. All the leaders of these organisations had in fact become SNC members while running their own small organisations. Evidence of their close relationship can also be gleaned from the fact that Mary Ramsay offered the Edinburgh Group of the SNC the use of United Scotland's Hanover Street premises in Edinburgh.[21] Oliver Brown, as already mentioned, allowed his Scottish Socialist Party to be incorporated into the SNC, while Wendy Wood went the whole hog and went to jail for the SNC cause. The SNC was also on friendly terms with the Scottish Convention although it did not subscribe to its devolutionary model. In this way, it was the SNP that appeared uncooperative, obstinate and the outsider which failed to get along with its nationalist colleagues.

But it was not all bad for the SNP. The existence of the SNC was also beneficial to the SNP as it became a new home to many of the SNP's mavericks. Individuals like Lamont, Grieve, Wood, Wilkie, and Young, who had often created internal strife for the SNP, all became members of the new SNC organisation. The SNC's policy of civil disobedience with few rules or guidelines was a calling card for these and other maverick individuals as it provided them with an outlet for their nationalist expression without fear of suspicion or expulsion as had often occurred in the SNP. But with such a high density of mavericks and firebrands all under the one roof, the SNC itself soon became a constant battleground between members. They routinely exchanged fire with each other in letters and at meetings as backbiting became the order of the day. For example, Lamont attacked Ramsay for having communist connections, Ramsay avoided Wood believing that she had encouraged violence in the past,[22] Wood criticised Lamont for being a hot head, Lamont denounced Wilkie as an alcoholic, while the Greenock Group accused the Glasgow Group of holding too much power and resigned en masse. It was a fracas that made the SNP appear almost at one and in harmony with itself. Continual sniping between SNC members such as this took up as much time and effort as that actually used to implement the SNC's policy or expand its stagnant ranks. It also led to the paradox that the SNC was an organisation based on Gandhism and peace, yet at the same time its members were at war with each other. By housing these warring factions, the SNC's formation was extremely beneficial to the SNP as it cleared the Party of its insubordinates who had so often disrupted its proceedings, attempted to change its direction and at times brought embarrassment upon the Party. Although some still remained members of the SNP, their time devoted to SNC pursuits allowed them less time to disrupt SNP policy or influence its Party members.[23]

Not surprisingly, the SNC with its fractious band of members failed to achieve much in the way of membership or support and remained a small and ineffective organisation that posed no real threat to the SNP, or to the authorities for that matter. The SNC managed to establish only five groups, based in Glasgow, Edinburgh, Aberdeen, Dundee and Greenock, and even then Greenock broke away leaving just four. Low on numbers, it was unable to attract the speakers, organisers or activists it needed to shore up support for expansion or to mount successful demonstrations or campaigns. The SNC also lacked an adequate headquarters structure which was essential to manage individual Groups and provide a leadership role. When the SNC was established, it was structured so that each Group would become a small autonomous unit and as an organisation it would have 'as few rules as possible to enable Congress Groups through Scotland as much freedom as possible.'[24] But a consequence of this was that SNC Groups often used their autonomy to fight their own personal battles rather than the SNC's. For example, in the Edinburgh Group where pacifists like Lamont were based, the anti-war campaign seemed to be fought more rigorously than the self-government campaign. Also, fighting between members only escalated as it was not censored by Headquarters. A lack of Headquarters involvement and the insufficient direction it gave to the Groups was noted by Ramsay, who complained that:

> Here we suffer also from not having any kind of centre, so that a "public" or semi-public meeting (even if not much attended by outsiders!) is all we have and that once a month, which does not keep members very closely in touch with one another, yet seems to be all that is possible, and certainly entails a lot of work I am sure on the secretary.[25]

By not creating a strong centre and by failing to provide adequate leadership and guidance to its individual Groups, the SNC simply became a body of warring units which all too often pursued their own ends. The SNC's lack of members, support and general direction consequently posed minimum threat to the SNP.

Extra-Parliamentary Campaigns - The Stone of Destiny and EIIR Title

Despite the poor performance of nationalist bodies like the SNP and the SNC, the early fifties was actually a vibrant time for Scottish nationalism. The period witnessed a string of non-conventional campaigns undertaken by Scottish nationalists that kept the issue alive and burning in the national press. The signing of the Covenant, for example, had aroused Scottish national sentiment and the gathering of the Scottish National Assemblies had awakened press interest. Another event that stirred nationalism back to life in this era was the return of the Stone of Destiny to Scotland.

The Stone incident occurred on Christmas Day 1950, when four young nationalist students, led by Ian Hamilton, retrieved the Stone of Destiny from Westminster Abbey. The relic is thought to be the ancient Coronation Stone of Scotland's monarchs which had been taken from Scotland in 1296 by England's 'Hammer of the Scots', Edward I. When the discovery was made that it had been 'retrieved' by nationalists from Westminster Abbey, it became an international story overnight. Most of the Scottish press and public reacted with light-hearted humour at the prank nature of the incident and the embarrassment which it brought upon the authorities. There was joy amongst the nationalist community that the Stone was returning to Scotland, albeit illegally, after more than a 650-year absence. Those who had taken the Stone from Westminster became instant heroes amongst nationalists and were admired by the Scottish population at large. The Stone had after all been stolen from Scotland in the first place, so for most Scots, what was sauce for the goose was sauce for the gander. For the English press and public though, things were somewhat different as they looked upon the incident as nothing more than the theft of a national treasure. The Stone eventually turned up at Arbroath Abbey draped in the Saltire, more than three months after it was snatched. Within minutes of its arrival at Arbroath, it was in the custody of the local police and was then promptly sent southbound to take up its position once again underneath the Coronation Chair at Westminster Abbey.[26]

Unlike other nationalist organisations, the SNP failed to capitalise on the event. In its drive for respectability, the SNP was reluctant to praise the four nationalists who had taken the Stone for fear of being seen to glorify illegal acts.[27] But other nationalist organisations were quick to cash in on the event and praise the efforts of the young raiders who had returned Scotland's ancient relic. The SNC offered appreciation and support for their heroic efforts; such antics were a text book example of the non-violent moves it preached. The Scottish Patriots also spoke warmly of those responsible for taking the Stone whom it believed had done their country a proud service, while the Scottish Convention's leader, John MacCormick, had actually been in on the raid. He had known in advance of the plot, had contact with the raiders involved and had even found 'safe-houses' in which to keep the Stone hidden.[28] But for the SNP, little was said of those who had taken the Stone. Arthur Donaldson wrote a small light-hearted story for January's edition of the *Scots Independent* relating to the publicity of the affair, but little else surfaced on the incident from the SNP.[29] Only after prodding from its members, and gauging that the mood of the Scottish public was favourable to the individuals who had 'lifted' the Stone, did the SNP relent and formally praise the nationalists involved. In a press statement released in March, more than two months after the event, the SNP blamed the authorities for its removal and called for its retention in Scotland:

> There can now be no doubt that the public return of the Scottish Stone of Destiny to Scotland would be welcomed by the people as a whole. The persistent ignoring constitutionally for the return of the Stone has laid the responsibility for the manner of its recent removal from Westminster upon those who have held it in London. It is suggested that the Government should now facilitate the public return of the Stone to Scotland.[30]

The SNP's statement echoed the popular mood of Scots who wanted to see a formal return of the Stone to Scotland and no charges brought against the individuals who had taken it from Westminster. If anything, they should be praised. The SNP had finally realised that the Stone event was favourable to nationalism and realised the benefits to be gleaned from capitalising upon the affair. But the SNP's statement was too little too late as the Convention and other nationalist organisations had already become the mouthpiece of Scottish public opinion which had been in tune with popular mood from the start, not months after the event. Even the Church of Scotland's

Church and Nation Committee appeared more in keeping with nationalist sentiment when it recommended that the Stone be returned to Scotland and recognised those who had taken the Stone had done so for patriotic reasons rather than for personal gain.[31] As other nationalist organisations led the way and soaked up the support generated by the event, the SNP was simply left playing catch-up.

However, when the next major incident erupted over the issue of the Queen's title, the SNP was determined not to make the same mistake twice. The death of George VI in 1952, which led to the succession of Elizabeth, caused a furore in Scotland when 'Elizabeth II' was chosen for the monarch's new title. For the Scots, this was inaccurate as Scotland had never had an Elizabeth I. Some within the nationalist community also pointed out that as James VI of Scotland had become James I of England, it was unfair to impose a different numerical method on the Scots. Letters from all walks of life and from all political persuasions flooded the press-sheets, the BBC, the Government and even the Queen herself to protest against the new title that was being forced upon the Scots. In a letter sent to the BBC by ex-Provost W. D. Kerr, for instance, Kerr complained:

> What is the reason of this disregard of Scots' rights, in what is after all a question of simple arithmetic? With the Union of the Crowns, apart from the Union of Parliaments, the reckoning of monarchs began anew. James VI of the Scots became quite properly James I of the U.K. But the arrogance of the Sassenach demands a different method of calculation when it comes to English monarchs. That is the Sassenach idea of Justice, the English bulldog's motto:- "What we've got we'll hold."[32]

But when letters of complaint failed to achieve a reconsideration of the Queen's numeral, a string of campaigns spread over various parts of Scotland in protest. In Glasgow, for example, a rally of around 5,000 people met to protest against the new monarch's title.[33] On the streets of Aberdeen, posters were pinned up promising a '£2,000 reward for information leading to the identification of Elizabeth I of Scotland dead or alive';[34] And in Edinburgh, two elderly sisters found themselves in court because of their refusal to pay income tax in protest at the Queen's designation.[35] Covenant leaders, John MacCormick and Ian Robertson, went one step further and raised a court case of their own by petitioning the Court of Session against the Queen's titling.

MacCormick and Robertson's petition to the Lord Advocate argued that the Queen's numeral was incorrect in fact and was a breach of the first Article of the 1707 Treaty of Union.[36] Their petition also set out to break down the doctrines of Professor Albert Dicey's famous theory on constitutional law,[37] which claimed that parliamentary sovereignty is absolute, that laws passed by Parliament cannot be challenged in court, that no Act of Parliament is binding to successive Parliaments and that the 1707 Act of Union is no more significant in constitutional terms than any other Act passed by Parliament.[38] MacCormick and Robertson's case, however, was dismissed by Session court judges on various grounds. First, Lord Guthrie declared that the Court of Session had to apply the rule of law as set out in the new Royal Titles Act of 1953, which gave assent to the Queen to apply any style and title she saw fit which had been agreed by government representatives, and that, in keeping with Dicey, no Act of Parliament should be challengeable in any court.[39] Second, Lord Russell determined that as one of the first Acts of the new UK Parliament was to provide only one Privy Council whose powers were to be the same as those of the English Privy Council, the custom was for the Accession Council to proclaim new monarchs and the right of the Accession Council had never been questioned by the courts. Only Parliament, Lord Russell argued, should challenge it.[40] Finally, Lord Cooper ruled that there was 'no specific reference to the Royal style in Article One' of the Treaty of Union whereas Article Two referred to 'King William the Third', who by Scotland's standards should only have been William the Second. Although, on the positive side for the petitioners, Lord Cooper did agree that the notion of parliamentary sovereignty was an English doctrine which had no basis in Scottish constitutional law. [41] On various counts then MacCormick and Hamilton's petition failed. But despite failing to convince the court of its line of argument, except Lord Cooper's determination on parliamentary sovereignty, it did strike a chord with many ordinary members of the Scottish public who claimed a moral victory.

The Scottish Republican Army?

As the new Queen's title penetrated the mainstream and confronted Scots increasingly through areas such as merchandise and logos, the protests took on a more sinister nature. At the end of 1952, the first pillar box in Edinburgh to bear the EIIR cipher came under attack. Only a day after it had been erected, it was vandalised by tar which the perpetrators used to cover over the offending EIIR sign. The following week, a letter bomb was found inside addressed to the Postmaster General, followed by more vandalism a few weeks later when the EIIR sign was smeared with paint. When the authorities cleaned the paint away to reveal a pristine EIIR sign once again, a stick of gelignite was then placed inside the box in an effort to permanently destroy it and its sign, though it failed to detonate. Despite the concern of local residents, many of whom naturally stayed clear of the box, and the fear of postal workers who actually had to collect mail from it, the authorities refused to yield and remove the sign. Predictably the pillar box was attacked again a few weeks later, this time with a hammer which damaged its cipher and casting. Still the authorities remained resolute. The box was simply dug out, repaired and replaced on its concrete base. The perpetrators retaliated the same day by targeting the box with another stick of gelignite, only this time it did detonate and blew it up leaving it beyond repair. The authorities relented and replaced the pillar box with another without the offending cipher.[42] The terrorists had won the day.

The SNP responded quickly to the situation, afraid of not maximising the publicity from the affair as had happened over the Stone of Destiny. It condemned the new Queen's title and blamed the authorities for forcing the symbol upon Scotland. In an effort to distance itself from violence, the Party also condemned the use of violent actions in pursuit of nationalist aspirations and made a statement to this effect, but it let itself down by seeming to blame the Government for the situation and not those actually responsible for acts of violence. In a statement published in the Scotsman, McIntyre declared:

> It is of greatest importance that no element of terrorism enters into the Scottish Movement, but, unless the Government gives due weight to the representations of responsible people, we are powerless to prevent the actions of those who feel frustrated by the present implacable hostility of the Government towards Scottish sentiment.
> The National Party have never approved of violent methods. I hope, however, that the Government will not be so childish as to return this symbol to which so many people take exception.
> The present Unionist Government had encouraged the people of Scotland during the election to suppose that remote control from London would be eased. Those pledges have been broken. That kind of thing could not be done without consequences which nobody desired.[43]

McIntyre's condemnation of the Government rather than the individuals responsible did little to clean up the name of nationalism which was becoming increasingly associated with acts of violence during this time. By not wholeheartedly condemning individuals taking part in criminal acts but criticising the actions of the Government instead, the SNP came across as rather sympathetic towards those responsible for illegal acts.

During the pillar box affair, reports began to appear in the press of a so-called Scottish Republican Army taking hold in Scotland that was behind the pillar box bombing and other attacks. In fact, the pillar box attacks were just part of a string of violent attacks carried out in the name of Scottish nationalism at the time. In a bold move, one nationalist blackened his face in disguise and broke into the barracks of the Royal Scots battalion where he vandalised a notice board bearing the EIIR symbol.[44] Shops selling EIIR merchandise also became targets. In one instance, James Martin, who was Secretary of the St Andrews Branch of the SNP, was charged and convicted of threatening a painter and decorator for exhibiting EIIR window displays in his shop. His younger brother, also an SNP member, was subsequently convicted of breaking the same shopkeeper's window, his alleged justification was: '[it was] the only way to accomplish the legitimate aims of my party.'[45] Other reported incidents included young extreme nationalists raiding ammunition dumps, which had been scattered over Scotland in the wake of the war, and arming themselves to the hilt for the Scottish nationalist cause. One nationalist was sentenced to six months imprisonment following the theft of rifles and ammunition from such a dump in Johnstone.[46] Unsurprisingly, the Irish connection also surfaced with allegations arising of weaponry being smuggled by the IRA to arm extreme supporters of the Scottish national movement. The *Sunday Pictorial* also wrote of an alleged joint plot between the IRA and SRA to attack power stations in the North of England and knock out pylons linking the Scottish and English grids, which, according to the *Pictorial*, was foiled by undercover Orangemen.[47]

Some extremists had success from their activities. Many shops became wary of stocking EIIR memorabilia for fear of attacks whereas merchandise bearing the 'EIR' sign increasingly appeared on sale; the latter proved a big hit with mainstream nationalists. Some shops which had refused to bow down to extremist threats were eventually forced to yield when their insurance companies became reluctant to cover them while they remained 'sitting ducks'. One Glasgow shop had to resort to taking down its EIIR plaques after being refused insurance cover following the threat of a possible attack.[48] As a result of the pillar box attack, EIIR signage on pillar boxes and postal vans were also dropped while the Postmaster General agreed to allow Scottish business firms to be supplied with GVIR franking machine dies instead of EIIR.[49] The extremists also achieved more mainstream press coverage than the SNP had ever mustered from legitimate constitutional methods and strategies. The lesson to learn, it seemed, was that terrorism worked.

Throughout 1953, accounts of the existence of a Scottish Republican Army were reported routinely in the Scottish press. This reached fever pitch at the end of the year when four Edinburgh nationalists went on trial accused of attempting to overthrow the Government. The 'Conspiracy Trial', as it became known, uncovered an alleged nationalist plot to bomb St Andrew's House, Scotland's seat of power, in a bid to topple the Government. The four young men accused were Owen Gillan, Robert Watt, Raymond Forbes and Malcolm MacAlister, who each faced two charges of possessing explosives with intent and conspiracy to overthrow the Government after unwittingly colluding with undercover agent, John Cullen. Cullen had flushed them out at a nationalist rally after pretending to be an extremist when he shouted to the speaker - 'Constitutional means having failed to get Scotland self-government, it was high time that more extreme measures were taken.'[50] The four took the bait and began discussing terror activities with Cullen, resulting in the St Andrew's House plot being hatched. Cullen provided them with some of the weaponry they needed for the plot but when the time came to carry it out, the police pounced. The case was whipped into a frenzy and became sensationalised in the mainstream press as claims of bomb plots, agents provocateurs and a Scottish Republican Army ran wild. In court, an arsenal of weaponry, inflammable liquids and explosives were exhibited which only dramatised the case further and showed just how close St Andrew's House had come to destruction at the hands of nationalists, according to the prosecution.[51] The defence of the four men was that they had known all along that Cullen was an undercover officer and that they were playing him along in order to expose police methods and that they also sought to bring the nationalist cause into open court and into the wider public domain. It did not wash with the jury, however, who found each of them guilty of possessing gelignite with 'intent to do violence'. Though on the much more serious charge of conspiring to overthrow the Government, the jury delivered a 'not guilty' verdict, perhaps as a show of reproach at the police methods used in the case which were heavily criticised, and which some nationalists argued amounted to entrapment. All four men received a 12-month sentence and instantly became martyrs amongst a large body of the nationalist community for sacrificing their freedom for the cause. Cullen, on the other hand, was vilified and faced a 500-strong mob hurling abuse at him when he left court surrounded by a ring of police, and then had to lie low for a long time afterwards.[52]

An important aspect of this case was that it gave credence to the idea that a Scottish Republican Army, modelled on the Irish version, actually existed in Scotland. The press reported cases of minor attacks on property and threats wielded against Scotland's 'enemies' by so-called members of the SRA long after the trial. A series of articles by Richard Haliburton, son of the Countess of Mayo, also appeared in *The People* in October 1954, in which Haliburton claimed to be a member of the Porch Club in Edinburgh, which he alleged was a front for the illegal activities of the SRA. In his week by week account, Haliburton produced a series of stories that named alleged SRA members and their illegal activities, such as alcohol bootlegging, gunrunning and bomb plots. He also claimed that the SRA had hundreds of members with cells operating throughout Scotland and that its Executive members received 'advanced training' in Ireland.[53] Some members of the Scottish National Congress had also taken to stamping bank notes with 'Join the SRA' as well as their more peaceful slogans, which only added to fears of the existence of a possible SRA.[54]

But for all the claims, it is highly unlikely that such an organisation actually existed. For a start, there is no evidence to support the contention that an organised movement of nationalists seeking an independent republican Scotland through terrorism was in operation, other than a few statements made by some young extreme individuals. Indeed, given that ammunition was so easy to come by in the 1950s in the wake of the Second World War, particularly with scarcely protected ammunition dumps littering the countryside, if such an organised group did exist then more attacks could have been expected. The notoriety of the SRA name was in fact largely the result of the press linking individual violent incidents of a nationalist nature and labelling them as suspected SRA activities in order to sensationalise them. As the name grew, so did the number of nationalist threats and attacks by individuals purporting to be members of the so-called SRA, who used the name to glorify their violent actions. But in terms of an organised band of members with an actual chain of command, no such organisation operated in fifties Scotland.

Real or imagined, the SRA's effect on the SNP was damaging as it tarnished the name of nationalism as a whole. Increasingly, members of the public began to associate alleged SRA activities with the SNP as those convicted of such attacks were often SNP members or members of other legitimate nationalist organisations. The SNP even began receiving letters from members of the public enquiring as to how they could join the SRA such was the association between them.[55] The authorities also became suspicious and police plants were placed in various SNP branches to monitor their activities. In one instance, Detective-Constable Malcolm Watson Thompson, who had given evidence at the Conspiracy Trial, was expelled from the SNP for 'conduct inimical to the interests of the National Party' on account that he was a police spy and had joined the Party under false pretences including using a false name.[56] In other cases, some employers were informed of the political persuasion of their employees who held SNP membership, which proved a real bone of contention as sackings sometimes followed. McIntyre responded to the State's unwelcome interest in the Party by writing to all Scottish MPs in which he accused the authorities of infiltrating the SNP by means of agents provocateurs and called for a public inquiry to look into police tactics surrounding the Conspiracy case.[57] His call for a public inquiry was promptly declined by the Secretary of State for Scotland who rejected any notion of agents provocateurs in the Conspiracy case.[58] Although feeling a sense of victimisation, the Party had done itself no favours by taking the corner of individuals associated with nationalist attacks all too often. Supporting these individuals only gave rise to suspicions in the first place that the SNP was linked to, or at least sympathetic towards, nationalist acts of violence or terrorism.

The SNP was certainly naïve at best when it came to the handling of suspected SRA incidents. Reaction to the EIIR pillar box case set the tone whereby the Party was quick to denounce the Government for causing misguided individuals to take drastic action, but the individuals themselves were not condemned with any degree of conviction. In the case of the Conspiracy Trial, the Party acted with incredible folly when it appeared to applaud the actions of the four young men who had plotted the attack. During the four's incarceration, for example, the Party circulated a petition calling for their early release while the Party Executive kept in regular contact with their families.[59] On their release, the Executive Committee of the Party also called on McIntyre and Gibson as Chairman and President to write to the four wishing them well and to enclose a memento and a small amount of money on behalf of the Party.[60] If that was not enough, the Party also helped make martyrs of them by contributing towards the cost of silver medals, inscribed with the famous Declaration of Arbroath passage 'For Liberty Alone', which were presented to the four at a dinner held in their honour following their release.[61] The SNP's poor judgement over this case simply compounded the perceived connection between nationalism and terrorism. With some of its own members directly involved in illegal acts and the Party's lack of condemnation, even adulation in the case of the Conspiracy Four, it is perhaps no surprise that the police did place some of its officers in the Party's midst to monitor its internal activities. In this way, the SNP only contributed to the dark cloud that hung over nationalism at the time.

SNP office-bearer, Muirhead, did little to shake off the Party's terrorist link either as his SNC organisation appeared to condone terror activities even more so than the SNP. The SNC refused wholeheartedly to condemn individuals wishing to take part in acts of violence in pursuit of nationalist aims and simply viewed their actions as the Government's fault for its refusal to implement a Scottish parliament:

> As you know Congress does not encourage or advocate violence. On the other hand it is not for us to denounce those who do use violence in support of the demand for Scottish freedom. So long as the British Government fail to act justly to Scotland some people are likely to use violence but we should denounce the Government for refusing to give Scotland her freedom and in that way discourage violent methods.[62]

Moreover, the SNC frequently rallied to the cause of those charged or convicted of violence or other criminal activities in the name of nationalism. It had been more proactive in assisting the Conspiracy Four by way of providing financial aid and moral support to the four and their families than had the SNP or any other nationalist organisation. Oliver Brown, who was President of the SNC, was also given a helping hand by the SNC when he fought and lost a court case against the *Scottish Daily Mail* which had stated that he supported the bombing of the EIIR pillar box.[63] The publication arose following a humorous statement Brown had made to a journalist which was taken out of turn. Brown, as a pacifist, was offended and brought a damages action for £3,000.[64] A fund was soon established by the SNC for Brown who had been left with crippling debts after losing the case.

Muirhead also tainted the national movement via his Scottish Mutual Aid Committee which bailed out individuals charged with illegal activities of a nationalist nature. The Scottish Mutual Aid Committee was established by Muirhead with the purpose of providing assistance to Scottish nationalists or their dependents who faced financial difficulties due to their nationalist pursuits. It was an organisation that did not judge the actions of those requiring its support, rather only that they required financial support owing to their nationalist activities.[65] In most cases, the Committee would pay the fines of nationalists who had been charged with minor offences, like fly-posting nationalist propaganda or breach of the peace offences. In one instance, the Committee paid a fine of £10 on behalf of a nationalist who had been called before Guildhall Magistrates Court. He was convicted of insulting behaviour at the unveiling of a memorial plaque in honour of William Wallace, near the spot where Wallace was executed. He had scaled the platform and protested against the singing of the national anthem.[66] However, in other cases, the Committee came to the aid of individuals linked with more serious offences, such as when it paid the fines of two brothers who had threatened and damaged the property of a shopkeeper selling EIIR goods. For the SNP, Muirhead's association with these extremists with offers of help via the SNC and Scottish Mutual Aid Committee was damaging to the Party. By having a high profile individual such as Muirhead in the SNP, who sat on the National Council, who pumped financial aid into the Party's coffers and who had been its President in the past, but who also headed other organisations that supported the nationalist criminal, the SNP was inevitably tainted by the chain that linked it with Muirhead, his organisations, and nationalist criminality.

The 1951 General Election

Only 20 months after the SNP's poor performance at the 1950 General Election, the Party was confronted with more electoral campaigning when the Labour Government announced it was taking the country to the polls on 25 October 1951. The Labour Government had been coerced by King George VI into calling an early election due to its precarious position in the House of Commons where it held a majority of just five seats. With British troops fighting in Korea, the Cold War under way and post-war optimism flagging, the King had been eager to clear up the issue of government instability before he left for his tour of Australia and New Zealand at the beginning of 1952, but the timing was far from perfect for the SNP. The Party was still reeling from the disastrous results of the previous year's General Election which had eaten into its accounts and had deflated Party morale. The Party had also failed to field candidates at two by-elections following the General Election due to a lack of resources and will, and was ill-prepared for the uphill struggle of mounting a whole new campaign at record speed. It did not bode well for the SNP.

In defeatist mode, the Party mustered only two candidates for the Election, McIntyre for Perth and East Perthshire, and Calum Maclean for the Western Isles. It was the lowest number of candidates the SNP had fielded at a General Election since its inception, which sent out the signal that the Party had given up even before it had begun. In some ways it had as the Party knew that it had little hope of attracting ballots while the dominant issue of electing the next Labour or Tory government, which was too close to call and needed all the votes of their respective supporters, loomed over the electorate. One notable difference at this election was the SNP's choice of seats. McIntyre abandoned his traditional urban constituency of Motherwell and Wishaw, where he had fought and won the 1945 by-election and where he had contested the previous two General Elections, to stand in the more rural setting of Perthshire. McIntyre's vote at Motherwell and Wishaw had been on the wane since his by-election heyday as the constituency changed its rainbow colours of the pre-war period to the socialist shade of red. Perth on the other hand was a much safer bet as it was not an industrial heartland of Labour. Moreover, the SNP had a strong organisation already in place there, with Perth Branch boasting the Party's largest branch membership. The choice of Perth, which had a large rural base, was also consistent with the SNP's policies which sought to protect and promote Scotland's rural economy and rural life. The SNP's Western Isles candidate similarly signified the Party's shift from the industrial belt to the rural environment. However, with just two candidates in place, the Party failed to convince the electorate it was a serious political contender and it obtained a poor result of just 7,299 votes in total. McIntyre made up the lion's share with his tally of 6,479 votes, that for the Party was fairly decent as it amounted to almost 15 per cent of the vote and was enough at least to save McIntyre his deposit. Maclean received only a meagre 820 votes, a poor showing by anyone's standards, which worked out at less than five per cent of the vote, and, so needless-to-say, he lost his deposit.[67] The results of the election were not just bad news for the SNP, the Liberals had gone into meltdown with their negligible return of just six seats, and due to a quirk of the UK's First-Past-the-Post electoral system, Labour also lost the election despite winning the popular vote by 200,000 as the Unionists took 26 more seats. Labour had focused its campaign on its achievements since coming to power in 1945 with the successes of full employment and the welfare state splashed across its manifesto sheets. But it was not enough to stave off the opposition threat as the Unionists' promises of tackling spiralling prices, cutting taxes and building 300,000 new homes a year helped it win the Election.[68]

Although the contest was largely about Labour versus Unionist given the margin between them, the climate had actually been favourable towards nationalism with incidents like the Stone of Destiny and the Covenant stirring the nationalist consciousness, while the negative association from so-called Scottish Republican Army events had yet to surface. Given the favourable climate, the question arises why did the SNP not perform better at the Election than it did? The SNP's lack of preparedness to fight the sudden General Election was part of the reason, but, like previous elections, a lack of organisation was the key to its failure.

The post-mortem that followed the Party's 1950 election defeat identified organisation as a crucial area which needed to be tackled if the SNP's share of the vote at future elections was to improve. In Neil Mathieson's Report to the Party on the topic, Party organisation was found to be unsatisfactory and lacking 'cohesion and purpose at all levels.' In his Report, Mathieson prescribed a number of remedies including the need for the Organisation Committee to meet more often, at least once a month, and for it to offer the National Organiser more help and guidance. Mathieson also believed that parliamentary candidates should be adopted in every constituency immediately, even where branches could not afford to run a contest, because, according to Mathieson, having a candidate ready would give branches a sense of purpose while the candidate in turn would likely act as unpaid organiser for the Party. The workload between branch members also required a better split according to Mathieson's Report, which promoted the idea that certain members should concentrate on certain duties in order for branches to become more efficient fighting machines. The Report also identified the need for the Party Executive to become more pro-active and involved in energising flagging branches. Finally, it proposed that branches should be encouraged to contest all local elections.[69] Mathieson hoped that adopting his suggestions would provide a springboard from which the Party could leap and grow. But far from following his advice, the Party chose to restrict organisation even further by disposing of the services of the National Organiser the following year in order to make savings with the result of harming its electoral contests even more.[70] The SNP blamed its poor financial position for the situation, which after two General Elections in quick succession had understandably placed the Party under tremendous strain. But by choosing to cut back on organisation over other areas demonstrated that the Party had not grasped the seriousness of its poor organisation nor the dire effect it had on electoral contests. The Party had simply failed to learn its lesson from previous contests.

The Party also failed to improve organisation within its own Headquarters after an internal audit uncovered its administration system to be wholly inadequate and in need of immediate attention. The audit revealed that the filing system was made up of four main parts headed Headquarter Membership, the Scots Independent, the Party Newsletter, and Donations, but each section was found to be illogical and flawed. Membership, which was riddled with duplications, misfiling, and inconsistencies, was the worst of all, as noted by the audit:

> The method of enrolling names was to list in the card index all members joining at headquarters, until recently with no note indicating whether they had been directed to any branch or not. No reminders were sent out in the vast majority of cases, and there is no easy way of ensuring that they had joined branches; the very great majority of members joining the party seem to have been lost track of through the party's own fault; the files no longer correspond to reality, and the majority of names on them are of lapsed members.[71]

Such disorganisation and maladministration did nothing to retain members who were simply forgotten about once they had joined. For those members who donated to Headquarters' worthy causes, some of their donations were not even noted by the Party, let alone acknowledged. This could only have discouraged generous donors from digging deeper into their pockets and giving to Headquarters' funds in future. For those who subscribed to the *Scots Independent*, some were sent two copies or more due to duplication, while others were sent reminders for overdue subscriptions yet still received copies of the journal. A complete overhaul of the filing system was required but such a suggestion was swiftly refused by Party leaders who opted for a quick patch-up job instead.[72] The Party's failure to tackle even the basic problem of its own internal organisation and filing procedures meant that it had little hope of achieving improvement or growth let alone winning elections.

The different results of the SNP's two candidates were also indicative of the importance of organisation. For McIntyre, the result was respectable which was due in large part to the efforts of the well-organised branch of Perth where members and activists were strong in number. Having a high profile candidate like McIntyre fighting the constituency also aided the efforts of local activists and spurred other members on to begin actively campaigning. But for Maclean, very little in the way of organisation existed in the Western Isles where there was no strong band of activists or members in place. The constituency had the added logistical problem of covering a large scattered area that required island-hopping to reach the electorate. Maclean was also a non-native of the constituency who had been drafted in at short notice to replace Donald Stewart after he withdrew his candidacy. Consequently, Maclean had only a week of canvassing time to visit the various islands and win over the hearts and minds of the islanders, a difficult task even with a robust organisation in place.[73]

The Party also continued to experience difficulty raising the revenue it required to build an effective organisation and conduct proper electoral contests. In the accounting year of 1951-1952, the National Treasurer reported that the SNP's lack of revenue had hindered the Party's functionality despite two bequests in that year boosting the Party's accounts.[74] The sorry state of the Party's accounts was partly caused by the accrual of debt resulting from the 1950 election campaign. With the Party's disastrous results in that poll, some members were also put off from contributing towards the Party's 1951 General Election Fighting Fund. The SNP's dire financial position also took its toll on the post of National Treasurer which was occupied by three people in 1951 alone, a sign in itself of the poor state of the Party's financial affairs. Alexander Aitken resigned from the post first in that year and was replaced by H. A. Barr before Arthur Donaldson eventually took on the role, which did nothing for consistency or financial strategy.[75] The *Scots Independent* was also still proving to be a prickly thorn in the SNP's balance sheet. Attempts to get fresh blood on board to contribute items to its pages had become increasingly difficult as the same old writers and their uninspiring articles filled its sheets. Much was also written by the Editor himself just in order to get the journal out on time.[76] With its lack of impact on home turf, the *Scots Independent* hardly surprisingly failed to grab the foreign market either. George MacGregor, the Party's Overseas Secretary who was tasked with the difficult job of promoting the Party abroad, blamed the paper for hampering his work as its lacklustre nature and amateurish configuration was no match for the foreign press.[77] With a lack of finance in place to produce quality journals or to build and improve organisation at all levels, the Party had scant hope of making any real mark at the polls. For the most part, its campaigns simply went unnoticed by a majority of Scottish voters at election time.

The Catto and Balfour Investigations

During the elections of 1950 and 1951, the Labour Government announced the setting up of a Committee of Inquiry to look into the possibility of producing financial and trading returns between Scotland and the rest of the UK. A Committee headed by Lord Catto was appointed on 4 July 1950, charged with the task of advising on the feasibility of separate returns for Scotland's revenue from government expenditure and on her balance of revenue and balance of payments. The Government had been spurred on by nationalist events such as the popular Covenant campaign and the Scottish National Assemblies and hoped that the establishment of such a committee would help turn the nationalist tide. To some extent it did as some Home Rulers believed the Committee was an important first step on the road to Home Rule because it could lead to financial data being compiled which could then be used for the promotion of a Home Rule Bill.[78] The SNP was sceptical though and viewed it as a diversionary tactic that side-stepped the real issue of self-government. It also feared information gathered by the Committee could be used to impede self-government if the 'subsidy-junkie' argument arose; that is to say that Scotland could not exist on its own and required England to financially prop it up.[79] In its submission to the Catto Committee, the Party warned that information uncovered by the Committee should be taken in the context of that resulting from Westminster policies and was in no way indicative of the effects that a Scottish parliament's policies would have had on Scotland.[80] It was a good get-out clause for the Party if the Committee's findings were not to its liking.

On 24 July 1952, the Committee published its long-awaited Report. It declared that separate returns for revenue from government expenditure and balance of revenues from general expenditure could be displayed separately for Scotland, but that no such separation could be made for imports and exports or for Scotland's balance of payments. The Committee argued that the main stumbling block to this lay with the fact that Scotland's economy was intrinsically integrated with that of the UK:

> We have found it possible to suggest methods by which a valid fiscal comparison can be made between Scotland and England and we have explained in detail the obstacles to the ascertainment of Scotland's share in the external trade of the United Kingdom and of Scotland's balance of payments. These obstacles all spring from the inherent difficulty of attempting to analyse the economies of two countries which under existing constitutional arrangements are component parts of one unified economic system and enjoy complete freedom of intercourse by rail, road, sea and air.[81]

The SNP strongly criticised the Report arguing that it only proposed tinkering around the edges of the current system of recording Scotland's fiscal data rather than recommending a complete overhaul which was required. As well as wasting an opportunity, the SNP also criticised the Report for, as it saw it, exaggerating the difficulties of separating some of Scotland's trade and balance of payments, which, the Report claimed, was due to the UK's highly centralised economy based in London. The SNP argued that Scotland should have been considered as an economic unit in its own right and that its economy should not have been viewed as interlocked with the UK economy for all time. The Party went on to argue that too many items fell under the heading of 'general' whereas in many instances items could be divided between Scotland and the rest of the UK, but were not.[82] It also complained that items of expenditure such as 'museums and galleries', which were mostly spent on English institutions, were placed under a 'general' heading. Whereas in other cases headings such as 'education', where Scotland's share of expenditure was proportionally higher, were split yet no account was taken of Scotland supplying the English workforce with thousands of highly educated personnel annually, proportionally higher than well-educated English personnel migrating north. For the SNP, it was a lose-lose situation for Scotland.[83]

Other Home Rulers criticised the Report. The Scottish Covenant Association, which had recently formed following the merger of the Scottish Convention and the National Covenant Committee, also took issue with the 'general' expenditure category. The Covenant Association's National Secretary and Economic Adviser, James Porteous, argued that, overwhelmingly, government offices were based in England with around 98 per cent of expenditure spent there.[84] For Lady Glen-Coats, now Chairwoman of the Scottish Liberal Party, it lived up to the low expectations she had of it which she described as a 'maybe aye or maybe no' sort of affair.[85] There was some hope for self-government supporters, however, when a new investigation that would look into Scotland's system of government and administrative affairs was announced soon after the Catto Report was published. The promise of a Royal Commission on

Scottish Affairs at least gave solace to some downtrodden Home Rulers.

The Royal Commission on Scottish Affairs snapped on the heels of the Catto Report with its announcement coming the day after Catto's publication. It fulfilled an earlier commitment by the Unionist Party which had pledged a Royal Commission in its 1949 *Scottish Control of Scottish Affairs* booklet, and which it reaffirmed during its campaign at the 1951 General Election.[86] Like the Labour Government's Catto Inquiry, the Unionists' pledge was also a response to nationalist activities such as the Covenant campaign and had the underlying purpose of stultifying nationalism. The hope was that establishing a Royal Commission on Scottish Affairs would help serve as a delaying tactic by allowing the Government to avoid taking action on the Home Rule question until the Commission had concluded. By that time, the Unionists hoped that the Home Rule issue would have died down. However, it should be recognised that a genuine view also existed amongst Unionists that something should be done to protect Scotland from the over-centralised economy which had been developed by the previous Labour administrations. The setting up of a Royal Commission thus had the dual purpose of offering Scotland the best hope of counteracting the 'ills' of nationalisation while keeping the 'nationalist beast' at bay.

The Government was careful not to make the terms of the Commission too wide so as to give credence to the idea of a separate Scottish parliament. Its remit restricted commissioners to consider only administrative reforms to Scotland's system of government which did not extend to legislative devolution. The Government argued that this was a matter which only Parliament or Cabinet could decide and was no task for an unelected body. However, it did give Home Rulers some voice by allowing evidence relating to wider parliamentary reforms to be permissible in the Commission's terms of reference. At the helm of the Royal Commission was the Earl of Balfour whose portfolio included the former positions of Chairman of the Divisional Coal Board for Scotland, Chairman of the Scottish Special Housing Association and Scottish Controller of the Ministry of Fuel and Power. Other Commission members included Duncan Fraser, former Lord Provost of Aberdeen; J. Spencer Muirhead, President of the Law Society of Scotland and Sir Thomas Gardiner, Permanent Secretary of Home Security and former Director-General of the Post Office. They were joined by a number of individuals from industry, such as Sir William Gavin, Chairman of Scottish Agricultural Industries; Sir Hugh Chance, Chairman of Chance Brothers Limited and Baillie F. H. N. Walker, Chairman of General Scottish Trust Limited and Manager of Scottish American Investment Company Limited. Only two women made the grade on to the 15-strong list of Commissioners: Mrs J. Campbell, Chairwoman for Scotland of the Women's Voluntary Services and Lady Agnes Dollan, the wife of the former Lord Provost of Glasgow, Sir Patrick Dollan.[87] One striking feature of the named list of Commissioners is that none of the members were open proponents of Home Rule whereas some had been antagonistic towards it and were linked to organisations that publicly opposed it. Balfour was also from largely English stock and had lived the archetypical English aristocratic life while most other Commissioners had at one time or another been educated in England.[88] It led many nationalists to conclude even before deliberations had begun that nothing radical would result from the Commission.

The SNP was certainly critical of the Balfour Commission from the outset, which it claimed was just another time-wasting tactic that dodged the issue of Home Rule. Though critical of its existence, the SNP still took the opportunity to be heard and presented both written and oral testimony to the Commission. In its written evidence, the Party presented Balfour with a 39-point memorandum which set out the need for constitutional reform. It asserted that the Treaty of Union had been trampled upon to the point that it was a 'legal fiction' and that the Houses of Parliament were just a continuation of the English pre-1707 system, which still practised pre-1707 English customs. It also claimed that the symbols of the realm represented England rather than the United Kingdom, and that the Government operated primarily as an English government for the benefit of England rather than for the benefit of the rest of its Kingdom. Another main thread of the SNP's testimony was the remoteness of government from Scotland. It stated that decisions taken about Scotland several hundreds of miles away in another nation's city only weakened the Scots attitude of responsibility and their ability to identify with government decisions, which in turn, the Party claimed, made government policies less effective. The SNP also complained that Scotland did not receive her fair share of government departmental expenditure. According to the SNP, an unfair proportion of government contracts and establishments went to England and only when there was no alterative were government tenders or establishments sought north of the border. For example, the British Tourist Board, the SNP complained, was funded by the public purse yet its activities concerned only England, whereas a Scottish Tourist Board had to be set up voluntarily in Scotland. For the SNP, this was simply double taxation on the Scots. The SNP equally criticised the Government's failure to deal adequately with the rural economy and emigration which affected Scotland proportionally more. In its submission, the SNP also scorned broadcasting, which, it claimed, was skewed in favour of English programming and called for the establishment of an independent broadcasting authority for Scotland.[89]

Expanding on its written evidence, the SNP met with Commissioners in April 1953 to provide oral testimony to the Commission. McIntyre, Gibson and Yeaman represented the Party and used the opportunity as an open forum to plug the Party's aims and policies. Predictably, the Party reiterated its demand for a free democratic Scottish parliament which it declared was absolutely vital if the Scottish nation was to continue to exist. It pointed out that Home Rule Bill after Home Rule Bill presented to the House of Commons had shown that a majority of Scottish parliamentarians were in favour of some form of self-government yet governments had consistently failed to act other than to provide broken electoral promises. McIntyre went on to declare that over 65 per cent of the Scottish population backed the demand for constitutional reform, while 25 per cent subscribed to the SNP's own particular brand of reform.[90] But when pressed by Commissioners for the Party's own membership figures, McIntyre declined to answer.[91] This could have been as much due to ignorance on McIntyre's part as any coyness to reveal low numbers given the deplorable state of administration at SNP HQ. Nevertheless, McIntyre's lack of candour failed to impress Balfour and his Commissioners or provide weight to the Party's testimony.

The Scottish National Congress reported to the Commission on a similar note by stating that Scotland should become fully self-governing and should only enter into sovereignty agreements as the Scottish people might decide. A main theme of the SNC's argument was that Scotland was rich in natural resources, like coal, iron, oil shale, agriculture, forestry, and hydro-electricity. The SNC believed that Scotland should use her natural reserves for her own material benefit to significantly improve her economic position rather than allowing the UK Treasury to make a return on them. The money accruing as a result, the SNC argued, could be used to provide Scotland's population with better housing, healthcare, and social standards. Another main tenet of the SNC's evidence was its anti-war stance. The SNC believed that Scotland's foreign policy should be modelled on Sweden and Switzerland whereby she should remain neutral in times of warfare. The SNC also believed that an independent Scotland should be self-supporting and non-reliant upon imports which would help her to remain neutral during imperial power struggles and future wars. Also, the SNC contended that Scotland was being 'swindled' out of hundreds of millions of pounds annually, largely through Scotland's contribution to the armed services. It used the example of government expenditure on aircraft in the UK, which it claimed amounted to £90 million in 1949, yet Scotland's government expenditure share of this was only £4 million, which was less than half her proportional share. The SNC did concede though that Scotland should take on her fair share of the British national debt on her transition to independence. However, it also believed that Scotland should be compensated for being dragged into wars that were of little benefit to her and for the hampering of her industries like sulphurous acid and the manufacture of the motor car. So by the SNC's reckoning, Scotland's share of the national debt was already paid whereas Westminster should be sending Scotland an IOU.[92]

The Scottish Covenant Association also called for a Scottish parliament in its submission to Balfour, but as expected, one with more moderate powers. It advanced a number of arguments for a parliament in Scotland in its memorandum which it later published under the name of *The Case for Scottish Devolution*.[93] It testified that Scotland was an effective national unit and that some Scottish institutions were already notable for the amount of autonomy they had. In terms of economics, it argued that an efficient Scottish government could reverse the situation of national income in Scotland being lower than that of England and that Scotland had already shown great fortitude in respect of her post-war economic recovery which she had achieved in spite of, rather than because of, her system of government. The Covenant Association also reiterated its view that Scotland should remain a partner of the United Kingdom and that no severance of Scottish MPs should take place from the House of Commons. Developing upon this view, it also called for reform of the House of Lords to include Scottish representation on a national basis. Although, interestingly enough on a more radical note, it did call for Berwick-upon-Tweed to be reunited with Scotland by way of transferring Berwick-upon-Tweed from the County of Northumberland to the County of Berwickshire.[94] It was a demand more befitting the SNP or SNC than would normally be associated with the more moderate Covenant Association. It was perhaps indicative of the fact that the Covenant Association was no longer the major player in Scottish nationalist politics that it had been and was more willing to adopt a radical position because it now had less broad appeal.

Other organisations giving evidence to the Commission called for more modest reforms to Scotland's system of government. The Convention of Royal Burghs, which represented 197 towns in Scotland, criticised the Scottish Grand Committee and other consultative and advisory committees that were used to administer Scotland. The Edinburgh and South of Scotland Chambers of Commerce spoke in similar vein and argued for greater devolved control. The South of Scotland Chamber of Commerce in particular asserted the need for greater devolved power and viewed devolution as an escape route for the Scottish economy in order to cast off its London-based shackles: 'Scotland's economy differs radically from that of the rest of Britain and suffers from past attempts to squeeze it into the same mould.'[95] The Association of Scientific Workers also agreed that more direct control by Scots of their own affairs was necessary to deal with distinctive Scottish problems. It argued that Scotland suffered as a result of UK policies that were based on UK averages whereas fundamentally different problems existed between Scotland and England. It viewed Westminster as too overburdened to deal adequately with Scotland's own particular set of problems.[96]

A large swathe of the business community, on the other hand, were content with the status quo and argued for uniformity between Scotland and the rest of the UK to help trade. The British Employers' Confederation, which was made up of around 60 employer groups, argued to this effect and viewed any divergence of Scotland from the UK as 'a retrograde step contrary to the best interests of industry as a whole.' According to the *Scots Independent*, the Confederation simply feared that a Scottish parliament would be more socialist than its Westminster counterpart and would likely introduce laws to protect workers and consumers where Westminster would not.[97]

After much deliberation, the Royal Commission eventually published its report in July 1954. It acknowledged that Scotland was a nation and that a problem did exist with the current administrative set-up between Scotland and England. It acknowledged the negative associations which many Scots had come to make of the Union because of this. But despite these acknowledgements and the evidence presented by various Home Rule groups, it made for grim reading for Home Rule supporters. Balfour and his Committee viewed the cause of the problem as resulting from the vast expansion in government centralisation based in London and by the economic differences occurring between Scotland and England with Scotland lagging behind England. The Commission believed that insensitivity on the part of English politicians played a factor in the resentment felt by many Scots, but it also believed that there was a general lack of knowledge of the existing devolved structures already in place which could be used to better effect in Scotland. The Commission refuted the suggestion that Westminster was overloaded and concluded that it had enough free capacity to deal effectively with Scottish Bills. The Balfour Report prescribed only limited change to Scotland's system of government by recommending some fairly minor administrative reforms. Nowhere in its provision did it allow for legislative reforms. In its list of recommendations, it advised that the administration of diseases of animals, highway matters and the appointment of Justices of the Peace in Scotland should all become the responsibility of the Secretary of State for Scotland. But it rejected other relatively moderate demands like the Scottish Standing Committee sitting in Edinburgh rather than London. The practicalities of such a move, the Commission argued, outweighed any potential gains. It also rejected the suggestion of establishing a Highland Development Authority. It argued that such a body would not improve administration in the Highlands and that the Minister of State was already tasked with the job of co-ordinating affairs in the Highlands. It also argued against any reshuffle of duties amongst Scotland's four departments. The Report did acknowledge that the Commission had received several requests for Home Rule but emphasised that these were in the minority with the majority of its submissions voicing opinion against a Scottish parliament.[98] In effect, Balfour prescribed more sensitivity towards the Scots which translated into very minor and limited tangible benefits. With little achieved after two long years of investigation, Home Rulers were, to say the least, riled by the Report.

The SNP was particularly incensed, not just by the lack of action to come out of the Report, but by its misrepresentation of the Party. The Report had claimed that the SNP desired self-government along the same lines as the Republic of Ireland. But McIntyre was quick to write and complain to Balfour that this was not the case and that in no instance had the Party desired self-government on a republican model, but that it did and would remain loyal to the Crown:

My Executive are very surprised to read in the Report of the Royal

Commission on Scottish Affairs of which you were Chairman that the Scottish National Party desires self-government on the same pattern as Eire. The Scottish National Party is not and never has been a republican body. The Party advocates self-government in Scotland under the Crown and within the Commonwealth and has always done so...

We regard this as a most serious mis-statement of fact which distorts before the public in an official publication expected to be accurate the views of many thousands of people.[99]

SNP officialdom was always keen to advertise its monarchist support, even though many members and some officials, like Muirhead, were republicans themselves. Most were prepared to suppress their republican leanings for the greater good of obtaining a Scottish parliament which was the number one priority, whereas the symbolic nature of the Crown was a minor affair in comparison. Republicanism was a fight for another day after the right to self-determination had been won. The SNP was also generally keen to steer clear of Irish comparisons with bloodshed of the Irish fight for self-government still in living memory and at a time of brewing troubles in Ulster, the Party preferred to use the Scandinavian and Swiss models of successful small European self-governing countries instead. The SNP also challenged the Report's contention that only a minority desired a Scottish parliament. The SNP pointed to episodes like the Covenant petition and the Kirriemuir and Scotstoun plebiscites as indicators of the overwhelming evidence of Home Rule support, rather than the business dominated self-interested organisations that gave evidence to Balfour.[100]

The SNC also cried foul of the Report, though its denunciation took on a more direct approach. It publicly burned a copy at the Tron Church at Glasgow Cross, the same spot where protesters had gathered in 1706 to condemn the Articles of the Treaty of Union.[101] The SNC not only criticised the lack of action suggested by the Report but it also found it to be disingenuous. For example, the Report suggested that English government departments should be more considerate when referring to Scotland and should classify her as a nation, not a province, but then fell into the same trap itself by suggesting that Scotland was simply a part of 'the country as a whole'.[102] The SNC also criticised the Commissioners themselves as some were associated with organisations that opposed Home Rule while none of them were known to be supportive of it, therefore, their appointment made the Royal Commission appear rigged even before it had begun.[103]

The Scottish Covenant Association joined in the condemnation of the Report but focused its argument on the limited scope of the Commission's terms. It described the Report's recommendations as 'wholly inadequate' and called for a national plebiscite to be carried out in order to move the Home Rule debate on. The

Covenant Association reiterated this point in a resolution it put before the Eighth National Assembly in October 1954 when it called for a national plebiscite to be undertaken and resolved to do this by way of petitioning Westminster.[104] However, similar means had been tried and tested by its predecessor in the past and had ultimately failed. By proposing a scheme comparable in nature, the Covenant Association seemed to lack good judgement, vision, or new ideas, although it did add to the weight of criticism already levelled against the Royal Commission and its Report.

Overall, the Royal Commission was a resounding disappointment to all shades of Home Rulers as it had taken so long to report then delivered so little. Even some non-nationalist organisations criticised the Report, like the Church of Scotland, whose executive body, the Church and Nation Committee of the General Assembly, likened it to a 'wee bit tinkering' that 'will not satisfy those who have caught the vision of Scotland.'[105] Like the Catto Report before, it had thrown a bone to hopeful Home Rulers, led them on and then let them down. Its remit to allow Home Rule evidence to be heard had lured some nationalists into a false sense of security of hoping that the Commission would make more of the evidence it received from various groups and individuals supportive of self-government. For other nationalists, particularly amongst the SNP, there was no such illusion. Balfour's two-year investigation simply enabled the Government to avoid confronting the debate while Balfour and his Commissioners were in deliberations. In this respect, it was merely a time-wasting exercise. Other nationalists, particularly those in the SNC, went a step further and viewed the Commission as an attempt to skew the evidence altogether by the appointment of an unfair selection of Commissioners not known for their Home Rule leanings. The business community, conversely, welcomed the Report with open arms as it did not threaten to restrict trade by allowing advances towards nationalism. On the contrary, its findings simply signalled business as usual. For the Unionist Party, the Royal Commission was a victory as it had achieved its underlying objective of delivering very little for the Home Rule camp while staving off nationalist agitation spawned from the Covenant. The setting up of the Royal Commission and its disappointing findings for nationalists also meant that the Unionist Party could take the moral high ground of claiming to listen to and to act upon nationalist concerns by means of establishing a Royal Commission, but without the drawback of actual delivery. It was a triumph for unionism.

SNP and Policy

While the Balfour deliberations were underway, the SNP put policy back on the agenda by issuing a supplementary statement to a special Conference on policy in the winter of 1952. The special Conference was an attempt by the Party to update and expand upon its basic principles and ideals which had been set out in its ground-breaking 1946 policy statement. It was also designed to tackle the day-to-day needs of the country, which, as the SNP saw them, centred around education, housing and fishing.

In its policy addendum, the Party complained that Scotland's education had become too anglicised and that Scottish history was suppressed in the classroom while Oxford and Cambridge were often looked upon as the finishing schools of Scottish education. On housing, the Party demanded the immediate suspension of all direct and indirect taxation by central government on housing developments as a means of tackling Scotland's slums and housing shortage. It reiterated the need to repopulate the Highlands and called for rural housing to be prioritised and for further rural industry and transport developments to take place to help achieve this. In terms of fishing, the Party's supplementary statement demanded that historical territorial water limits be enforced to keep out foreign trawlers and that this position be defended if need be in the International Court of Justice at the Hague, just as the Norwegian Government had done to protect its fishing industry. The Party's support for Scottish fishing would also help Scotland to be self-sufficient in respect of her food supply. Other areas were also picked out for special attention, like ownership of industry, which the SNP believed should not be in the hands of the few but in the hands of the many. To accomplish this, the Party proposed to encourage employee share ownership schemes and to make such schemes a protected right of the employee for organisations over a particular size. It hoped that such a policy would create a closer relationship between the worker, industry and the local community.[106]

The policy supplement reinforced the SNP's left-of-centre position which aimed at a redistribution of wealth and greater social harmony. It also cemented the SNP's aspirations for improvements to the rural economy and for an increase in the size of the rural population. This was an area of policy which the Party was increasingly taking an interest in, especially now that its electoral campaigns were shifting from urban to more rural constituencies. The Party also maintained its view that government intervention should not be overly applied but used when needed. For example, the SNP was not averse to nationalisation per se, but it did not seek it as a matter of principle and believed that it should only be used when the economic case was made for it.

As with previous policies, the Party's new statement concentrated on social and economic issues and avoided the cultural aspect. The SNP was well aware that socio-economic arguments must take precedence in its Home Rule bid if it was to be taken seriously by voters. Labouring the cultural side would simply be seen as retrograde and damaging to the cause. But the Party's lack of cultural emphasis left a void for some members who sought some romanticism amongst the hard facts and figures. Such a gap prompted the formation of the cultural group, the Young Scots National League, by a number of young SNP romantics. The League's brief included promoting the Gaelic language, supporting Scottish songs, hosting ceilidhs and co-operating with other Celts through study visits to other Celtic nations.[107] It played to the backward-looking and romantic notions that many voters had of Scottish nationalism at the time, but far from discouraging its activities the SNP recognised the benefits of the League and lent its support, dubbing it the youth arm of the Party.[108] The Party realised that the League offered its youth a cultural outlet whilst at the same time it also helped enrol new members as some apolitical young Scots became attracted to the League for its cultural appeal only to be politicised and graduate to full SNP status.[109] For SNP members who were too old to join the Young Scots National League, groups like the Saltire Society and Scottish Centre helped fill the cultural gap.

One notable difference of the SNP's new supplementary policy compared to its original 1946 statement was the reaction it evoked from party members. The Party's original statement had caused upset amongst some SNP members as the debate took place as to whether the Party should have a policy at all or simply exist as an 'interest-group' type party. The Party's Executive had been at odds over the issue as individuals such as Muirhead, and ex-leader Young, disagreed with the need to formulate any type of policy (see Chapter One). The announcement of the Party's new supplementary statement six years later caused no such debate and in fact attracted very little attention at all. This may have been because Party members had become used to having a party policy so being faced with proposals for a supplementary part was no big deal. Having an up-to-date statement was also surely an improvement on any outmoded version. Furthermore, with individuals like Young, who had opposed the introduction of a policy statement, no longer a member of the Party, and Muirhead, who was so wrapped up in his own SNC organisation to take that much notice of the SNP's activities, there was less likelihood of opposition arising to any new tag-on policy statement.

As the SNP became more aware of the importance of policy, its strategy became increasingly advanced and it began to focus on single issue initiatives. One such initiative was its 'Ten X Ten Plan' which was launched in 1954 and proposed significant investment in the country's transport system. The Party called for capital investment to be ploughed into Scotland's transport infrastructure in an effort to improve Scotland's economy which would promote a faster flow of goods, services and people. It argued for improvements to be made to rural and central networks because, it claimed, rural areas were 'wasting away' while the industrial belt was burdened with congestion. The Ten X Ten Plan simplistically proposed that an average of £10 million should be spent on transport annually in Scotland over a 10 year period. Such investment, the Party argued, would allow speedier works to be carried out on ventures like the Forth Road Bridge and the Clyde Tunnel and would secure the go-ahead of many more major projects. The Plan also called for planning cohesion between local authorities by proposing that development schemes be co-ordinated in order that work could take place in some areas while preliminary work got underway in other areas to spread out material and labour demands and avoid undue competition between districts. In terms of finance, the SNP argued that the Plan was affordable and feasible as it only amounted to a fraction of what Scots already paid out on road, car fuel and new vehicle purchase taxes.[110] But despite the Party's arguments, the Plan failed to capture the interest of SNP members let alone generate notice or influence from outside its ranks and, as a policy, it was soon dead. McIntyre blamed the Plan's failure on there being a lack of SNP officials and activists who were able to promote it as well as a general lack of direction given on how best to advance it.[111] But regardless of its failure, it was still a significant move for the SNP in terms of policy-making as it marked an important shift in the Party away from its usual reactionary policy announcements towards a more proactive planning and development stage.

The Party had also developed a more international feel to its policy with some policy announcements levelled at the international stage rather than confined to domestic issues. In June 1950, for instance, McIntyre sent a statement to the French Foreign Secretary, Robert Schuman, in which he expressed the SNP's support for the Schuman Plan while condemning the British Government's more insular approach:

> It cannot be taken that responsible Scottish opinion support the British Government in its policy of non-co-operation in Europe and insistence on absolute sovereignty. This latest manifestation of English National Socialism and Isolation is deplored. We look forward to the future co-operation of Scotland with other free countries of Europe.[112]

Later in the year, the Party also issued a statement on Korea in which it declared its support for the action taken by the United Nations Organisation in attempting to stop communist aggression.[113] These announcements, and similar ones that were geared towards the international field, displayed evidence that the Party was serious about a wide number of policy aspects, national and international, and exemplified that the Party was not the inward-looking organisation some of its critics made it out to be. By looking beyond its own borders and raising policy issues on an array of home and foreign matters, the SNP demonstrated that it was serious about policy-making and was no longer the single issue Party it had once been in the past, trumpeting self-government and nothing much else. Its policies also offered the electorate in Scotland an alternative to the political consensus that was emerging between the two main parties in British politics at the time. From having no official policy before 1946, the Party had come a long way in its policy affairs in just a few short years.

Conclusion

On the face of it, the SNP had made little progress between 1950 and 1954. It had reached the mid-fifties on a similar footing as it had entered the decade, with few supporters, members or financial resources to propel the Party forward. The Party also appeared as splintered as ever with the arrival of Muirhead's SNC which simply added to the number of Scottish nationalist groups. The SNP had also failed to tackle the problem of poor organisation within the Party which continued to hinder its performance at election time and lose it much needed members and support. Reports of so-called SRA activities in the press, and the SNP's response to them, only added a new dynamic to the Party's set of problems and its ability to fight the nationalist cause. However, the Party did make some progress in these years, particularly in the field of policy where it had developed and improved upon its 1946 policy statement. The introduction of its policy addendum in 1952 displayed evidence that it was serious about policy issues while its advancement in foreign policy and strategy of single issue initiatives equally enhanced its policy development. Producing memoranda for the Catto and Balfour investigations also helped develop the Party's policy skills by forcing it to focus on key policy issues. Furthermore, despite the difficulties arising from alleged SRA activities, incidents like the taking of the Stone of Destiny and the EIIR title controversy revealed that a groundswell of potential nationalist support did exist in Scotland which, under the right conditions, could be captured by the Party. The SNP was also freed in this era from several hard-line dissenters who now called the SNC their party home which enabled the SNP to get on with the job of promoting its aims and policies rather than battling against its members. In this light, the SNP experienced some small but significant improvements in the 1950-54 era which were important in shaping its future course. But the period also remained one of stagnation and inactivity for the Party in terms of its supporters, membership and electoral performance. It clearly had a long way to go.

4

The Age of Unionism - 1955-59

The General Election of 1955 and the Rise of Unionism

The General Election of 1955 spelled more disaster for the SNP in the electoral arena when only two candidates were put forward to fight the Party's cause. McIntyre was picked for Perth and East Perthshire again, while James Halliday was chosen to fight Stirling and Falkirk Burghs. Although McIntyre - who by now was well established in the constituency - was able to increase his share of the vote to 9,227 votes which was 22.8 per cent and achieved second position knocking the Labour candidate into third place, Halliday's result was less than impressive with just 2,885 votes gained which worked out at only 6.7 per cent.[1] Like the 1951 General Election, the Party's lack of candidates exemplified its inadequacy as an electoral force from the outset. As the cost of standing candidates largely fell to branches rather than Headquarters, most branches were simply unable to afford parliamentary contests in their constituencies. A flood of letters from various branches to the SNP's Election Committee highlighted this point as they expressed their inability to put up parliamentary candidates mainly due to a lack of finance, followed by other important issues like a lack of organisation, election agents, and grass root support in their areas.[2] Some branches only consisted of around 20 members and were simply too few in numbers to shoulder the financial burden. HQ's move to dispense with the services of its National Organiser two years prior to the Election as part of a cost-cutting exercise, despite the vital role of the post to electoral contests, did nothing either to help the Party's electoral chances. Even when HQ did offer the sum of £50 towards Stirling and Falkirk and Perth and East Perthshire Constituency Associations' electoral expenses,[3] it did so several months after the contests had been fought whereas receiving the sum would have proved far more useful during the actual campaigns. HQ for its part, though, could provide little in the way of practical help to branches given its own deplorable state. The small membership of the Party, which remained stagnant at around 1,300 members, brought in few dues or donations vital for the upkeep of HQ. According to a report produced by HQ just prior to the Election, only 49 branches were in existence with a combined total of just 1,315 members listed. This worked out at less than 27 members on average to a branch.[4] Even then this figure may have been inflated with some names still appearing on the membership roll whose membership had expired.[5] As well as being low on numbers, an anti-election element also existed within the Party and some of those who did give generously to Party funds did not wish their contributions to go towards electioneering. For example, one supporter left the Party £500 from her Estate just prior to the 1955 General Election on the condition that the sum would not be used for parliamentary elections.[6] This was good news for the National Treasurer but not for the Party's electoral performance. The Party's overall lack of membership and financial support impeded its ability to organise and campaign effectively and resulted in its meagre electoral return. However, though the Party was much to blame for its own electoral performance, external forces also account for its paltry result.

The political climate in Scotland during this decade had become increasingly receptive to the Unionist Party as unionism became the order of the day. This was demonstrated at the 1955 General Election when a large swathe of the Scottish electorate became convinced that the Unionist Party was the most apt to deliver for Scotland and gave it 50.1 per cent of its vote. It was an excellent result for the Unionist Party in Scotland, which was even higher than the UK average of 49.3 per cent, and helped retain the Party in Government. It was also the first and only time that the Unionist Party had gained an overall majority of Scottish votes at a General Election.[7] The result is even more remarkable when viewed in the context of the socio-economic set up in Scotland which was more conducive towards Labour voting. Given this conundrum and the Party's domination of Scottish politics in the fifties, it is important to explore why the Unionist Party was so successful in Scotland during this period.

One important factor was the Unionist Party's ability to play the Scottish card and appear the most Scottish of the British parties. This was done to great effect by the Unionist Party with its criticism of Labour's nationalisation programme which it dressed up as being anti-Scottish for transferring power away from the Scots and into the hands of Whitehall bureaucrats. The Unionists' policy of greater devolved administration on the other hand was presented as an antidote which would restore power back to Scotland. Its establishment of the Balfour Commission to look into Scottish affairs and its commitment to implement Balfour's administrative recommendations that would see the transferral of Animal Health, Justices of the Peace and some transport functions from London to Edinburgh played along to this tune.[8] The Unionist Party also wore tartan on its sleeve by flying the Saltire at election contests and its Scottish conferences and by using Scottish symbolism generally to promote its image as Scotland's Party. Speeches made by its leaders also echoed the Party's appeal to Scottish sentimentality and its desire to safeguard Scottish interests and traditions. For example, Churchill espoused that he 'should never adopt the view that Scotland should be forced into the serfdom of socialism as the result of a vote in the House of Commons.'[9] The Unionist Party's 1955 General Election manifesto, *United for Peace and Progress*, continued along the Scottish serenading line as a large dedicated section to Scottish affairs appeared in it. This included the Party's outline to promote Scottish industry and employment, agriculture and the Highlands, and to expand its building and infrastructure programmes in Scotland.[10]

Labour by comparison only made a fleeting reference to Scotland in its *Forward with Labour* manifesto, and even then clumped Scotland in together with Wales and Northern Ireland.[11] Even though for the Unionists trumpeting the Scottish card was simply a dress-making exercise to help win votes and the Party harboured no commitment to Scottish self-government, its proclamation of all things Scottish nevertheless ensured it was perceived as the most Scottish of the British parties and accordingly secured it the largest share of the Scottish vote.

Another factor accounting for Unionist success in the fifties was a general rise in prosperity which led Scots to conclude that the Union was delivering for Scotland and that the Unionist Party was the best vehicle to continue its delivery. When the Unionists were returned to power in 1951, it marked an end to austerity with the repeal of rationing which Labour had retained after the war. House building also began in earnest under Unionist rule as more building materials became available due to post-war recovery. 'Homes fit for heroes' had now become a reality for many Scots as the Unionists' house building programme ran ahead of target with some 38,000 new houses built in 1954 alone.[12] It was a world apart from Labour's programme of austerity which it had pursued in government largely out of necessity due to post-war shortages. The Unionists also cashed in on Labour policies such as the National Health Service and the expansion of the welfare state which Labour had driven through in its 1945-50 term of government. Such policies were a major triumph for Labour and remain a major achievement in the Party's history, but at the time the full benefits of these policies were not fully felt by the general population while taxation to service them was. The Unionists on the other hand were fortunate enough to be in power at a time when the bedding-in period of Labour's socio-economic programme had ended and the public began to fully realise its benefits. Soon the health of the nation was improving and there was a general rise in living standards in a relatively short period of time after the Unionist Party came to power. It was the Unionists that the public therefore associated with prosperity and looked to as the Party most capable of providing the goods while ignoring Labour as the driving force behind them. The Scottish public was also given the message loud and clear in the fifties that Scotland was doing rather well out of the Union with the success of policies like the welfare state and the Special Areas Act[13] which affected Scotland disproportionately more. The publication of the Catto Committee Report in 1952 reinforced this message with its claim that Scotland got more out of the British pot than she put in. For many Scots then, the view was that the Union worked well to Scotland's advantage and that the Unionist Party was the best medium in which to bring about its benefits.

As well as gaining on the back of Labour policies, the Unionists also gained from an increased sense of British identity felt in Scottish society during this period. With the advent of British planning and the nationalisation of Britain's key industries, a sense of British identity may have strengthened as more Scots became exposed to and used to the term 'British'. For example, the nationalisation of the rail industry in 1948 meant that the names of rail companies such as London, Midland and Scottish (LMS) and London and North Eastern Railway (LNER) were replaced with British Railways. In the gas industry, municipal names such as Glasgow Corporation and Edinburgh Corporation and private companies like Coatbridge Burgh Gas Company and East Linton Gas Light Company gave way to British Gas following its nationalisation, also in 1948. These changes increasingly exposed Scots to the term 'British' as industry names and logos bearing the word 'British' were now branded on everyday items such as tickets, bills and information materials, which may have instilled a stronger sense of British identity and Unionism amongst the Scottish people. The success of British-wide policies like the National Health Service and the expansion of the corporate economy, which brought tangible benefits to the everyday lives of Scots, also meant that Scots themselves looked more kindly towards the British State and were more inclined to identify with it. Association with the British State and British identity was also increased in the fifties with the Coronation of Queen Elizabeth II. Despite the numerical objection by some Scots, the vast majority did not blame the Queen herself and joined with other Britons in celebrating the new monarch's reign. The televising of the event for the first time only added to the sense of unity it evoked. The Empire, despite being on the wane, still remained a significant unifying force to a sense of 'Britishness' amongst Scots, particularly so as Scots had punched above their weight in building it. This growing sense of British identity and unity felt within Scottish society can be partly attributed to the Unionist Party's success as well as the nationalists' failure.

A final factor accounting for Unionist success in Scotland was a lack of adequate opposition able to counter the Unionist Party during this era. By the time the 1950s arrived, Labour had fulfilled most of its main policies such as the nationalisation of key industries and the introduction of free health care, and was left in the rather curious position of having little further to offer the electorate. In a way, the Labour Party had become a victim of its own success in terms of policy delivery and now lacked direction or new initiative. The British Labour leadership was also in discord during this period as charismatic left-winger, Nye Bevan, resigned as Labour Minister for Health in 1951 and was then almost expelled from the Party. The ageing Attlee, as Party leader, also had little appeal to a now consumer-driven society and left the House of Commons for the upper chamber of the Lords. The Liberals, as mentioned in the previous chapter, had gone into meltdown at the 1951 General Election and showed little sign of recovery in 1955 with just 110 seats contested. A lack of adequate opposition from the main British parties only helped facilitate the success of the Unionist Party in this period.

While the success of unionism rose, nationalism by contrast declined and slipped off the radar as incidents like the Scottish Covenant, the Scottish National Assemblies and the taking of the Stone of Destiny now appeared distant memories by the mid-fifties. What little publicity the nationalists did receive was also often negatively portrayed with the reporting of so-called Scottish Republican Army episodes and the depiction of nationalism's political masters pursuing isolationist policies that would leave Scotland on her own and worse off without the safety net of the Union. As long as the Union continued to deliver for Scotland and so long as Scots continued to perceive themselves as better off within it, nationalism was and would remain nothing more than a minor distraction to unionism. It was a bleak period for the SNP operating in an unfavourable external climate which afforded the Party few supporters or opportunities for growth. It was also in this climate that the SNP was confronted with its next major hurdle when the biggest threat to the Party since the split of 1942 began to erupt.

The Nationalist Party of Scotland

Around the time of the 1955 General Election, the SNP was faced with dissent amongst its ranks when a number of simmering issues within the Party finally reached boiling point. Tensions arose soon after James Glendinning had become editor of the *Scots Independent* in Autumn 1954 and had instigated a series of attacks against the Party's leadership. Glendinning did not like McIntyre's style of leadership which he saw as dull and uninspiring and believed that McIntyre had delivered little for the Party after almost a decade in the Chair. Glendinning also harboured anti-English feeling which was at odds with McIntyre's own view and contrary to the Party line. Highly critical of the Party leadership and the lack of progress the Party was making, Glendinning joined forces with Sam Shields, H. A. Barr, Donald Stewart (not the SNP's future President) and Violet Sinclair in drafting and circulating a statement to the Party's 1955 Annual Conference which accused the current leadership of inefficiency, maladministration and dirty tactics. On the first charge, the rebel five alleged that the Party's Headquarters had been allowed to descend into 'administrative chaos' and that its closed door and secretive approach did not allow members to freely investigate the Party's state of affairs. On the second charge, the rebels accused the Party leadership of the more serious allegation of gerrymandering by allowing 11 new branches to be created to ensure certain office-bearers stayed in office. The rebels claimed that Perth Branch, which was the constituency of McIntyre, had been divided into nine separate wards just prior to the Annual Conference. They also claimed that both Aberdeen South and Kelvin Groups had received branch recognition only a month before the 1955 Conference, and contrary to constitutional rules, they had been allowed voting rights at the Conference. For the rebels, the reason for this was simple - 'to ensure the re-election of certain office-bearers.' On the final charge, the rebels accused some Party officials of undertaking smear campaigns in an effort to throw off any threat or opposition to their leadership.[14] The statement did not mention any individual names but it was clear to all and sundry at the Conference that McIntyre, who had been a vocal opponent of Glendinning's antics and had hampered his editorial control of the *Scots Independent* on many occasions, was implicated in the reference. Glendinning and Sam Shields also made a play for Party leadership at the Conference; Glendinning as a contender to McIntyre for the Chair and Shields as a challenger to Tom Gibson for the Presidency. Both did so in an effort to revitalise the Party with fresh blood and to steer it in the direction they wanted the Party to go. But their efforts were in vain as McIntyre was returned to the Chair and Tom Gibson to the Presidency while most of the old leadership retained their posts too.

Days after the Conference, Glendinning was sacked from his editorial position by the Board of the *Scots Independent* for what it claimed was his unsatisfactory standard of work at the Party journal.[15] In reality, Glendinning's antics at the Conference and his unsavoury attacks on the Party leadership had far more to do with his sacking, but firing an incompetent editor was less controversial. The Board was by no means unanimous in its dismissal of Glendinning as Muirhead, Wilkie and Barr all dissented, splitting the Board's decision in half.[16] Muirhead had long disagreed with the SNP leadership over tactics and had a history of refusing to take action against controversial figures within the Party. Wilkie shared a similar stance and had himself rebelled against the Party and was expelled in 1948. He had only been allowed to rejoin after a 1954 Annual Conference ruling accepted his assurances that he would conform to party rules – a decision the Party would later regret.[17] As for Barr, he was of a similar mind to Glendinning on certain points of view and had indeed been one of the five rebels who had signed the 1955 Conference circular which was highly critical of the Executive. Unfortunately for Glendinning, however, it was McIntyre who was Chair of the Board and he used his casting vote to ensure Glendinning's departure from the journal. But the ramifications soon came back to haunt McIntyre when Glendinning resurfaced a couple of weeks later as leader of a new faction named the 55 Group.

The 55 Group emerged as a protest group operating within the Party against what it saw as the incompetent and dictatorial leadership of the SNP. Founded by Glendinning, Douglas Henderson and Donald Munro, the new Group saw its role as something of an information organ to report to SNP members the activities of the Party at the national level in the hope of rousing a change in leadership and direction. It also provided an outlet for the racist views of its members, many of whom harboured strong anti-English sentiment and used the Group to express their Anglophobic views and even urge violence. From the outset, the Group made claims of controlling and undemocratic behaviour by some Party leaders. In its first newssheet, it accused several office-bearers of conducting a secret meeting at the home of Party Vice-Chairman, M. B. Shaw, at which it alleged they analysed Annual Conference documents including ballots to ascertain who had opposed them.[18] In its third edition, the Group also accused office-bearers of using 'dictatorial methods' in order to 'stifle free discussion or criticism of any kind' and even referred to some leaders (without naming anyone directly) as 'a small clique of petty Hitlers striving desperately to hang on to their positions by crushing all opposition.'[19] The Group also alleged tyrannical conduct at a National Council meeting which took place in June, at which McIntyre had raised doubts over Glendinning's right to be present and Shaw had motioned (unsuccessfully) to suspend the five rebels who had circulated their statement at the 1955 Annual Conference.[20] The Group cried foul again when McIntyre, George Leask and Murdo Young gate-crashed a private meeting in Stirling between local SNP nationalists and some 55 Group members. At the meeting, discussions took place on the different methods advocated by both camps and it was accepted by all attendees that the differences in the Party were about method rather than policy. But when the Chairman of Stirling Branch, James Ellis, sought for an understanding to be reached, Glendinning quickly accepted while McIntyre did not.[21] For the 55 Group, it was just another example of the despotic actions of McIntyre and other SNP office-bearers in their bid to retain power at all costs.

To a certain extent, McIntyre had himself to blame for the emergence of the Group and its attacks on him because up to a point he was a controlling figure as Party leader. For example, he prevented James Glendinning from opening some mail that was addressed to him in his capacity as editor of the *Scots Independent*. As Chair of the Board, McIntyre also denied Glendinning a large measure of freedom in which to edit the Party periodical, a scenario which triggered tensions between both men in the first place.[22] As mentioned above, he had also arrived uninvited at a private meeting in Stirling where Glendinning and other 55 Group members were present. As a leader, McIntyre also lacked charisma and good oratory skills and had a reputation for doggedness. However, it would be unfair to level any significant degree of blame at McIntyre's door, for though he acted in a controlling way in some circumstances and was no match for MacCormick's charisma or oratory skills, his tenacity was what the Party required in keeping it focussed on the long road ahead as gimmicks and quick fixes had been shown to fail in the past. As Chairman, McIntyre also had the responsibility of overseeing the Party and had a duty to tackle issues arising and promote unity and harmony; if anything, he could be accused of neglecting his duties by giving Glendinning too much rein to undermine the Executive. McIntyre also endured much criticism without reacting to it. Indeed, the fact that Glendinning and others within the 55 Group were still able to operate within the Party and were not suspended or expelled is evidence in itself of McIntyre's and other office-bearers' tolerant leadership approach, the antithesis of being dictatorial.

The 55 Group was not born solely out of frustration at the Party's leadership in any case, it was also a response to the SNP's poor electoral showing. The Group was made up of mostly younger members of the Party who had become dissatisfied with its sluggish performance and its inability to contest more than a couple of candidates at a General Election. Most lacked the patience of older SNP veterans who tended to take a long-term approach and knuckled down to the prospects of a lengthy struggle, unlike members of the new Group who were spurred into forming during the Party's 1955 electoral campaign. The Group looked upon the 1955 General Election as a missed opportunity by the Party to capture a larger share of Labour's declining vote which it believed could have been achieved by contesting more seats and by adopting a more radical line. The Group also complained that, after two decades of electioneering, the SNP was gaining fewer votes now than it had in the 1930s when the Party was first formed.[23] For the Group, this record of the SNP's retrograde performance was an indictment of its management and strategy style and was a powerful motivator in its own efforts to bring about a change at the top to turn the Party's performance around. However, what it failed to mention or take into account was the completely different external climate the Party and its Executive were now operating in, one that was far less receptive to nationalism than it had been back in the 1930s.

As the 55 Group continued its vocal campaign against the Party Executive and stepped up its Anglophobic and violent expressions, the National Council was finally compelled to act. It realised that its attempts to ignore the Group in the hope that it would fade into oblivion had failed as the Group had only become more radical and had gained more members along the way. Accordingly, the National Council passed a motion by 31 votes to four in September 1955 which stressed that racial hatred and the incitement of violence were contrary to the policy of the SNP.[24] It would have wide-reaching effects for the Party. Less than a fortnight later, on 5 October, 55 Group co-founder, Douglas Henderson, was expelled by the National Executive for contravening the motion.[25] Henderson, a 23-year old student who was Secretary of Edinburgh Branch and Area Council Secretary for the Party, had been the most outspoken of all the 55 Group members in his taunts of racial hatred and violence, even more so than Glendinning. His expulsion triggered the resignation of dozens of Party members, many of whom were 55 Group members, who felt that the time was now right to leave the Party and start afresh outwith its confining rules and ineffective methods. In a statement by Violet Sinclair and Donald Stewart, they argued that 'a more virile policy is necessary if we are to retrieve our Scottish nationhood.'[26] The first wave of resignations came from Richard Strachan, David Smith, Hamish Fergusson, Andrew Currie, Nancy Christie and Archibald McPherson, most of whom held branch office-bearer positions.[27] They were soon joined by a host of others when 32 members of the Edinburgh Central Branch (which housed the largest number of 55 Group members) left en masse, followed by members of the other smaller Edinburgh branches of South, West, East and George Square. Individuals from Glasgow Scotstoun and Alva Branches also left the Party.[28] Soon after the first set of resignations, a meeting was convened by Glendinning and Henderson on the 30 October at which a packed audience of around 300 attended. The aim was to advertise and recruit members for a new political organisation to be known as the Nationalist Party of Scotland (NPS) that would replace the 55 Group.

At the meeting in Glasgow's Central Halls, Glendinning was announced as the NPS President, Alastair McCallum became Chairman while Henderson took on his usual role as Secretary. Despite McCallum holding the Chair, Glendinning and Henderson took the lead and spoke on the platform along similar lines to the 55 Group with chants of racial hatred but on a more heightened scale. Henderson was more verbal in his Anglophobic attacks which frequently implied violence:

> If there are any English here tonight, I say if they have any sense they will get out of Scotland now while the going is still good.
> It may not be so good in a few years' time. They should get out when they are still in one piece.
> It may be that if the English adopt the same tactics here as they have used in every one of their colonial territories, we too may be forced to use the methods that the nationalists in Cyprus have been forced to use today.[29]

The meeting was attended by many nationalists who held bigoted beliefs and responded well to Henderson and Glendinning's racist tones. When SNP National Secretary, John Smart, spoke out at the meeting against Henderson's Anglophobic speech, he was indeed heckled and jeered by the audience. It was apparent from this and the tone of the rest of the meeting that the new Party and its members were not concerned in the least with promoting a respectable image of nationalism which the SNP had been striving so hard to achieve, but were more concerned with the advancement of anti-English sentiment and Anglophobic ploys to regain Scotland's statehood. No longer impeded by the SNP's rules and directives, its members were now free to speak and act how they pleased no matter how unsavoury they came across.

The new Party wasted no time at all in showing the extent of its Anglophobia. At a follow-up meeting in Edinburgh a couple of weeks later, Glendinning, Henderson and McCallum all made speeches condemning the English who they saw as 'the enemy' and argued for England to be stopped in what they viewed as its subjugation of Scotland. As ever, Henderson was most forthright in his address when referring to the English in Scotland:

> It is not the hand of friendship we should show the English, but the fist.
> The rallying cry of the party must be 'The English must go!' If the

English stay in Scotland this party cannot answer for what happens to them. We can't answer for their property, limbs, or life. If they want to get out they should get out now.[30]

Glendinning and McCallum were also frank in their lectures. Glendinning warned the audience that the NPS was out to make trouble and that it would not utter 'nice little platitudes acceptable to the House of Commons.' Rather, it would speak to the English in language they understood, which, accordingly to Glendinning, was not the language of reason. McCallum similarly spoke of the Party's intention to smash opposition and to 'use every means' to achieve its goal.[31]

The NPS's written communication was even more explicit in its attacks on all things English, particularly the publication of its pamphlet *The English Are They Human?*. In it, the Party stated a series of instances where alleged human rights abuses had been carried out by English individuals to foreign nationals. In one example, it claimed that English assailants, or 'Limeys' as it phrased it, had carried out an attack on an African nationalist who was doused in paraffin then set ablaze. In another example, it blamed the English for the death of a 19-year-old Chinese girl in Malaya who was allegedly murdered then strapped to a plank outside a police station. The NPS also portrayed convicted IRA terrorists in a glorified light as 'prisoners-of-war' in its pamphlet. It alleged the mistreatment of three such individuals in Wormwood Scrubs who, it claimed, were forced to go on hunger strike to obtain the same treatment from the English authorities as 'murderers and embezzlers'. Not pulling any punches, it then went on to describe English society as 'rotten and putrid to the core... with sexual perverts and shameless adulterers in high places.'[32] In similar vein, the NPS's newssheet, *Advance*, kept up the attack and in one edition called on Scots to blame the English people themselves rather than their political masters for England's treatment of Scotland: 'Some Scots still think that the English people should not be blamed for what their government is doing to Scotland, Wales, Cyprus and other territories where the English rule still prevails. This way of thinking is entirely wrong.'[33]

The philosophy of the NPS was spelled out in somewhat tamer terms when it published its manifesto in September 1956. It stated that the nation state was the 'natural human community' in which only the rights of individuals could be secured, and condemned imperialism as 'soulless and immoral'. It warned Scots that the single biggest threat to their existence was England's efforts to assimilate their country into its own, which, it claimed, was intensifying as England's power in the world was declining and its focus of attention was shifting to the UK's shores. Accordingly, it saw its own role as defender of Scotland which it viewed could only be achieved through complete separation from the English State. Even if the will of the people did not dictate full Scottish independence, the NPS still believed its duty was to seek and institute it as its responsibility was to the Scottish nation and not to 'the whims of any particular generation.'[34] Yet there was a clear contradiction in this view as its own establishment had largely come about following allegations of the use of dictatorial methods in the SNP, yet it was quite prepared to impose a new constitutional system on the Scottish people whether they wanted it or not. In terms of strategy, the NPS viewed itself as something of a revolutionary force whose members would use active resistance by any means possible in the struggle for independence. It resolved to turn the tide of English settlement in Scotland, which, it claimed, was Anglicising the Scottish people and undermining their very culture and traditions.[35] It also encouraged Scottish patriots to perform their 'national service' to society by joining its ranks in fighting for their nation's freedom and it threatened 'unwavering resistance' to any form of English control.[36]

The kind of tactics the NPS actually pursued, however, were relatively low-key and did not live up to its fighting talk. It became involved in organising the innocuous Wallace Day event, for example, where nationalist pilgrims met annually at Elderslie to commemorate their national hero. It also focused on developing its own internal organisation in order to widen its message and attract more members (something the SNP would have been wise to emulate). It employed Donald Munro as full-time Organiser on 4 January 1956 and set up a fund from which to meet his salary. Muirhead, who was wealthy, had a strong record of donating to nationalist causes and did not always see eye to eye with the SNP, was pressed for a donation.[37] Another tactic it pursued was entry into local politics where it hoped to influence councils. It established a separate fund for this purpose and was able to put forward three of its members, Douglas Stafford, Ian Nicholson and Helen King, as municipal candidates in Edinburgh's 1956 local elections. A fourth member, Alistair McSwan, attempted to stand in Glasgow but was refused when his nomination paper was turned down by the Town Clerk Deputy.[38] A handful of pursuits undertaken by NPS members, however, were of a more subversive nature. In one incident, an army recruitment centre's window was smashed with a brick which had the slogan 'Throw the Limeys out' wrapped around it.[39] In another episode, three NPS members were charged with fly posting bills in Ayr town centre which protested at the use of so-called 'Limey Law' in cases involving Scots military personnel. The bills were posted in response to the trial of two Scottish soldiers in Ayr who were court-martialled under English law and were also used as a protest against the wider issue of English law used in courts-martial involving Scottish troops. Two of the three NPS members charged with the offence were defended by outspoken Party Secretary, Douglas Henderson, who was a law student at Edinburgh University. His defence seemed to do them little good, however, as both were fined £1 while the third accused who was not defended by him was admonished.[40] Illegal incidents carried out by NPS members were relatively rare, however, and minor in nature as members and leaders talked a better game than the actions they actually pursued.

The SNP's response to the NPS was firm and unequivocal. Immediately after its formation, John Smart released a number of statements to the press in his capacity as National Secretary in which he distanced the SNP from the new Party and condemned its racist outlook. In his first statement, Smart highlighted the ruling passed by the SNP's National Council in September 1955 which prohibited members from partaking in racial hate propaganda or violence and officially disclosed Henderson's expulsion for flouting the rule. He confirmed that some members associated with Henderson had resigned, but on a positive spin he stressed that the SNP was glad to see the back of them and that it was better off without them:

> They now relieve the Scottish National Party of the burden of their presence and, as such, this is the more welcome, as it will consolidate the party in its advance, unhampered, to new strength on democratic lines, fighting by all rightful methods for the full freedom of the nations.
>
> This is their first real contribution to the well-being of the party.[41]

In another statement a week later, he accused the new faction of harming the wider self-government cause and declared that as the NPS was a political organisation no SNP member could also be a member of it; this was as much a warning shot to SNP members thinking about joining the new grouping as it was about dissociation from it.[42] Others within the SNP shared in the condemnation. In more hard-hitting language, the Glasgow Area Council of the SNP described members of the NPS as 'Teddy-boy rebels' and pledged its loyalty to the leadership of the SNP.[43] George Dott also denounced the new Party and labelled its members 'the Nappies' because their age group was almost exclusively below 30. Glendinning, whom Dott referred to as 'the Führer', was in his thirties and was the exception.[44] Internal memos were also passed from Smart to branches warning members against any involvement in the new faction and to refrain from any sort of propaganda that could bring the Party into disrepute. In his first letter to members warning them of the Council's racial hate ban, Smart also informed branches to ensure that only speakers who could be relied upon to present the Party's policy in a dignified light should be allowed to speak at public meetings. In instances where this did not occur, members were advised to contact HQ.[45] In another letter passed by Smart to all branches and groups, it described the policy of the NPS as fascism and then, in a psychological show of being over the split, focussed on the SNP's new campaign which aimed to stand 36 candidates at the next General Election.[46]

In other circulars and announcements, the SNP's tone remained emphatically against the new Party. In public and in private it was steadfast in its denunciation of the NPS and in its dissociation from it, but despite its robust approach, the SNP made the vital error of not responding soon enough to the new faction. When Glendinning first set up the 55 Group after his attempt for the SNP leadership had failed at the Annual Conference, the Executive of the SNP neither acknowledged or condemned it. Instead it viewed the Group as too small and insignificant to bother about, whereas taking action against its members would only grant it attention and status which it did not deserve. The SNP leadership naïvely thought that by ignoring the Group it would simply fade and disappear. Even after Henderson's expulsion in October, some Council members still held this view and worried that the Party's actions against the Group would simply glorify it. George Dott was one such member who took the view that ignoring the Group was the best policy and argued such in a letter to McIntyre: 'There is no substance in them and left to themselves they will fall to pieces.'[47] But for others in the Party, they had finally come to realise that their strategy of not acting was wrong, and in the six month period of inaction after the Group was formed, they had simply given it carte blanche in which to grow and fester within the SNP's midst. Tom Gibson expanded on this point in a memorandum which criticised the SNP for showing too much tolerance to members of nationalist factions, and not just 55 Group members:

> Our trouble has arisen from the fact that we have not kept aloof enough from them, and not otherwise. Any member of the National Party who is a member of one or more of these outside organisations, or any member of these outside organisations who desire also to become a member of the National Party, cannot believe in the policy of the National Party, and is therefore a disloyal member of the National Party, a trouble maker, and a weakness and a nuisance. What may I ask is the use of making members sign the following declaration: "I endorse the Aims of the Scottish National Party, agree to abide by its Rules", and at the same time allow them to remain members of other political organisations whose Aims, Policy, Direction, Constitution and Rules are all different from that of the National Party, and mostly conflict with them.[48]

By not acting against the Group when it first emerged, the SNP lost more members to it by allowing it to develop and gain strength. It was also a PR nightmare for the Party as the Group had developed amongst its membership, and no amount of distancing could change this fact.

The NPS's effect on the SNP was damaging in several ways. One obvious effect was that it reduced the SNP's already small membership when members left in droves to join with Glendinning and Henderson in the latest outfit. Over 100 left to form the new NPS, no small figure given that the SNP's total membership was only around 1,300 at best, and amounted to more than seven per cent of its total membership figure. To add to this, most resignations and expulsions also came from members in Edinburgh which was a part of the Central Belt already under-represented by the SNP. Members in Edinburgh who were not connected with the faction and wished to remain members of the SNP were also left with no branch when the SNP suspended all of its Edinburgh branches which were at the heart of Glendinning and Henderson's support base. This essentially meant that the SNP was wiped out in Scotland's Capital. Similarly, other areas suffered proportionately more, like Renfrew and Greenock in the West, where a higher percentage of members had been expelled or had opted to resign. Many of them in this area had been disgruntled by the SNP's decision not to co-operate with other nationalist bodies in organising the 1955 Wallace Day event at Elderslie in Renfrewshire which they viewed as an insult to Scotland's national hero on the 650th anniversary of his death.[49] Three of the five rebels who challenged the SNP leadership at the 1955 Annual Conference had been members of Renfrew Branch. As well as the number of members who left the SNP, the Party also suffered in terms of the loss of calibre in some of the members it lost to the NPS. The establishment of the NPS took talented individuals away from the SNP, like Henderson, who had real aptitude and leadership abilities which the SNP could scarcely do without. The SNP also lost a disproportionate percentage of its youth to the NPS due to the young age group of the new organisation along with their fresh appeal, enthusiasm, and energetic support.

The Anglophobic nature of the NPS was also damaging to the SNP as it sent out a harmful image of nationalism which was still reeling from association with alleged Scottish Republican Army plots. The arrival of a new nationalist organisation with its rhetoric to drive the English out of Scotland using all possible means and its production of literature such as the pamphlet *The English Are They Human?* blew any respectability earned by the national movement out of the water. It was also alleged that Special Branch was monitoring NPS activities which did nothing either to portray the national movement in a credible light.[50] The NPS's damaging image also rubbed off on the SNP more than any other nationalist organisation, not least because it had originated from the SNP, but also because of the similarity in names which frequently resulted in confusion. The SNP was often referred to as the National Party by the press, by the outside world and even by the Party itself. When the new faction chose the name 'Nationalist Party of Scotland', it too was regularly referred to as the National Party or the Nationalist Party resulting in obvious misunderstandings. To make matters worse, the SNP's forerunner, the National Party of Scotland, was almost identical in title to the Nationalist Party of Scotland causing even more confusion. To the uninformed eye, the SNP and NPS were simply one and the same. It was a major bone of contention for the SNP to be associated with, never mind known as, 'the NPS', and it feared mistaken identity issues could arise, such as funds and legacies going to the NPS which were intended for the SNP, or for supporters to join the NPS thinking they were actually joining the SNP. Such was its concern, the SNP took legal advice on the matter and looked into court proceedings to force the NPS to change its name although it abandoned this course of action when its legal counsel advised against it.[51] The Party was simply forced to live with the name association of the NPS and any harmful effects it had.

But despite the negative effects mentioned above, it is important to highlight that the NPS's overall impact was limited. For a start, its racist outlook meant that it appealed to very few people. The NPS had initially gained around 100 members from the SNP when it started up, but beyond this it failed to capture a wider audience. The NPS claimed to have attracted around 400 members, but this appears to be an inflated figure put out by its leadership to give the impression that it was a larger and more important organisation than it actually was. It falsely claimed to have taken members from the SNP on more than one occasion. In Glasgow, for example, it alleged to have taken Govan Branch from the SNP but no SNP Govan Branch actually existed at that time. It also claimed to have taken control of Scotstoun Branch but only five members of this Branch had resigned from the SNP.[52] NPS support was also localised around the Edinburgh area where SNP support had been weak anyway, so it was less damaging to the Party than if it had emerged in an area like Perth, the SNP's heartland. Furthermore, the SNP claimed that some former Edinburgh members had only joined the SNP to infiltrate it and bolster 55 Group support, and of all the Edinburgh branches that were suspended, only one had existed for more than a year prior to the NPS being formed.[53] In this circumstance, the effect on the SNP was less than if it had been SNP traditionalists leaving the Party to join the NPS. Soon after the split, the SNP also got to work in re-establishing the small number of branches which had been suspended. In Edinburgh East, for instance, a new Branch Secretary was appointed in November 1955 to help restore the Branch.[54] By quickly getting to work in rebuilding the areas affected by the NPS, the SNP was able to minimise its negative effects. NPS activities were also hampered when it came under attack for its extreme views. Its office based in Glasgow was broken into on several occasions over a short period of time, which disrupted NPS operations and limited the damage it wrought on the SNP.[55] On balance, the NPS did prove to be a headache for the national movement and for the SNP in particular with its language of racial hatred and intolerance which gave nationalism a bad name. But the NPS's small membership and limited support also reduced its harmful effect which meant that although it was damaging to the SNP and the wider nationalist community, its impact was not disastrous.

Halliday's 1956 Leadership Takeover – 'A Year of Consolidation'?

At the SNP's Annual Conference in May 1956, the Party was determined to make the year ahead much brighter than the disappointing one it had left behind. It began by projecting a fresher image of itself when it elected a new and younger leader as National Chairman, James Halliday. Halliday, a school teacher by profession, became the Party's youngest Chairman at the age of just 28 and seemed a breath of fresh air following McIntyre's nine-year tenure. Halliday had joined the SNP as a student and quickly rose through the ranks, becoming Convenor of the Election Committee before taking on the role as Chairman. He had also fought the Stirling and Falkirk Burgh constituency at the 1955 General Election as one of only two candidates fielded by the Party, the other being McIntyre. Halliday had many of the key leadership attributes necessary to make a good Party leader. He had excellent oratorical skills which he had proved during his student years at Glasgow University where he had obtained the prize for best speaker in Union Debates. He had also been joint Chairman of the successful Campaign Committee which won John MacCormick the Rectorial Election at Glasgow University in October 1950.[56] As Halliday took the Chair, McIntyre moved to the more symbolic role of President. It was a shift that suited all concerned. McIntyre had become increasingly unpopular amongst some ordinary members who had seen few tangible results under his leadership and plenty of internal discord. McIntyre himself wanted to stand down following the establishment of the 55 Group and the NPS and duly passed the torch to his younger colleague.[57] The timing also suited McIntyre as he had just fought and won the Stirling Municipal election in May 1956, which meant that his somewhat lighter duties as Party President would afford him more time to devote to his councillor activities where he could put the Party's case forward in the local political arena. Halliday was also given the rare opportunity to lead and shape the Party at a very young age and was able to bring to the table his own fresh style and direction. In his first year, he hoped to unite the Party by focussing its attention on primary Party concerns such as policy issues and new initiatives in what was to become a 'Year of Consolidation'.[58] With a brand new young leader in post, McIntyre elected to local government and no major internal wrangles taking place, things were already looking up for the Party.

Before long, the Party began to focus its attention outwardly on a range of current affair issues. One area it became involved in was the issue of shale oil, which the Party argued was in danger of terminal decline in Scotland due to the Government's taxation policy. The shale oil industry in Scotland employed around 3,000 people and was used in the manufacture of products such as motor spirit, paraffin wax and detergents. Increased tax levies imposed by the Government, however, were destroying the industry in Scotland while at the same time more money was being spent on imports, according to the SNP.[59] The Party also argued that the Government's oil policy favoured England over Scotland when it came to certain oil products. For example, in an article in the *Scots Independent*, Arthur Donaldson pointed out that there was higher consumption of diesel in Scotland proportionate to England and that a rise in taxation on this product would affect Scotland adversely more than England;

yet in England there was greater demand for fuel oil for industrial and heating purposes and a cut in supply in this product was not necessary north of the border.[60]
The Party surmised that if a Scottish government existed, it would have made different decisions to Westminster when it came to shale oil products as it would only
have had Scotland to take into account rather than the UK as a whole. It also argued
that a Scottish government would harness and promote the industry more effectively
than its Westminster counterpart.

The SNP also became involved in the topical issue of New Towns which were being
built around the periphery of Scotland's cities. New Towns were created in the post-
war period to alleviate overcrowding in Scotland's major cities and involved housing
people from largely crowded areas of the cities into new settlements on the outskirts.
The idea had been promoted by *The Clyde Valley Regional Plan* of 1946, which argued
for the establishment of such towns to provide 'a better distribution of the population
and of industry' and to relieve communication and transportation networks.[61] Glasgow was the most overcrowded of the four cities in Scotland but its problem was not
unique and New Towns were built across central Scotland. East Kilbride was the first
to be designated a New Town in Scotland in 1947, followed by Glenrothes in 1948,
Cumbernauld in 1955, Livingston in 1962 and Irvine in 1966. Despite their somewhat drab concrete appearance now, the development of New Towns proved popular at the time amongst many city dwellers who were finally afforded the opportunity
to move from their often cramped, damp tenement quarters into more spacious and
multiple-room accommodation in new houses and flats. New Towns also came with
their own town centres, amenities and industrial estates which provided residents
with everything they required right on their door steps. Having a clean spacious
new home with new facilities and job opportunities in a recently developed area led
to a significant rise in the standard of living of many New Town settlers almost
overnight. But despite the popularity of the developments and the significant rise in
living standards they afforded many Scots, the SNP objected to the Government's
overspill policy. For the SNP, creating new large urban areas close to cities failed to
tackle the problem of population density in the Central Belt and only served as a
short-term solution to the problem of overcrowding in Scotland's cities. In a statement it issued on the subject, the SNP advocated a policy of dispersing people to districts throughout Scotland, particularly to villages and towns such as in the Highlands
which were suffering population decline. The SNP argued that this could be facilitated by the relocation and decentralisation of businesses, government departments
and nationalised industries to different parts of Scotland. Such a policy, it argued,
'would bring new life, and new opportunities, to many towns threatened with decline; would offer city dwellers the chance to return to a loving community instead
of an expensive new dormitory, and would make the best use of existing centres.'[62]

While construction work got underway at Cumbernauld, the SNP also criticised the Government for its different approach towards Glasgow and London's overspill programmes. It argued that Glasgow Corporation had been unfairly forced to subsidise its overspill while London had been more generously treated and had not been burdened by the building costs of several of its New Towns. It also argued that many businesses would be forcibly displaced or would fold from a lack of trade in areas of Glasgow affected most by the overspill policy and requested a government inquiry to look into the affair.[63] However, the SNP failed to mention that business closures and displacements would happen anyway if its own favoured policy of dispersing people more evenly over Scotland had been implemented. The Government promptly declined its request in any case with the line that firms were already moving voluntarily and any problems which did surface would be dealt with as they arose. But this was simply maladministration on the Government's part, according to the SNP, which it believed should have been taking preventative measures to avert difficulties arising in the first place rather than dealing with them as they appeared. Such a course of action, or rather inaction, it argued, would result in a high number of industrial casualties from the overspill policy.[64] Given the SNP's objection to the overspill programme, it is ironic to note that the SNP benefited rather well from it in later years as a number of its future supporters came from New Town areas.

As well as its involvement in topical issues, the SNP also embarked upon new initiatives in Halliday's first year of leadership such as its 'Choose Scotland Campaign'. This campaign was launched in 1956 with the aim of enrolling new members and supporters into the Party to capitalise on the forthcoming 250th anniversary of the 1707 Treaty of Union. The main plank of the campaign was to advance the issue of Scotland versus 'North Britain' and to encourage Scots to choose Scotland by joining the SNP. The scheme involved canvassers going into the field and compiling a register of those prepared to declare themselves as supporters of the aims of the SNP. Those willing to sign up were asked to pay 1/- for the privilege as a 'demonstration of sincerity' and all fees collected by branches were split equally between branch and Headquarters while those collected by Headquarters were wholly retained by Headquarters.[65] Branches were also encouraged to arrange meetings, dances and concerts to promote the scheme while HQ focussed on advertising. In launching such an initiative, the Party hoped to capitalise on sentimental emotions which the 250th anniversary of Scotland's nationhood might stir up. It also hoped to gain the signatures (and the 1/- fee) of people who were sympathetic towards the Party but who did not necessarily want to become members of it.[66]

But despite this initiative and the topical debates it became embroiled in, including a record number of press releases it had issued over the course of the year, not everything was positive for the Party under Halliday's new direction. The SNP's 'Choose Scotland Campaign' in fact attracted few supporters and fell far short of the 1,000 new members that it had optimistically hoped for. One reason for this was that it faced stiff competition from other nationalist bodies who had banded together to run their own 250th anniversary scheme. The 250th Anniversary Committee, which was formed at the instigation of the SNC, proved to be a more popular and successful scheme. It was set up in order to mark the Union anniversary with high-visibility events and was largely made up of SNC and NPS members with Robert Blair Wilkie taking on the role as Chair.[67] The SNP had been invited to participate too, but given the bad blood between itself and the NPS, not to mention the fact that it had expelled many members sitting on the Committee at some point or another, including Chairman Wilkie, it turned down the offer and launched its own campaign instead. The tactics which the 250th Anniversary Committee adopted followed along SNC lines despite its multi-group make-up, which included organised functions and protests in various cities and towns throughout Scotland. It culminated in a National Demonstration being held in May 1957 at the symbolic location of Parliament Square in Edinburgh, just yards from where the Union had received Royal Assent. This demonstration, with the help of a lone piper, passionate nationalist speeches and the burning of the Treaty of Union (an old tried and tested tactic of the SNC), helped enthuse an audience of hundreds and overshadowed the anniversary work carried out by the SNP.[68]

Another problem the SNP faced under Halliday's first year of leadership was the persistent blame culture shown by the Party towards its rank and file which did nothing for Party consolidation or morale. The most glaring example of this was the publication of an article headlined 'Blame Yourselves' in the SNP's internal newssheet. This article, published in March 1957, took a dim view of the Party membership which it accused of not doing enough to advance the SNP's cause. The article also acknowledged that sales of the *Scots Independent* had increased on the one hand, but blamed ordinary members for not selling more on the other. It made it clear that it blamed members themselves rather than Party officials for not doing enough for the Party:

> Who is to blame? Many will turn and point accusingly at the officials: they always do when a job is not being done well – always blame someone else.
> Blame yourselves! It's you, the ordinary rank and file, who are to blame. The officials are doing their job as well as they are able with the support given to them. If they are not, who put them in the jobs? You did! If they are trying but are not getting support, who is dodging the issue? You are![69]

This was a slap in the face to the Party's already hard-pressed members, particularly those who involved themselves in branch work, often after a full day's work, or gave up their weekends only then to be criticised in the Party's newssheet for not securing more members or selling more *Scots Independents*. Statements such as the above only served to demoralise ordinary members and to create a 'them' and 'us' attitude between members and officials which was detrimental to the unity of the Party. This statement was also published during the 'Choose Scotland Campaign' launch which would have done little either to encourage members to sacrifice more of their free time for the scheme for what seemed an ungrateful leadership. George Dott went one step further and blamed the wider Scottish people for the lack of progress towards independence rather than simply SNP members alone. In a letter he wrote at the beginning of 1956, he accused Scots of being the principle reason why there was a lack of progress in the movement due to their unwillingness to work for it:

> I tell you the reason for failure is neither in policy nor in leadership; - it is in the fundamental political dishonesty of the Scottish people. One could give much chapter and verse but let it suffice that more than two million of them signed an undertaking [The Scottish Covenant] to do "all in their power" to achieve self government. If even half of them had been sincere we should have succeeded...
> The plain truth is that the Scottish people are too lazy and too vain to admit that anyone can teach them anything and they will not support any political policy which requires sustained effort.[70]

Dott's statement and the attitude of some Party officials that the problems of the SNP lay elsewhere than with its leadership or policies reflected badly on the Party. It may have also hampered any meaningful evaluation being carried out by the SNP on areas such as leadership or policy as the perception from these statements was that all was well in these areas. It is interesting to note that Dott's statement was later echoed in the nineties by SNP patriot, Jim Sillars, who also blamed the Scottish people for the Party's lack of progress at the polls by referring to them as 'ninety minute patriots'. By this Sillars meant that the Scottish people were passionate nationalists for events such as the World Cup but when it came to staying the course in the political field, they faltered. Sillars may have had a point, but such statements did nothing to boost Party support then or back in the fifties. Halliday's first year of leadership was not a runaway success then when it came to consolidation or unity with articles such as 'Blame Yourselves' appearing in the Party's newssheets. Halliday was successful, however, in terms of shifting the Party's focus more outwardly and towards current topical issues as well as keeping the Party's finger far more on the pulse in respect of Scottish politics. Engaging members in projects such as the unsuccessful 'Choose Scotland Campaign' still united some in working together for the common cause of the Party and provided participants with useful lesson-learning experiences which could be utilised in future campaigns. It may not have been the turn-around which Halliday or the Party had hoped for, but one year on under new leadership, the SNP had at least begun to recover from its 1955 position.

Party Political Broadcasting

In the second half of the fifties, the subject of party political broadcasting for smaller parties increasingly came to occupy the attention of the SNP. Broadcasting had long been a grievance of the SNP. It complained that too few broadcasts had a Scottish slant while the amount spent on Scottish programming fell significantly short of the fees collected from licence holders in Scotland. It objected to the term 'regional' which was given to denote the various broadcasting areas in Britain and which was used to depict Scotland as a whole. It protested that Scotland was only permitted the same powers through its Broadcasting Council as those given to English regions and it alleged that the BBC was used as a tool to promote 'uniformity and anglicisation' and demanded that Scotland be given complete control of broadcasting within her own border territory.[71] The Party was momentarily heartened when the Broadcasting Council for Wales decided to allow Plaid Cymru party political broadcasts for the first time in 1955. This came about following repeated demands by Plaid to change the broadcast allocation in Wales, particularly after 1950 when the qualifying number of candidates which political parties must stand at elections to receive broadcasting time rose from 20 to 50. For Plaid, this was completely unreasonable as the number of constituencies in Wales only amounted to 36 which meant that it could never obtain broadcasting time even if it stood candidates in every constituency in Wales. Under pressure from Plaid and other bodies within Welsh society, the Welsh Broadcasting Council decided to institute a fairer broadcasting policy in Wales which would reduce proportionally the qualifying number of candidates political parties must stand to one twelfth of Welsh seats.[72] Under this plan, Plaid qualified for broadcasting time and the SNP was happy with the precedent it set as it could prompt a change in broadcasting policy in Scotland resulting in the SNP gaining broadcasting time for the first time also. But the Welsh Council's decision provoked protest from the Government and the Opposition who prompted the Postmaster General (PMG) to issue a directive in July 1955 repealing the Council's decision which effectively banned political broadcasts by the smaller parties. In his letter to the BBC outlining the repeal, Dr Charles Hill, the PMG, called into question the interpretation of Article 12 (4) (a) of the BBC Charter which appeared to allow Broadcasting Councils the right to permit 'regional' political broadcasts. Hill advised that this had not been the intention of the Article when it was written. He illustrated the point that if the Welsh Council's proposal went ahead then any group calling itself a party which had put up at least three candidates at a previous general election would be eligible for two 15-minute political broadcasts annually. This could mean, Hill added, a party obtaining a total of 30 minutes broadcasting time a year for the sum of just £450. He consequently directed the BBC to refrain from transmitting so called 'controversial' party political broadcasts, as he termed it, by smaller parties other than those agreed to by the main political parties.[73]

The SNP's reaction to the PMG's veto was naturally hostile. It viewed it as a broadcasting attempt by the Government and Opposition to throw off any potential challenges to their positions from smaller parties. It declared the decision to be illegal and in breach of the BBC's Charter and accused the PMG of stooping to underhand tactics with the Government and Opposition to keep the smaller parties off the air.[74] Plaid Cymru naturally cried foul too and mirrored the SNP's damning views while the Broadcasting Councils for Wales and Scotland also protested against the PMG's unwelcome intrusion and interpretation of the BBC Charter. The *Glasgow Herald*, known for being an opponent of Home Rule, uncharacteristically felt the need to criticise too. Its political correspondent called into question the undemocratic implications of the decision which effectively enabled the Government and Opposition to keep smaller parties from party political broadcasting and determine the interpretation of the Charter:

> ...it is permissible to wonder whether it is really democratic that the two 'monster' parties should be able simply by a ukase agreed between themselves to keep others off the air in their own regions.
> 'One may even wonder whether it is legal. If Parliament approved a charter which gave the national broadcasting councils power to put on political broadcasts, it is surely a matter for Parliament to decide whether that power should be taken away. There is something distasteful about the notion that the 'usual channels' can get together and decide that Parliament did not really intend to do what it did.[75]

These democratic implications so lucidly depicted in the *Glasgow Herald* and the whole notion that the major parties could, with the PMG facilitating, prevent smaller parties from obtaining party broadcasts, truly riled the SNP. In the wake of the PMG's decision, the SNP became embroiled, even fixated, with the issue and engaged in a number of strategies to bring about a change to broadcasting policy.

One of the first strategies it adopted was to establish a BBC Committee within its own sub-Committee structure which was given the task of updating and pushing forward the Party's broadcasting policy. David Rollo became the Committee's Convener and he and the other Committee members began to flesh out the Party's broadcasting objectives. By May 1956, a memorandum titled 'Scottish Political Broadcasting' was produced and sent to the PMG which declared that Scotland had distinctive problems and issues which needed to be discussed on a national basis in Scotland and on an equal footing by parties involved in Scottish politics. As such it called for the qualification of party broadcasts in Scotland to be made on a Scottish rather than a UK basis with the number of qualifying seats at the Scottish level reduced accordingly to reflect a fairer share. Parties would also need to hold annual 'policy-making' conferences and have contested seats at the previous three general elections to qualify.[76] As well as its memorandum, the Party's BBC Committee also got to work in putting together a series of policy proposals on broadcasting for adoption by the Party. These proposals were reported to the Party's 1957 Annual Conference and included an appeal for news bulletins for the Scottish Home Service to be prepared in Scotland and a call for Scotland to be given a higher profile in the BBC's external services. But these were only the short-term proposals. The BBC Committee also put together the Party's longer-term broadcasting strategy which recognised that no fundamental change to broadcasting could be made until Scotland obtained her own Parliament. It asserted that a Scottish Broadcasting Corporation was a necessity if Scotland was to continue as a nation and that 'one of the first and most obvious duties of our Parliament would be to set up such a Corporation.'[77] The Committee also drew attention to the fact that Lord Balfour was now Chairman of the Scottish BBC Council and Scottish Governor of the BBC. Balfour had chaired the Royal Commission on Scottish Affairs only a few years previously which firmly stated that Scotland was a nation. The SNP's Committee now expected Balfour to ensure that Scotland was treated as a nation in respect of her broadcasting, though given the rest of Balfour's findings back in 1954, the Committee held out little hope that this would be the case.[78]

While strengthening its broadcasting policy, the SNP also joined forces with other parties to protest against the PMG's broadcasting ruling. It turned to public demonstration in Spring 1956, alongside Plaid Cymru, Common Wealth (a socialist organisation which called for common ownership and morality in politics),[79] and the Independent Labour Party (ILP), which were all small parties affected or potentially affected by the ruling. The four parties gathered in Trafalgar Square under the banner of the 'Three Nations Rally' where representatives from each Party took to the stage to vocally protest on behalf of their parties. The speakers were Alderman Gwynfor Evans for Plaid Cymru, H. Stanley Kirkett for the ILP, W. J. Taylor for Common Wealth and James Halliday for the SNP.[80] The speeches they made reflected the characteristics of their various parties and were used to advertise their parties' policies as well as to state their protests. In Kirkett's speech, he called for industry to be run by the workers and claimed that the BBC and nationalisation were just forms of 'state capitalism':

> Now look at us here – the representatives of four left wing organisations complaining at the unfairness of the BBC – a nationalised industry. The BBC bosses won't let us speak on the wireless so we have to come free enterprising into Trafalgar Square.
>
> No, nationalisation is not peoples' ownership. Nationalisation is only a method of dealing with certain industries. The Labour Party took over certain industries that had failed, because they had failed. There was no new principle involved. The Tories had already nationalised the BBC and the Post Office. The nationalised industries

with their Boards of Directors, their Major-Generals and Trade Union Bosses are no more under popular control than the Boards of any other big financial or industrial monopoly. The nationalised industries are just a form of State Capitalism. They are not socialist at all.

Industry must be owned and controlled by the people and we mean the people not just bureaucratic boards. We believe that the workers in industry should take over and run industry.[81]

In similar fashion, Taylor's speech lamented the unfairness of smaller parties being kept from the airwaves but it also plugged his Party's own policies:

Has it ever occurred to you how basically unjust –un-English – it is that parties that have arrived politically, whose leaders have only got to open their mouths to be reported in the newspapers, are allowed to speak regularly on the nation-wide radio programmes at no expense to themselves; whereas the representatives of small, relatively unknown parties, no matter how constructive their policies, and which really need free publicity to make headway, are excluded?

…We join with the Nationalist parties partly because we agree with many of the things their people stand for, but also because we fervently believe in their right to be heard. Anyone who listened to the arguments of Welsh or Scottish nationalism for the first time today must have had their prejudices profoundly shaken. Common Wealth believe that many of the advantages the Welsh and Scots think they can get from self-government would also be within the reach of English people under a more decentralised system of government… Common Wealth also believes with the I.L.P. that the trumpets must be sounded against that strongest of all the bastions of authoritarianism in this country – the workplace. Whether a man work for private or public industry, in a workshop or in an office; whether a women is a clippie or a nurse; all are entitled to a much bigger say in the way not only their job, but the industry or service of which it forms a part is run.[82]

The joint effort of the Rally attracted more attention for the parties than they could have hoped for if they had worked alone. After the Rally, the parties maintained their working relationship of lobbying for a change in broadcasting policy and were joined by another small party, the Fellowship Party, to become the 'Five-Party Committee'. This Committee engaged in correspondence with the PMG and the major parties and put to them its collective proposals for better broadcasting representation by minority parties.[83] The parties also encouraged their members to write to MPs and the press, which had some result when Scottish Liberal MP, Jo Grimond, agreed to raise the question in Parliament.[84] Although, beyond this, the Committee's case largely fell on deaf ears as it was not in the major parties' interests to grant air time to their smaller rivals.

A less conventional strategy which the SNP adopted was pirate broadcasting. This came about when a small group of Scottish nationalists illegally tapped into a BBC television newscast on the 24 November 1956, and asked viewers to remain tuned for the first pirate broadcast of Radio Free Scotland.[85] During its 20-minute broadcast, Radio Free Scotland treated viewers (or technically listeners as there was no picture to accompany the sound) to a burst of 'Scotland the Brave' followed by an explanation of the reasons of why it had illegally taken to the air, namely, because of the directive that had been imposed by the PMG which, it declared, kept nationalists off the air. It stated the economic case against Union and appealed for contributions for the St Andrew's Day Fund before closing to the tune of 'Scots Wha Hae'.[86] The broadcast only reached some parts of Central Scotland but it did capture peoples' attention as many stayed tuned in to listen to it out of sheer curiosity and were exposed to the issues facing Scottish nationalists from the nationalists' own perspective. The SNP was not directly responsible for the new pirate Station but it had played a part in its establishment. Its BBC Committee Convener, David Rollo, was an electrical engineer by profession and had helped build its transmitter.[87] The Party was impressed with the Station's first broadcast and it was happy to receive a request from its operators who sought supervision by the SNP as 'a guarantee of responsibility'.[88] This request from Radio Free Scotland for some degree of regulation and control by the SNP was an attempt to claim legitimacy within the nationalist community. The Party unanimously agreed at its next National Council meeting to officially back the Station which it saw as a shrewd way to break the broadcasting ban.[89]

Radio Free Scotland soon became one of the SNP's main tools in the battle over broadcasting policy. It conducted pirate broadcasts throughout Scotland, notably in urban areas such as Glasgow, Edinburgh, Dundee, Stirling, Falkirk and Kilmarnock, where population density was higher and more listeners could be reached. It also managed to build another transmitter with the help of David Rollo which enabled its transmission network to widen.[90] In its broadcasts, it covered important contemporary issues like emigration, the export industry and shale oil, in which it put forward the SNP's policies and point of view. It transmitted recorded interviews with prominent members of the SNP such as James Halliday and Arthur Donaldson, and those of other nationalists like Plaid Cymru's President, Gwynfor Evans.[91] It played popular Scottish songs like 'Scots Wha Hae' to stir up the national consciousness and to add zest to its programmes. Its broadcasts gained some publicity in the local press. The Glasgow *Evening Times*, for example, wrote a front page editorial about the new station.[92] Radio Free Scotland also deployed a number of techniques to escape the unwanted interference of the authorities. It conducted some of its broadcasts from nationalists' lofts and used different homes to keep on the move. It made use of a mobile van which was able to make a quick escape if the authorities happened to pick up its position. It even used a boat to deliver some broadcasts which put it outside the three-mile coastal limit and safely out of reach of the long arm of the law.[93] But despite its endeavours, Radio Free Scotland failed in the fifties to make an impact on broadcasting policy. For one, the illegality of its broadcasts meant that they were haphazard and sporadic with its transmitter constantly on the move in a cat and mouse game to avoid the potential threat of jams or raids. Working underground also meant that it was unable to advertise its next programme to listeners and it could only sign off with the promise to reappear at some place and at some point in the future. Any faithful audience base it may have built up never knew when to tune in again for the next instalment. As expected, it also attracted a higher proportion of nationalist listeners to its programmes so its broadcasts tended to preach to the converted. Crucially, it failed to cut any ice with the PMG too into making a u-turn ruling in the fifties, which was the principal reason why it had taken to the air in the first place.

The arrival of Scottish Television (STV) in 1957, however, seemed to offer the SNP new hope when it came to broadcasting. When it was announced that Scottish Television was coming on air, the SNP eagerly awaited its arrival in the expectation that it would provide viewers with a more balanced picture of Scottish life and Scottish affairs and would offer more sections of the Scottish community representation on programmes screened in Scotland. The SNP had itself in mind when it came to discussion programmes. The Party also saw the advent of Scottish Television as a way to improve the BBC's television service in Scotland as the BBC's monopoly would be broken as it would become subject to competition. It also saw an opportunity for budding Scottish artists and production workers to be employed in Scotland rather than having to make the journey south to advance in their careers.[94] It was a high set of expectations that the SNP had for the new commercial station as it excitedly anticipated its arrival.

When STV came on air, however, it failed to live up to the Party's high hopes. The SNP complained that the programming which STV broadcast made little use of Scottish artists whereas 'canned' American and English shows were the main substance of its air time. It complained that STV had failed to produce any Scottish plays or even plays from Scotland more than a year after it first took to the air.[95] Moreover, the SNP's hope of gaining broadcasting time on the new station failed to materialise when STV did not invite it to participate in a series of political broadcasts which the Labour, Unionist and Liberal parties were asked to take part in. The SNP claimed that this was unfair as it was being denied access to equal broadcasting facilities in the constituencies where it stood candidates. The SNP also bitterly complained when it was refused the right to buy advertising time on STV. It highlighted the paradox that it was not considered a political party for the purposes of party political broadcasts on the BBC yet when it tried to acquire advertising time on STV it was denied it because it was classed as a political party.[96] It was a no win situation as far as the SNP was concerned. The arrival of commercial Scottish television, the SNP's joint action with other parties and the activities of Radio Free Scotland had all proved futile in delivering the SNP's broadcasting policy or gaining it any significant degree of broadcasting exposure. It was only in the sixties that the Party would begin to experience a change in its broadcasting fortunes.

Scottish National Congress Membership Ban

Despite the SNP's preoccupation with broadcasting in the second half of the fifties, the Party still found time to outlaw Scottish National Congress members from its ranks. Since 1948, the SNP had a ruling in place banning members from dual membership of other political parties. But when the SNC was established in 1950, this ruling was not applied to the new organisation, leaving SNP members free to hold SNC membership if they so desired. The SNP's failure to classify the SNC as a political party was partly due to the fact that Muirhead had founded the new body but he also remained a significant figure within the SNP, particularly in terms of providing financial support. Categorising the SNC as a political party would have automatically barred Muirhead, whereas the SNC was such a small and insignificant organisation anyway that it was hardly worth bothering about. As the years rolled on, however, the SNP became increasingly concerned with the SNC's pursuits and ever more weary of association with it. The final straw came when the SNC made an appeal to the USSR in 1958 asking it to raise the issue of the Treaty of Union with the United Nations Organisation. The SNC appealed on the grounds that the Treaty's Articles had been breached by Westminster and should be brought before the International Court of Justice at The Hague. This so-called 'Russia Resolution' by the SNC was the end of the line for the SNP who considered the USSR to be a colonising power which acted against the interests of smaller nations. The SNP had long been a public critic of the USSR's colonial conquests. It had issued a press statement in 1956, for example, expressing its sympathy with the Hungarian people following the USSR's invasion and welcomed Hungarian 'refugees' to live and work in Scotland until their homeland had been liberated.[97] The SNP looked upon the SNC's request for USSR support therefore as incompatible with its own policy and consequently banned its members from holding SNC membership under the terms of its constitution at a National Council meeting in March 1958.[98] The effect of this ruling banned outright all existing members unwilling to forgo their SNC allegiance, including Muirhead, the 'grand old man' of nationalism himself.

The SNC deplored the ruling. In a letter from its Chairman to the SNP's National Secretary, the SNC warned that the decision would fracture the movement further and hinder joint action from taking place in the future. Its Chairman, Wilkie, also argued that the SNP's decision was erroneous because the SNC was not a political party as it did not seek to contest elections and asked the SNP to reconsider its position with these arguments in mind.[99] The SNC also justified its reasons for approaching the USSR. It made the case that it had already appealed to other nations within the Commonwealth, Scandinavia and the European Coal and Steel Community to have the Treaty of Union brought before the United Nations Organisation but all to no avail. It had also ruled out the USA because its chances were negligible due to the 'special relationship' which existed between Britain and the USA and because the USA was unlikely to jeopardise its missile base plan that it had for Scotland at the time. The USSR, on the other hand, was unlikely to be as accommodating to British diplomacy as other nations had been and seemed like the best prospect.[100] But despite its reasoning, the SNP maintained its decision to outlaw SNC members. The USSR issue had simply been the straw that broke the camel's back in determining its decision.

Other issues bubbling below the surface had already tempted the SNP to confront the issue of SNC membership. The death of former Scottish Secretary, Walter Elliot, in January that year had sparked a by-election at Kelvingrove which took place in March and resulted in friction between the organisations during the campaigning phase and in the run-up to the ban. SNP HQ had initially hoped to contest the seat as it would provide valuable experience and publicity for members in preparation for the General Election. A branch also existed in the area while resources could be pumped into the contest from other areas. But the Party decided not to contest the seat when it was informed of the lack of preliminary work, the lack of funds available and the weakness of the local organisation in the area after seeking the advice of the area's Kelvingrove Branch Secretary, Miss Miller, and the Glasgow Area Organiser, Mr Mackie.[101] With no SNP candidate put forward to fight the by-election, a member of the SNC, David Murray, came forward to contest the seat as an independent instead. Murray was a supporter of an independent Scotland but in his election campaign he watered down his constitutional aspirations for the electorate and came out in favour of a federal Britain and agreed to take the Liberal whip if elected. With no candidate of their own, many local SNP members rallied round Murray to help his by-election campaign, including David Rollo, the SNP's Treasurer and BBC Committee Convener. They were also joined by members from the SNC, Liberal and Scottish Covenant parties.[102] With some local SNP members backing Murray, statements such as 'S.N.P. full support for Murray' soon appeared as part of his electoral campaign. When word got back to SNP HQ, it was far from amused to discover unofficial statements had been put out or that local members were in cahoots with members of other parties to support an SNC member as an independent candidate who only spoke in favour of a federal Britain. Halliday took a cautious approach and said nothing in public about the unofficial and incorrect reports of the SNP backing Murray's candidature in order not to harm the self-government vote, but behind closed doors he criticised the support which some of his Party members had given to Murray and circulated a letter to all Executive members warning that only SNP members should be supported at electoral contests:

> Mr. Murray may be a non-party candidate. Certainly he is not a Scottish National Party candidate, and I believe that S.N.P. members working for anyone other than an S.N.P. candidate are guilty of a serious breach of discipline. If they worked for Labour, Unionist or Liberal candidates their position would be obvious. In my opinion they have offended just as seriously by working for Mr. Murray.[103]

David Rollo, in response to the circular, justified his own reasons for supporting Murray on the basis that he believed Murray to be a devoted Home Ruler who would not be swayed in Westminster and that taking the Liberal Whip would not amount to much. Rollo also shared similar views to Murray on the policy areas of industry and housing.[104] Rollo's explanation seemed to suffice and he managed to escape disciplinary action arising out of the affair. A small handful of members who had played a more prominent role in Murray's campaign and had close links with the SNC were not so fortunate and were expelled from the Party.[105] Murray himself failed to secure his deposit on polling day in a three-sided race with Labour and the Unionists leaving the activists with egg on their faces.

SNP relations had also been strained with the SNC over the issue of Muirhead and the *Scots Independent*. The *Scots Independent* had always been in a precarious position from a financial point of view. It failed to pay its way and had to rely on subsidy from the SNP and donations from individuals like Muirhead to keep it in print. As a monthly journal, it was unfit for the purpose of keeping nationalists abreast of current issues as stories would often break just after its monthly edition had gone to press leaving the editor having to wait till the following month to report on them and, by which time, events had moved on. To plug the gap and help counter the large propaganda machines of the major parties, the paper was run as a weekly from 30 January 1954. It was hoped that a new weekly edition would also widen the journal's circulation and influence which had been limited as a monthly.[106] But by increasing its publication a different approach had to be taken to help finance it, which resulted in the paper being published by Muirhead's Scottish Secretariat company under the direction of a Joint Board of nationalists made up of the SNP and Scottish Secretariat.[107] This relationship proved stormy, though, with incidents such as Glendinning's sacking as editor splitting the Board down the middle. The SNP believed that it had lost too much control over the journal with Secretariat now publishing it and with Muirhead and other SNC members on the Board favouring greater coverage of the SNC and other nationalist views. Muirhead and Secretariat on the other hand believed McIntyre's position as Chairman of the Board gave the SNP too much say and clout over how it was run. It was not a match made in heaven and the tempestuous relationship only lasted 21 months before the Joint Board was dissolved in November 1955 to make way for a new private limited company. As arrangements were made to establish the new company, the SNP resumed control of the journal and proceeded to set the terms of the new body. It began canvassing for shareholders, which were limited to 50 in law, and enabled the SNP to target the investor market it favoured most.[108] As the SNP moved full steam ahead, it became clear that Muirhead had taken his eye off the ball by agreeing to dissolve the Joint Board in favour of a new company without agreeing to terms and conditions beforehand. He had effectively given the SNP a free hand to dictate the terms of the new company and had allowed it full control in the interim. Out of courtesy, Muirhead was given the opportunity by the SNP to purchase shares in the new company but he did not take up the offer, disgruntled at not being consulted after the Joint Board had been disbanded and by the journal's lack of an independent appearance under the SNP's control.[109] He made a claim to control the new company as chief creditor on account of the losses Scottish Secretariat had incurred when publishing the *Scots Independent*, a claim which was quickly rejected by the SNP.[110] The battle over the *Scots Independent* led Muirhead to retreat from SNP affairs and to concentrate on other activities like starting up his own paper, *Forward Scotland*, which represented the policies and points of view of the SNC. Its first edition ran in September 1957 but it was too small in scale to pose any significant threat to the *Scots Independent* and it also had Archie Lamont editing it who seemed to preoccupy himself with offending those involved in the paper, like Muirhead and Wilkie and even the printers.[111] The friction over the *Scots Independent* lowered the SNP's tolerance towards Muirhead and the SNC and brought it closer to acting on the opinions of those in the Party who called for the issue of SNC membership to be addressed.[112] Muirhead's attention and financial support towards the SNP also tailed off and his sphere of influence over the Party correspondingly petered out. With the issue of SNC membership finally resolved by 1958, the SNP was able to turn its time and attention towards preparing for its next major venture, the 1959 General Election.

The 1959 General Election

The SNP entered the 1959 electoral race more prepared than it had been for any previous General Election in the post-war period. The Party had initially decided to stand a majority of candidates in the wake of the 1955 contest, but it set its goals more realistically by 1959 by aiming to contest around half a dozen seats and to move from its current position as Scotland's fifth Party to at least fourth place ahead of the Communists.[113] By January 1959, it had three confirmed candidates for the constituencies of Perth and East Perthshire, Kinross and West Perthshire and Stirling and

Falkirk Burghs, and it soon hoped to have a further three candidates in place for the constituencies of Aberdeen, Dumfries and Hamilton. Contesting these seats formed the basis of the Party's National Election Plan which was produced at the beginning of 1959 to enhance its electoral chances. It outlined a number of action points to be implemented by the Party to aid it in its campaigning efforts. One point instructed the Party to appeal for election funds from outwith the Party including appeal statements to the press highlighting the importance of the Party to Scotland while emphasising the large resources which the Labour and Unionist Parties would have access to with the aid of trade union and business donations. Another point required senior SNP officials to make themselves available on a rota basis to work in HQ Office throughout the campaigning period to offer advice, handle enquiries and assist with and facilitate the Party's campaign generally. Leaving this task to the regular office staff was deemed unsuitable because they were already swamped with their routine work duties and they did not necessarily have the political and campaigning knowledge of senior officials. Another action point of the Plan called for more communication to flow between candidates and HQ and between fellow candidates themselves. This would enable HQ to co-ordinate the campaign more effectively on a national basis and help candidates become knowledgeable of each others' activities. The Plan also set out arrangements for an Election Conference to be held on 21 February with the purpose of ensuring all delegates knew what they had to do in the forthcoming campaign and were briefed on the facilities available to them. At this Conference, branches not directly involved in the campaign were also allocated to individual candidates who they were asked to support and undertake specific duties for as required.[114] Presumably the rationale for this was that it would personalise the relationship between branch and candidate, leading branches to work harder for 'their' candidate than if they worked for the SNP's campaign as a whole. The Plan also instructed an election manifesto to be issued to clearly show the policy of the Party to voters.

The SNP's policy manifesto, *This Can be the New Scotland*, was duly published in time for the campaign. It comprised of a booklet which offered voters a more comprehensive view of SNP policy than the policy leaflets that had been issued at election time in the past. It was devised from the Party's existing policy and from various reports which Halliday, McIntyre and Donaldson had prepared for the Party's Annual Conferences but it only concentrated on the SNP's long-term objectives of what it planned to achieve once self-government was instituted.[115] Another smaller manifesto, however, was produced that concentrated on what the Party sought to achieve in the short-term if it became a minority Party within the House of Commons. The Party realised that it was prudent to state what its short-term policies were at the Election given that it was only standing a handful of candidates and had no way of delivering on its long-term objectives. As part of its short-term measures, it promised to push for the establishment of a separate Scottish Board of Trade based in

Hamilton to help revive the Scottish economy. It also promised to seek the decentralisation of other government departments and base them in Scotland. This included the establishment of a Scottish Pensions and Insurance Ministry in Perth, a Scottish Mint in Stirling and a Revenue Department in Falkirk, amongst others. In education, it supported the scrapping of the unpopular Fourth Year Certificates and promised to promote more research, while on health it called for improved maternity services and for the rules governing radioactivity to be extended. It also set out its short-term goals on the issues it had become heavily involved in over the years. On shale oil, for example, it promised to push for the abolition of taxation, and for broadcasting, it would strive for more money to be spent on Scottish programming and for a third television service of a Scottish nature to be established.[116] These were just some of the areas the Party proposed to tackle as a quick fix to Scotland in the short-term if its candidates were returned at the polls.

Equipped with its manifestos, the Party took the Government to task on a number of policy areas as a central part of its campaigning programme. One of the issues it attacked the Government on was the economy in Scotland, which, the SNP argued, was different from England's and had suffered as a result of economic policies designed for England being forced upon it. It accused the Government of causing a deliberate depression in Scotland with its credit squeeze deflationary policies which were applied to the UK economy as a whole when industry in England was overheated, only then to be reversed to inflationary policies when England experienced a downturn. The Government's so-called 'stop-go' policies, the SNP argued, may have helped tackle the problem in England but it negatively impacted upon Scotland's industry where over-expansion was not an issue and inflationary policies were largely required.[117] The Party also negatively campaigned on the Government's 'Dreadnought' defence programme which it criticised for being too small in size to keep pace with advancements made by other countries. The SNP complained that Dreadnought, which was the name given to the Government's nuclear powered submarine programme, had only been commissioned on an initial 'one-off' development basis despite it being a copy of the USA's 'Skipjack' programme which had essentially provided the research and testing already. The SNP argued that the Dreadnought programme was wholly inadequate and needed to be massively extended to keep the Royal Navy from lagging further behind other states and to help counterbalance the USSR's enormous submarine fleet. The SNP also highlighted the economic advantage of extending the programme which could inject new life into Scotland's ailing shipbuilding industry.[118] While calling for a much expanded Dreadnought programme, the SNP, however, remained firmly opposed to a nuclear bomb policy.

As well as attacking the Government, the SNP also directed its campaigning criticisms towards the Labour Party. The SNP attacked an 83-page booklet devised by

Labour named *Let Scotland Prosper*, which was submitted to a Special Conference on Scottish Affairs held by the Scottish Council of the Labour Party on 13 and 14 September 1958.[119] The SNP complained that the booklet made no concessions to self-government for Scotland because it focussed on planning and controls on a UK basis which would mean Scotland being directed from London.[120] The SNP then complained of the apparent contradictory policy at Labour's Special Conference when Labour also presented a report by its Scottish Executive named *Scottish Government*, which seemingly supported some element of self-government:

> We declare our belief in the principle of the maximum possible self-government for Scotland, consistent with the right to remain in the United Kingdom Parliament and continue full Scottish representation there...
>
> We suggest a Special Committee or Speaker's Conference to examine and consider the question of Scottish Government as part of the wider question of the United Kingdom Government.[121]

For the SNP, this was simply evidence that the Labour Party only masqueraded to be a proponent of self-government to gain Scottish votes but would revert back to its centralising planning policies from London once in power as outlined in its 83-page policy booklet.[122] The SNP only had to look at Labour's track record in office during 1945-51 when it introduced a host of planned economic policies directed from London on a grand scale despite its long history of supporting devolution.

As a major plank of its campaign, the SNP also claimed that there was no real difference between the Labour and Unionist parties and it presented itself as a radical alternative instead. The lack of variation in policy between the Government and Opposition, the SNP claimed, offered voters little choice between parties at the polls and Labour's lack of support to its earlier devolution pledges meant that it had now become a Unionist party with no radical edge. A statement by the Party's National Secretary, John Smart, lamented:

> The Labour Party has ceased to offer any constructive radical alternative to the policies of the Conservative and Unionist Party. Indeed the Labour and Tory Parties are now equally unionist, and almost equally conservative. The Scottish National Party believes that the issue of Scottish self-government is the major political question for the Scottish people today, and will remain so until either self-government is achieved through the policies of the S.N.P., or Scotland is finally submerged through a continuation of misgovernment by one or other of the two London Parties.[123]

The so-termed 'Post-War Consensus', where similar policies were pursued by the major parties, led the SNP to present itself as a distinctive Party at the Election which offered the electorate different and radical policies to the other parties. The Labour and the Unionist parties were simply 'the two faces of a devalued Bank of England note – differing in appearance, but identical in effect' as far as the SNP was concerned.[124] The SNP also argued that it was Scotland's only true party as only it spoke and operated exclusively for Scotland. By presenting itself in this way, the SNP hoped to capture the votes of those who desired a different choice at the Election and sway any disgruntled Labour voters who may be supportive of self-government.

Some new procedures were also implemented by the SNP to aid its campaigning efforts. The National Council ruled that SNP literature would be made available to branches free of charge as far as funds would permit, which was successful in clearing dusty propaganda off HQ shelves and into circulation during the election period.[125] Business Reply Cards were also used to make it easier for the general public to contact the SNP if they wished to find out more information about the Party. These postage paid Reply Cards were distributed with the Party's manifesto and other pieces of literature while the brochure, *Introduction to the Scottish National Party*, was printed to answer frequently asked questions arising from returned Reply Card enquiries.[126] The procedure for allocating branch dues was also revised so that dues were no longer charged on the basis of the number of members branches had. A new scheme was introduced at the beginning of 1959 instead whereby a fixed fee of £1 per month was levied against each branch regardless of size and an annual affiliation fee of 1/- per member was charged. This new scheme was introduced to encourage branches to increase their membership without fear of facing high branch dues.[127]

When polling day arrived, the results of its campaigning efforts seemed disappointing for the SNP. Of the six seats the Party hoped to contest only five were fought, and of these three were lost deposits. Aberdeen North was the Party's lowest return at just 5.8 per cent of the vote, followed by Hamilton at 6.2 per cent then Stirling and Falkirk Burghs at 6.6 per cent. Of the two saved deposits, Perth and East Perthshire polled the highest with 23.1 per cent while Kinross and West Perthshire managed 15 per cent. It was a far cry from the majority number of seats which the Party had initially hoped to contest and saving just two deposits was hardly a ringing endorsement from the Scottish electorate. However, the results were an improvement from previous General Elections since 1945 and they were also an important springboard for later SNP successes.

With five candidates standing, the Party had also more than doubled its number of contested seats from the previous two General Elections where only two candidates had been put forward. In the constituency of Perth and East Perthshire where

McIntyre stood, the Party had gained an impressive result once again which was slightly up from the previous election by 0.3 per cent and had knocked the Labour candidate into third place for a second time. This showed that support for the Party in this constituency was solid and consistent. In the neighbouring constituency of Kinross and West Perthshire where Donaldson stood, the result was also impressive considering that this seat had not been contested by the Party before, yet Donaldson managed to save his deposit polling just 1.8 per cent behind Labour.[128] The fact that no Liberal candidate stood in these constituencies significantly benefited the SNP. Even in the constituency with the lowest SNP poll, Aberdeen North, the result was not as disastrous as first seemed when taken into account that the constituency had not been contested by the Party since 1945 and did not have the same level of organisation in place as Perthshire. The Party's result at Stirling and Falkirk Burgh where it obtained just over six and a half per cent was perhaps the most disappointing. Although not the lowest, it was slightly down from the previous election result despite three SNP members winning local election seats and McIntyre previously winning his town council seat in 1956, which had accustomed electors to voting for the SNP in this constituency.[129] It would seem from this that the electorate in Stirling may have voted tactically to obtain SNP representation at the local level, perhaps in the hope of wringing concessions from the Labour dominated Council, while staying with Labour, the Party of its choice, at the Westminster level. Nevertheless, Stirling aside, the Party's campaigning efforts of preparing early for the Election, adopting manifestos and new procedures and fighting on key issues such as the economy, had gained it more votes than any of its previous electoral endeavours in the fifties. The Party's contests at Aberdeen North and Hamilton in this Election were also significant in highlighting its focus on urban areas again and its efforts to pick up Labour votes, like dressing itself up as a radical new alternative Party. Even though the margins were small, the General Election of 1959 marked the beginning of a turning point in the electoral fortunes of the SNP.

Conclusion

The latter half of the fifties was a difficult time for the SNP as it still failed to attract significant support. Its pitiful performance at the 1955 General Election graphically illustrated its lack of popularity while it emphasised that unionism was what most voters actually wanted. Its internal divisions which led to the formation of the Nationalist Party of Scotland also damaged the Party's reputation and lost it a significant percentage of its younger and more talented members. Furthermore, its endeavours to change broadcasting policy came to nothing and tied up a considerable amount of Party time while it pursued the issue. But despite its tribulations, some positive developments did occur for the SNP in this period. Halliday's new Chairmanship in 1956 brought a fresher and younger appeal to the Party while the departure of 55 Group members enabled the SNP to concentrate on current issues and initiatives rather than internal dispute. The SNP also addressed the issue of banning Muirhead and SNC membership which meant that the Party was less likely to be harmed in future by association. The results of the 1959 General Election also displayed evidence that the SNP was making progress, albeit small, in the electoral field. Its early preparatory work for the Election and the adoption of its manifestos were also important strategies for future elections. On balance, however, the fifties were bleak years for the SNP with few encouraging results recorded by the Party. Its biggest accomplishment was perhaps simply its ability to stay the course in the face of chronic stagnation without compromising its fundamental aims or principles. The small progress which the Party did make in this period was vastly overshadowed by its failure to grow in members or supporters and it concluded the decade much the same as it had entered it – as a small and insignificant Party surviving on the fringes. But that was all about to change. In only a few short years the SNP would undergo unprecedented growth and support which would see it transform from its fringe Party status into a serious political force.

National Covenant Committee, c1950 (back row l to r) unknown, J M Rollo, unknown, Sir John Cameron , KC, Michael Byrne, unknown, unknown, Nigel Tranter, Andrew Hadden (is in the back row one or other side of Nigel Tranter), unknown, John Bayne, Robin Orr, J J Campbell. (Front row l to r) Dr John MacDonald, W Ross MacLean QC, William Power, John MacCormick, Robert Gray, Prof A Dewar Gibb, unknown.

Above: John MacCormick as Rector of Glasgow University - 1951. Right: Scottish Patriots' founder Wendy Wood. Photo: Scottish Political Archive

Jimmy Halliday at the podium at SNP conference. (Inset) Robert McIntyre speaks at SNP conference. (Both photos: Gordon Wright)

Robert McIntyre and Arthur Donaldson at Bannockburn (Photo: Gordon Wright)

Robert McIntyre (Photo: Gordon Wright)

Billy Wolfe in celebratory mood, (Photo: Scottish Political Archive)

All those who attended the SNP Conference 1956 at the Allan Water Hotel, Bridge of Allan. **Front row**: *George Leask, Bruce Watson, Arthur Donaldson, Tom Gibson, Fiona Smart, Helen McIntosh, Olive Bruce, Vi Donaldson.* **Second row**: *Murdoch Young, Ian Howard, Olive Halliday, Robert McIntyre, Angus MacIntosh, David Rollo,* **Third row**: *William Gillespie, Russell Hill, James Halliday, John Frew, Andy Bruce (London), John Smart, Bobby Stevenson, unknown.* **Fourth row**: *Mr Nicholson, unknown, Mr McIntosh, unknown, Iain Smith, Eoin Grant. Hugh Watson.* **Back row**: *Robin Leask, John Gilchrist, unknown, Mrs Joanne Watson, unknown.*
Photo: D Ross Robertson

PARLIAMENTARY ELECTION, 1955

To the Electors of

STIRLING, FALKIRK AND GRANGEMOUTH BURGHS

JAMES HALLIDAY

JAMES HALLIDAY was brought up in the Scottish democratic tradition, to regard all men as brothers and to respect the views of others. He is a teacher of history in Lanarkshire, and can claim a knowledge of social problems in widely varied areas. He is able also to look at Scotland against a European background, and as a historian has an understanding of the origins of many present-day problems.

DOUGLAS YOUNG

to the

Electors

of the

Kirkcaldy Burghs,

1945

FREEDOM FOR THE SCOTTISH PEOPLE

to enjoy the life and wealth of Scotland—
That is the purpose of my campaign.

We are facing a crisis in our nation's affairs. The basic existence of our whole people is endangered. We have been warned.

From many varied examples—the Forth road bridge, Prestwick airport, Rosyth dockyard, the mid-Scotland ship-canal, the housing scandal, *Bevinism*, the coal-muddle, the fish-muddle, the oatmeal-muddle, the Education Bill, the Board of Trade's discrimination against the Fife linen-manufacturers, the anti-Scottish conduct of the B.B.C.—we can judge by results how the British Parliament and the London State-Departments sabotage practical schemes of Scottish betterment.

Our Local Authorities' plans for housing and public services, the projects of Scottish private enterprise, the reasoned demands of cultural associations such as the E.I.S. and the Saltire Society, even of the Churches—all alike are carelessly neglected or arrogantly prohibited by a government outside our borders over which we have no control.

Scotland must have a new system—or our people will perish.

Winnie Ewing on the Tartan Express after her famous victory in the Hamilton by-election in November 1967. (All photos on this page: Scottish Political Archive)

Pollok looks to.. LESLIE

Jimmy Halliday, Billy Wolfe, Robert McIntyre and Arthur Donaldson. (Photo: Scottish Political Archive)

Winnie poised for victory at Hamilton by-election in November 1967. (Photo: Scottish Political Archive)

5

Party on the Rise - 1960-64

The Scottish Economy

As Scotland entered the sixties, the SNP had no indication of the huge growth it would undergo over the next few years. The SNP had made a slight improvement in its performance by the end of the fifties, demonstrated by its modest advance at the 1959 General Election, but this was negligible compared with the accelerated rate of growth the SNP underwent in the sixties. An area which kick-started the SNP's rapid growth was the economy, an external factor which the SNP could claim no credit for. In the 1950s, the UK enjoyed a booming economy which faced little competition from other European nations whose economies had been ravaged by the effects of war. The UK had full employment and in Scotland the gap in wage levels had also narrowed with England which brought relative prosperity.[1] But by the late fifties, the tide was turning as war-ravaged countries like Germany began to recover their economic positions and outperform Scottish industries. Export industries in Scotland such as shipbuilding failed to modernise with the initial lack of competition and were left wanting when foreign competitors rose up and took over large shares of the markets. Issues like the Suez Crisis, which led to an increase in defence expenditure, also weakened the UK economy and resulted in deflation in 1957 followed by recession in 1958.[2]   Scotland fared particularly badly with her disproportionate number of traditional industries bearing the brunt of the UK's downturn, industries which were at the frontline of world markets and increased competition.[3]   Consequently, unemployment figures rose in Scotland disproportionately to England, reaching over 100,000 in 1958-59, the first time the 100,000 mark had been reached since the war.[4] Emigration also rose as over half a million Scots left Scotland for abroad or England during the fifties.[5] This exodus intensified as Scotland's economic situation worsened and prompted talented individuals like Billy Wolfe, future leader of the SNP, to join the Party. The growth of the media, including the advent of STV, only seemed to highlight the economic contrast between the prosperous South East of England and economically impotent Scotland, and show that Scotland was no longer doing well out of the Union.

The Tory Government made attempts from the late fifties to tackle Scotland's flagging industries and higher unemployment rate relative to the rest of the UK. Regional planning was set in train with government money given to companies like Wiggins Teape for a pulp and paper mill at Fort William, and Colvilles Limited for a new strip mill at Ravenscraig, despite Colvilles' objections.[6] Major projects like the construction of the Forth Road Bridge and the Clyde Tunnel also got underway around this time and an inquiry into the Scottish economy was established by the Scottish Council (Development and Industry) in 1960 with government support under the Convenership of John Toothill. Toothill, of Ferranti Limited, published his Report in 1961 which highlighted Scotland's over dependence on heavy industry and advised on the importance of diversification within the Scottish economy:

> Scotland is however relatively deficient in the science-based industries and in those producing consumers' durable goods. Notwithstanding the success achieved in attracting new industry the economy is still, directly and indirectly, dependent upon ship-building for the employment of one-seventh to one-sixth of the total number in manufacturing industry.
>
> More diversification is needed in order to spread the risks and to increase the representation of the more rapidly expanding types of production. If this is to be accomplished, more new firms must be attracted to Scotland.[7]

The Report also identified growth as a vital component to solving Scotland's economic problems rather than maintaining employment, and recommended an economic planning department be established within the Scottish Office to take over and streamline industrial and planning functions carried out by other Scottish Office departments. This was duly set up by the Government the following year when the Scottish Office underwent restructuring and established the Scottish Development Department, which became responsible for economic planning and development within Scotland.[8] Car manufacturing was also promoted with the opening of Rootes car plant based at Linwood near Paisley in 1963 (where the Hillman Imp was built), followed by the setting up of the British Motor Corporation at Bathgate in 1964,[9] both of which fed the demand for steel from Colvilles' newly constructed strip mill.

But despite this flurry of activity, the Government failed to adequately grapple with Scotland's economic condition and its regional policy efforts leaned towards heavy industries on which Scotland was already over-reliant. The SNP was quick to make political capital out of the Government's handling of the economy and attacked it for Scotland's poor performance compared to the rest of the UK, especially Scotland's higher unemployment rate which was twice the rate of England's.[10] The SNP also criticised the findings of Toothill, which it renamed 'Boothill', for failing to consider agriculture, fisheries and forestry in its Report, areas which particularly affected Scotland, and for the Government's failure to institute an economic policy tailored specifically to meet the needs of Scotland.[11] The Party also became involved in specific campaigns against Government policies such as the closure of Aberdeen's food research station in 1960 and Beeching's (Chairman of the Board of British Railways) various railway closures in the sixties which affected many Scottish towns.[12] The

SNP was able to score political points by attacking the Government in this way and its argument that Scotland should go it alone and devise her own economic strategy now seemed to resonate with more and more people. Interestingly enough, however, despite the Government's shortcomings over the Scottish economy, living standards did not actually decline in Scotland during this period from the previous decade and the unemployment rate still remained low in relative terms. The *Annual Survey of Economic Conditions in Scotland* by the Clydesdale and North of Scotland Bank in fact estimated that real income was 75 per cent higher in Scotland per head in its 1958 annual survey than it had been 25 years earlier when its surveys began.[13] However, Scots' expectations had risen above what the Government was able to deliver and the economic contrast between Scotland and England had only widened. The public's perception in Scotland was that they were worse off, or at least not any better off, than they had been a decade ago and some now looked to the SNP as a party through which to lodge their protest. This opportunity first presented itself at the Bridgeton by-election in November 1961.

Bridgeton and West Lothian By-Elections

Bridgeton was the first election that the SNP fought in the 1960s. The Party had been too weak locally to contest three other by-elections that had already taken place in Edinburgh North, Paisley and Fife East during 1960 and 1961 which were contested by the Liberals. At Bridgeton, a newcomer to the SNP named Ian Macdonald was put forward to contest the seat. Macdonald was a graduate in Agriculture from Glasgow University, where, like so many SNP activists before him, he had been exposed to the workings of the Glasgow University Scottish Nationalist Association (GUSNA) propaganda machine. On leaving University, Macdonald trained as a pilot in the RAF as part of his National Service, which, ironically, it is said, involved him transporting Britain's first H-Bomb across the Atlantic, which far from squared with SNP policy. On returning home, Macdonald took up farming on the pastures of Newmills in Ayrshire where he became heavily involved in SNP activities.[14] At just 26, he was chosen to fight the Glasgow Bridgeton by-election seat which had not been contested by the Party before. The prognosis was not good for the SNP at Bridgeton. Not only was it unchartered territory for the Party, it was also a Labour stronghold and SNP branch organisation in Glasgow was patchy. It came as a pleasant surprise to the Party then when Macdonald saved his deposit by polling an impressive 18.7 per cent of the vote (impressive by the SNP standards) which was just two per cent behind the Unionists' vote and could have been even greater had the ILP not fielded a candidate.[15] The poll was also amongst one of the best results which the SNP had had in the post-war period and it helped rejuvenate electioneering life into the Party. The result was also significant in terms of the effect it had on Macdonald. Inspired by the result, Macdonald sold his farm and offered his services to the Party on a full-

119

time basis. This offer was seized by the Party and on 1 June 1962, Macdonald began working full-time as the Party's National Organiser. [16] Before long, Macdonald would prove to be one the most capable and dynamic organisers the Party had ever seen in terms of increasing membership and support.

A few months later, the opportunity arose for the SNP to contest another by-election 30 miles east in the constituency of West Lothian. Like Bridgeton, West Lothian had never been contested by the Party before and a relative newcomer and novice to politics called Billy Wolfe was chosen to fight the seat. Wolfe had joined the SNP in 1959 as a response to Scotland's flagging economy and high emigration rate. He was a trained chartered accountant who worked in his family's manufacturing business and lived in the West Lothian village of Torphichen. Before joining the SNP, Wolfe had been a member of the Saltire Society where he had built up knowledge about Scotland and had found great satisfaction in its publications which for a period seemed to fulfil his cultural needs. But by the late fifties, he had become disillusioned with the work the Saltire Society exhorted and came to believe that Scotland's future lay in the political rather than the cultural field. [17] He realised that self-government was also a part of self-expression and that if Scotland was to survive as a nation and tackle issues such as her economy, then Scots must take on the duty of nationhood and govern themselves through the establishment of a Scottish parliament. [18] The by-election took place on 14 June 1962 and, like Bridgeton, the result was as much a surprise to the SNP as it was to other parties. Against expectations, Wolfe polled a startling 23.3 per cent and knocked the Unionist vote into third place. The swing was so great in fact that the Unionist candidate polled just 11.4 per cent and failed to save his deposit, which was as much news in itself as the SNP coming in second place. Wolfe's poll is even more remarkable when considering that it was a five-party electoral race with the Liberal and Communist Parties also putting forward candidates which gave voters much greater choice. The Liberals polled slightly below the Unionists with 10.8 per cent of the vote and the Communists' vote ran at just 3.6 per cent. [19] Labour had gained an outright majority with 50.9 per cent and now had the formidable figure of Tam Dalyell representing the constituency. He was an ardent opponent of Home Rule who would later be known for raising the West Lothian Question. [20] Although many were shocked by the SNP's result, the Party's relative success at West Lothian was not entirely unforeseen.

Wolfe had fought a strong campaign with his rag-tag army of campaigners who came from diverse occupational backgrounds and included a publican, a bank teller, a merchant seaman, a painter and decorator, a draughtsman, a surveyor, not to mention several others. Not one came with a political or campaigning background but they systematically took to the doorsteps and hammered home Wolfe's message, making up in enthusiasm what they lacked in experience. Wolfe's campaign message was 'Put Scotland First' which was an old slogan used by George Dott back in 1946 during his Kilmarnock by-election campaign but it was used by Wolfe to far greater effect in 1962. Wolfe campaigned on local issues like shale oil which was a key industry in the constituency that employed over 1,000 workers in Lothian alone but was under threat partly because of government taxation policy.[21] Wolfe also campaigned on the decline of the coal industry in West Lothian which was another important industry in the area and one which fed into shale oil. Wolfe also pointed out concerns about unemployment, emigration, the EEC and Scottish taxpayers' subsidy to England during his electioneering. His campaign was bolstered by the arrival of Ian Macdonald, the SNP's newly appointed National Organiser, who came to drum up support for him in the area. This job was made easier by the local organisation which already existed in West Lothian where long established branches worked together to promote Wolfe's candidature and a Constituency Association was also formed to co-ordinate branch activities during the election period. Wolfe was also a native of the constituency and was well known in the community which further aided his campaigning efforts, an advantage which Macdonald did not have at Bridgeton. Wolfe had been born and bred in the area and played an active role in the local community, notably in the Scout movement and in his local church. His roots and involvement in the constituency meant that some voters already knew who he was before campaigning began and were sympathetic towards him. Wolfe also started his campaign early in a bid to attract more support. He ran a press campaign from the end of March by placing adverts in the local papers in order to become more visible and to publicise his message. He also held his first public meeting on 4 April in the village of Dechmont, months before the election date.[22] By running such a strong campaign, Wolfe's result was, therefore, not just good fortune.

The election had an important effect on Wolfe and the Party. Like Macdonald at Bridgeton, Wolfe was encouraged by the result to devote more time to the Party and was quickly promoted to high office where he would prove to be a valuable asset. On attending the Party's first National Council meeting after the election, Wolfe was made Convener of the Economics Committee, a member of the Election Committee and a member of the National Executive Committee all in one day! From being an unknown in the Party only months before, Wolfe now held important office-bearer roles and would become an increasingly important figure in the SNP in the immediate years ahead, taking top office as Party Chairman in 1969. The result naturally had a positive effect on the Party too. Having achieved two respectable by-election results in a short space of time, SNP members believed that the Party had turned the corner and focused their attention on the important task of electioneering. The results also generated much needed publicity for the Party and helped boost its membership figures as well as helped motivate existing Party members. The benefits in West Lothian were even greater. The Party experienced a surge in its support and it developed its organisational procedures in the area. The West Lothian Constituency Association was established on a permanent basis which liaised, coordinated and improved branch organisation and it set about establishing a new weekly news-paper, *The Standard*, with a targeted circulation figure of around 8,000 copies.[23] The increased nationalist atmosphere in the constituency following Wolfe's contest may have also had a bearing on the young Alex Salmond, Scotland's present SNP leader and First Minister, who was born and raised in the West Lothian town of Linlithgow.

It was not all good news for the Party though on the by-election front. Other by-elections which took place during 1962-63 did not yield such promising results. In Glasgow Woodside, Alan Niven, who had been election agent for Macdonald at Bridgeton, obtained just 11.1 per cent in 1962. In 1963, the Party polled even less as Arthur Donaldson obtained a mere 7.3 per cent in the constituency of Kinross and West Perthshire, James Lee achieved just 7.4 per cent at Dundee West, and John Gair polled only 9.7 per cent in Dumfriesshire, in each case losing their deposit. At Glasgow Rutherglen the following year, the Party failed to contest the seat at all.[24] The presence of Liberal candidates at these elections (with the exception of Dundee West) who had been adopted and had organised their campaigns much sooner had a detrimental effect on the SNP's results. The well-known popular figure of Jack House, otherwise known as 'Mr Glasgow' because of his affection for and knowledge of the city, was an established Liberal candidate at Glasgow Woodside. The Liberal candidate in Dumfriesshire was also better known than the SNP's John Gair who, unlike Gair, had been active in the constituency for months before the by-election date. In Kinross and West Perthshire where the SNP's result had more than halved, the SNP, as well as fighting a local farmer who stood as the Liberal candidate, also suf-fered because Sir Alec Douglas-Home, who had just taken up the Premiership fol-lowing Harold Macmillan's resignation, also stood as the Unionist candidate. The SNP was consequently squeezed by the Liberals and the Unionists at this election. SNP candidates received a less favourable press at these by-elections in comparison to Wolfe at West Lothian which also operated against them.[25] With these by-election results, the SNP had by no means arrived.

Organisation within the SNP

Despite the SNP's sporadic performance on the electoral field, the SNP did see tremendous improvements in its organisation during this period. In 1963, Assistant Secretary, Gordon Wilson, undertook a review of the Party's internal structure in a bid to improve its operation. Wilson, a rising young light within the Party, who would later take the Chair in 1979, began his review at the end of November and completed it just weeks later in December. There were several reasons for carrying it out. Is-sues had arisen over the efficiency of the Party's Executive, the National Council and the National Executive Committee, to govern and lead effectively as many Council and Executive members complained that too much time was taken up by routine administration matters at the expense of policy and other executive issues. This was particularly the case for the National Council which was the SNP's governing body between Annual Conferences and only sat four times a year. It had over 80 attendees and rising, which also proved problematic for effective governance. Many also complained of the long hours which they spent at Executive meetings dealing with matters which could easily be dealt with by lower divisions of the Party without ever reaching Executive level. Long-serving member, Tom Gibson, resigned from his National Council and National Executive Committee posts for this reason a short time after Wilson began his review:

> My reasons for resigning are quite simple. I find that as time goes on I am becoming too impatient at having to spend so much time at both executive and council meetings with routine details which could quite well be done without my having to be present. As I am elected by the conference as a full member, I find it more and more difficult to carry out the obligations that go with such an appointment. I simply am not doing my job properly for which I was elected, and I want to be relieved of the necessity to attend the meetings.[26]

Problems had also surfaced with the SNP's committee structure which came under fire for being poorly supervised, often having unsuitable conveners in post and having remits which overlapped, or worse, omitted areas altogether. In the case of the SNP's Election Committee, this was criticised for being ad hoc and only operating when an election loomed rather than as a standing committee all the time. Its lack of preparedness was exposed during the series of by-elections in the early sixties in which the Party performed poorly. Various other committees were also deemed unfit for purpose, some of which operated as one-man bands like the Overseas Committee run by W. S. Orr, or had ceased functioning altogether such as the important Finance and Organisation Committees, which only added to the administrative strains of an overloaded Executive. Office efficiency was another internal area of concern which was slammed by the Report for adding to the problems of the Party's poor organisational structure. The SNP's HQ at 59 Elmbank Street in Glasgow was in a disorganised and inefficient state with no one in charge on a day-to-day basis. Office management had been the responsibility of the National Secretary, but with the appointment of Ian Macdonald as National Organiser in June 1962, this function transferred to him. Macdonald, however, had no previous office experience and was out in the field touring branches for large periods of time, which meant that little was provided in the way of office management at SNP HQ.[27]

Wilson's review proposed a number of reforms to tackle these issues, which was approved, with the exception of a few minor alterations, at a specially convened National Executive meeting in early 1964. To solve the problem of the Party's Executive, the National Council and the National Executive Committee were given clearer scopes in which to operate which placed more emphasis on policy decision-making, strategy and coordination while routine administration matters were left to the committees. To minimise duplication of work between the National Council and the National Executive Committee, the Executive Committee also took on a filtering role to screen out less important items so that they did not reach the National Council level. Moreover, the nature of the Party's two Vice-Chairman positions dramatically altered. The role of Vice-Chairmen had largely been ornamental in nature with their only duty being to preside over meetings in the Chairman's absence. Following reorganisation in 1964, these positions became vital functioning roles within the Party with clearly defined responsibilities. One post became Vice-Chairman for Publicity and Development, a role taken on by Billy Wolfe, while the other became Vice-Chairman for Organisation, filled by newcomer C. Douglas Drysdale. A Senior Vice-Chairman position was also created which took on the appearance of a deputy leadership role. The advantage for the Party in developing its Vice-Chairmen posts in this way was that it created additional fully functioning office-bearer roles to soak up the workload burden and place them directly in charge of key tasks facing the Party, that of organisation, growth, policy and of the increasing importance of external relations. Creating work splits between Vice-Chairmen also clearly defined their roles and reduced duplication.

The SNP's committee structure was also improved. Many committees which were moribund or had fallen away altogether were revitalised following reorganisation. The Finance Committee, for example, whose role was to raise funds, encourage branches to participate in financial ventures and to keep the Party's finances in the black, was resurrected and helped lessen the load of an overstretched National Organiser and National Treasurer. The status of the Election Committee also changed to become a standing committee within the committee structure which meant that it operated all year round rather than as and when required. This resulted in it becoming more prepared and pro-active in electoral issues rather than reactive which had often been the case in the past. It also began candidate vetting procedures and building up a bank of prospective candidates for future elections. Committees were also rationalised to complement the new Vice-Chairman roles. A new Publicity and Development Committee was set up and the Organisation Committee was re-established after a year of being out of action. The Party's committees also began issuing regular progress reports to the Party's Executive which were extremely beneficial, not only from a monitoring point of view for the Executive, but perhaps also encouraged committees to work harder in order that they could report that progress had been made in their areas in their monthly reports. The reports were also distributed in advance of Executive meetings which freed up more time for discussion of high level issues while at the same time they provided the Executive with an overview of the state of play of the Party. A growing number of people joining the SNP around the time of reorganisation also meant that the Party had an increased supply of members able to take part in the committees and keep them active.

Rationalisation was also instituted at the Party's HQ office to improve its efficiency. A new SNP office at North St. Andrew Street in Edinburgh began operating as the Party's Public Relations Department in 1965. It was run by newly appointed honorary Public Relations Secretary, Rosemary Hall, which took some of the administrative strain away from hard-pressed office staff in Glasgow.[28] The Department's opening and the appointment of a PR Secretary were important for developing the Party's external image in the latter half of the sixties. Some new office procedures were also introduced to create efficiency savings. For example, more standard-type letters were issued by HQ in reply to enquiries from the public rather than tailor-made answers which took up more time at the expense of other administrative duties. Standardising letters also became increasingly important as the decade wore on when the number of enquiries to HQ grew rapidly.

Although there were many benefits of reorganisation following Wilson's review, one important area was virtually ignored – the Party's branches. Historically HQ had been weak in its organisation of branches and had often failed to provide proper guidance and support to them, particularly when it came to electioneering which was the Party's primary device for bringing about its independence goal. Conflict also existed between branches and HQ as some branches were critical of the Executive's 'laissez-faire' stance and the inadequate way in which it dealt with branch grievances, while others looked on the Party's central organisation as unduly meddling and interfering. HQ's failure to strike the right balance between providing helpful information and unnecessary interfering was highlighted by one National Council member to Wilson during his review:

> ...there is a crisis of confidence in the quality of leadership and efficiency of the executive at this time – a crisis perhaps of long standing but brought to a head by the recent series of by-election reverses. The old branches nurse a distrust of Headquarters interference and mismanagement. The new branches feel that they have not received adequate advice and direction.[29]

But despite these points being raised, Wilson paid scant attention to branches in his Report and consequently there was no overhaul of the branch system to improve its linkage and relationship with HQ during the reorganisation. The only recommendation Wilson made on the issue was for more help to be given to branch treasurers and secretaries by way of providing them with standard accounting forms and advice on matters of procedure, and even then branches were expected to provide more information about their activities, funds, membership lists, meetings and attendances to HQ in return. Wilson also put responsibility for the state of the Party's HQ onto branches by arguing that it was ultimately them that pulled the strings:

> When all is said and done, it is the branches who, in the National Council or at National Conference exercise control over the National Party. It is they who elect the National Officebearers and Conveners of the standing or ad hoc committees. It is they who provide the finance and personnel on which the Party is run. While the leaders are responsible for the morale and good guidance of the Party, they are ultimately dependent on the goodwill and resources of the branches. As in industry, management and labour must work together if productivity is to be improved.[30]

Wilson's Report, however, failed to offer a more robust system in which 'management' and 'labour' could work more closely together. HQ's failure to tackle the branch system and improve its relationship with branches as part of its reorganisation would have implications for the Party in the latter part of the decade when branch organisation massively expanded (discussed in the next chapter).

In spite of its failings over branches, the Party's external organisation improved significantly during the period of reorganisation. Branch and membership growth began taking off around 1962 from the time when Ian Macdonald took up his appointment as National Organiser. The SNP had around 2,000 members in 20 branches when Macdonald began his tenure as National Organiser in June 1962. The following year, one year into his post, membership had doubled to 4,000 and the number of branches had more than doubled to 43. By June 1964, this figure had almost doubled again to 8,000 and 80 respectively.[31] The correlation between branch and membership growth and Macdonald's appointment was no coincidence. Macdonald was an extremely competent and diligent organiser who put his heart and soul into the role, sometimes working up to 80 hours a week. He concentrated his efforts on starting up new branches and offered advice, guidance and encouragement to them in order to keep them going and to increase their membership rolls. He also spent time breathing new life into some of the Party's older flagging branches and encouraged well-established branches to widen and form new branches in neighbouring areas. Macdonald toured all over the country successfully building up the Party's branch network and membership numbers, though his greatest success during 1962-64 was in the Lowlands where he was based. In Glasgow, for example, where only two branches existed in 1961, branch figures quickly increased to four, comprising Glasgow North, South, East and West, not long after Macdonald commenced his Organiser role, and by Spring 1964, Glasgow Scotstoun, Woodside, Maryhill, Springburn, Provan, Bridgeton, Pollok and Craigton had emerged as constituency branches with Cathcart, Shettleston, Govan and Hillhead also in the pipeline.[32] West Lothian also underwent significant expansion during this time, which was testimony to Wolfe's efforts as well as to Macdonald's organising labours. The number of branches in West Lothian when Wolfe fought his by-election campaign in 1962 was just two, but by the middle of the decade, this figure tripled to six with the existence of Whitburn, Blackburn, Broxburn, Westfield/Torphichen, Armadale and Bathgate. Wolfe's large by-election return and his activist pursuits had helped build this support while Macdonald's Organiser role facilitated it. Some areas of the North East also began to take off, such as in Aberdeen and Banff, though in the Highlands and in Orkney and Shetland, expansion was limited because of logistical problems arising from a small and scattered population. In the case of Orkney and Shetland, the Liberals were established as the leading Party making the SNP's task even more difficult. Areas around Perth and Stirling where the SNP had traditionally been strong also saw the Party's branch and membership activity increase thanks to the organising efforts of Macdonald.[33]

But it was not just down to Macdonald. The newly re-established Organisation Committee also played a part in the Party's grassroots expansion. It was convened by Alan Niven who was an experienced organiser who had acted as Macdonald's election agent at Bridgeton and who had stood himself at Woodside. The Committee recognised that branch growth was largely occurring in an accidental rather than planned way and set about forming a strategy for the Party's planned growth. The Committee did this by producing a survey of the SNP's state of play in each constituency in Scotland to ascertain where its support lay and where organisation should be targeted. From the completed survey, the Committee was able to determine the areas to which the Party's efforts should be directed, which included places where the Party's support was already strong or rising, such as in Banff, Aberdeen and Glasgow. Edinburgh North, East and Leith were also noted as target areas as the Party set its sights on the Capital even though its support in Edinburgh remained weak overall. Constituencies which had elderly MPs were also targeted as they had a higher probability of producing a by-election through the death of a sitting MP.[34] The work undertaken by the Organisation Committee in identifying priority areas of organisation was vitally important for improving the Party's support in key areas and greatly assisted the National Organiser operating in the field. Unfortunately for the Party, it was only put to the National Council in November 1964 and came too late for the October General Election of 1964. The Organisation Committee also helped in initiatives such as the Party's 'Meet the People' campaign, which saw numerous SNP canvassers patrolling Glasgow City Centre distributing tens of thousands of leaflets and business reply cards to Saturday shoppers, backed up by *Scots Independent* vendors, poster displays and speaker patrol vans.[35] This type of work by the Organisation Committee complemented the work of the National Organiser and helped in the overall organisational improvement and growth of the Party.

With improved organisation and rising support also came improved and rising finances. As the Party's membership rose, more revenue was made by HQ from branch dues. Between 1962 and 1964 branch dues in fact almost trebled from £275 to £849. Some branches were slow to pay so even more revenue was owed to HQ in outstanding dues. Membership fees paid directly to HQ also increased in this period from £64 in 1962 to £90 in 1964. This slower rate of growth is indicative of the fact that as the SNP's branch network spread, those who wanted to join the SNP could often now join a local branch which may not have existed before. But it was not just branch dues and membership fees to HQ that were increasing, revenue from other sources such as donations, appeal funds, literature and merchandise also rose with a growing membership to seek funds from and sell to. Income collected by the Party in 1962 for the St Andrew's Day Fund, for example, was £512 and for merchandise was £33. By 1964, the St Andrew's Day Fund generated a massive £2,224 and sales from merchandise brought in £318. These figures show that not only was the Party's membership growing, but that members were also spending more money per head on Party activities than ever before. The Party even began investing some of its income in shares such as taking out holdings in Scotia Securities Ltd, which were worth £1,100 in 1964. This in turn generated the Party a dividend which amounted to an investment income of £156 in 1964 alone. However, as the Party's income increased so did its expenditure. One obvious increase was the Party's tax bill which almost doubled between 1962 and 1964 from £53 to £91 for income tax alone. For local rates and insurance, a similar picture emerged increasing in the same period from £291 to £389. Party administration costs also rose from £1,972 to £3,463. Included in this was a steep rise in office salaries from £893 to £2,017, which reflected the general increase in work which the Party was now carrying out.[36] The Party's growing income and expenditure levels during this period, which displayed an increase in Party activity level overall, put the SNP on a stronger financial footing than it had been in the past. However, it is worth keeping in mind that the SNP still remained poor in relative terms compared to other political parties and it would later have to come up with some innovative ways and means in order to improve its financial standing and compete with the major parties.

Collapse of Nationalist Organisations in the 1960s

While the SNP's support began to climb in the 1960s, other nationalist organisations were not so fortunate. Some began to disappear from the national movement as it underwent a period of realignment. The Scottish Covenant Association, run by John MacCormick, experienced the greatest collapse when it went from being the largest nationalist body in the early fifties to extinction just a decade on. After the failure of the Covenant petition in 1951, the Covenant Association shifted its focus of attention from mounting petitions to pushing plebiscites and began lobbying political parties to introduce a nation-wide poll in Scotland. It believed that such a ploy would determine the Home Rule Question once and for all and would lead to a Scottish parliament being instituted. The results of the Kirriemuir plebiscite back in 1949, and its own postal poll in Scotstoun in 1950, had already shown overwhelming support for a Scottish parliament by this method and the Covenant Association believed that no government could refuse to implement a parliament if this was shown to be the determined will of the people. But by 1959, the Covenant Association had failed to convince consecutive governments to endorse its idea of a nation-wide referendum and it teamed up with the non-partisan Plebiscite Society to conduct its own poll in the Borders town of Peebles. Like Kirriemuir, voters were asked three questions: if they were in favour of an independent parliament in Scotland; a parliament which dealt with purely Scottish affairs; or no parliament at all? An overwhelming majority of 82 per cent recorded their desire for a Scottish parliament in an impressive turnout of over three-quarters. Of those desiring a parliament, most voted for a devolved structure in line with the Covenant Association's aim.[37] Inspired by the result, MacCormick began planning to recall a Scottish National Assembly in Edinburgh to obtain a 'strong expression of Scottish national opinion' and even toyed with the idea of pursuing a redeclaration of the Covenant petition as had been launched a decade ago,[38] possibly in a bid to recapture the support and glory days that the Covenant Association had once had.

But such pursuits only sounded the death knell of the Covenant Association. The Covenant Association's approach of using a national plebiscite was foolhardy because its previous policies had already demonstrated that the main political parties were unwilling to act on its non-parliamentary tactics. Its refusal to change direction and pursue a different strategy when this line of policy failed also showed a lack of dynamism and ability to operate within the political climate on the Covenant Association's part. Its plebiscite at Peebles, in association with the Plebiscite Society, also highlighted its lack of innovation as various individual polls, petitions and surveys had been conducted in the past which had already displayed overwhelming support for a Scottish parliament. Peebles was therefore simply a repeat of what had gone before and brought nothing new to the table. The Covenant Association also wasted precious resources in the process while the results at Peebles were predictably ignored again by both Government and Opposition. MacCormick's proposal to reconvene the Scottish National Assembly and redeclare the Covenant petition (neither of which actually got off the ground) were in a similar vein of repeating old failed policies and only succeeded in showing that the Covenant Association was going round in circles and getting nowhere. The Covenant Association's continued refusal to go down the parliamentary mandate route and contest elections to bring about its objectives remained its fundamental flaw. By not taking this route, the Covenant Association continued to deny itself the most effective weapon available in the fight to bring about its devolutionary aim. The closest it came to parliamentary politics was to encourage its members to vote for candidates at elections who came closest to its point of view. Beyond this, no parliamentary course of action was pursued and this was the Covenant Association's Achilles' heel.

By the 1960s, the Covenant Association had reached the end of the line with its petition and plebiscite campaigns. The press had lost interest in it as it failed to achieve any headway or offer anything new on which to report on. Political parties still refused to listen to it as it posed no ballot threat or risk to their party positions. Members had begun to desert it realising that it was going nowhere. The Covenant Association was on its last legs and its activities had all but dried up. The end was nigh and in October 1961 the crunch finally came when its founding father, John MacCormick, died. MacCormick's sudden death ushered in the end of the Covenant Association with no one waiting in the wings that could takeover the pivotal role MacCormick played or be the figurehead he symbolised. For some, MacCormick was simply the 'Scottish Covenant Association' and the much needed time, money and energy which he spent on the organisation was lost when he died. After MacCormick's death, the Covenant Association's office was swiftly sold off to pay off mounting debts and slash running costs. Attempts were made to keep the organisation going from the back office of Angus Gunn's business premises,[39] but with no driving force like MacCormick to steer it forward and shoulder the financial burden, it was eventually wound up. A list of suitable memorial schemes were drawn up to commemorate MacCormick with the small residue of £226 left over from Association funds. These included an inscribed tablet to be laid on his grave and framed photographs of him to be presented to his former school, Woodside Secondary School.[40]

The Scottish National Congress was more active in the 1960s than the Covenant Association had been but it too dropped off the political map during this decade. After the SNP's membership ban in 1958, the SNC concentrated its efforts on establishing an ad hoc constituent assembly in Scotland. Its plan was to form an assembly made up of representatives of all of Scotland's 71 constituencies which would adopt a Scottish constitution and then act as Scotland's unofficial parliament until parliamentary elections could be carried out, or so the theory went:

> After careful consideration Scottish National Congress has decided that the time is now ripe to form a permanent representative National Committee to have continually under its survey all matters affecting the welfare, security and status of this Nation, meeting regularly in Edinburgh or Glasgow, and proceeding constitutionally to debate and pronounce upon all affairs concerning Scotland. In other words, we propose, in face of the intolerable inertia of our present English-controlled representatives at Westminster to set up a SHADOW PARLIAMENT, pending the re-establishment in this land of democratic

self-government.[41]

The SNC invited selected individuals favourable to the national movement to take part in the scheme. The initial response was slow, but by October 1960, the SNC had enough individuals to hold a provisional constituent assembly meeting at which a new body named the Committee of Articles was formed. [42] This Committee was made up of individuals from a cross-section of the nationalist community though, true to form, the SNP refused to take part in it and individuals represented themselves rather than their nationalist organisations. The Committee got to work drafting a Scottish constitution and it also began gathering the names of nationalists prepared to become constituency representatives in an ad hoc Assembly. When enough names were gathered, a Provisional Assembly was held on 21 April 1962, at which 12 Commissioners were appointed to act as the Assembly's executive.[43] Their function was to get the Constituent Assembly up and running until such a time as Scottish elections could be conducted to install a democratically elected parliament. Commissioner, David Murray, justified the Assembly's initial undemocratic nature by pointing to other institutions which had begun life as unelected bodies then became democratised, like the first General Assembly of the Church of Scotland. For the Commissioners of this self-styled shadow cabinet, it was simply an undemocratic means to a democratic end and they had high hopes that the Assembly they had initiated would become the foundation stone on which a future democratically elected Scottish parliament would lie:

> This great Assembly I can assure you will be written into the history books as the Assembly which was as great as that that met in Liberty Hall in the United States in the year 1778. Future generations of school bairns will be deeved by as yet unborn teachers to remember that it was in the Adam Rooms, George Street, Edinburgh that our first Provisional Assembly was held.[44]

But it proved to be far from historic and only six months after the Assembly had been held it was suspended indefinitely owing to a lack of support. The Commissioners cited the SNP's failure to become involved and back the Assembly project as the main reason for its suspension. They conceded that without the support of the SNP as the principal self-government organisation in Scotland, the project had little authority amongst the national movement and was consequently isolated and doomed to failure.[45] But the SNP's refusal to become involved was hardly surprising given that its policy was one of electoral mandate. Many individuals involved in the scheme were also ex-SNP members who had parted company with the SNP on bad terms, such as Douglas Young, who had disagreed with the SNP's dual membership policy back in the forties then joined Labour, and James Glendinning, the 55 Group and Nationalist Party of Scotland leader, who was now Acting President of the Provisional Assembly. The SNC's strategy of launching the Assembly scheme without the backing of the main nationalist organisation and its failure to anticipate the implications of this showed a considerable lack of foresight on the SNC's part. The SNP's position as the largest of the nationalist organisations and its increasing growth also displayed clear evidence that the majority of nationalists desired a Scottish parliament fought for by an electoral strategy rather than non-mandate policies. Even if nationalist numbers had been on the SNC's side, decisions taken by an unofficial self-appointed Assembly could not be enforced nor would they be acceptable to a Westminster government or a Scottish electorate. The SNC's failure to recognise this proposition when launching and participating in the scheme highlighted its poor judgement and short-sightedness when it came to strategy and hastened its demise during this period.

A more lasting legacy of the scheme, however, was the framing of a Scottish constitution which was drafted by the Committee of Articles in 1964. This Constitution consisted of 97 Articles and was framed around the assumption of an independent Scotland operating within the context of the Commonwealth. Article 1 predictably guaranteed the sovereignty of Scotland as an independent nation: 'Scotland is, under God, a free, independent, democratic nation, the power to rule being vested in the Scottish people and exercised by them through a National Assembly appointed by a free vote of its citizens.' The other 96 Articles covered an array of areas from the rights of citizens, the powers of political institutions, land and resources, business and industry, to culture and the colour of the National Flag. It was based on a unicameral system of government and a proportional representation system of voting by way of the single transferable vote. It also rejected the notion of parliamentary sovereignty as outlined by Dicey and emphasised the importance of sovereignty residing with the people. The document was largely the work of Matthew Somerville, Catherine Snodgrass and John D. MacLean, although contributions were received from Dr Victor MacKinnon, a lecturer in constitutional law at Edinburgh University, and Andrew Dewar Gibb, a former Chair of Scots Law at Glasgow University and former SNP leader back in the 1930s.[46] It was a significant piece of work which was conducted over a two-year period and provided the SNC and Assembly supporters with a glimpse of what an independent Scottish state could look like if implemented. However, in the absence of an Assembly to put the Constitution before, it could not be adopted and it was simply shelved in the hope that the Assembly would be resurrected at a future time, which, of course, never came. The democratic principles of the Constitution also flew in the face of the Assembly which had not been initiated by the democratic will of the Scottish people and was therefore an anomaly. With no Assembly existing and a rapidly declining SNC unable to provide further support by the time it was produced, the Constitution was stillborn.

The Assembly scheme was not the SNC's only shortcoming during the sixties. The SNC also became deeply entrenched with the anti-war campaign to the detriment of its organisation. Since its inception in 1950, the SNC had displayed strong anti-war sentiments and its opposition to nuclear weapons became more vocal as the decade moved on. By the onset of the 1960s, SNC members were at the forefront of various anti-nuclear campaigns and had played a key part in the formation of the Scottish Peace Congress in 1960, which was established to oppose the Polaris nuclear base at the Holy Loch. Congress also took part in anti-war demonstrations, like the Campaign for Nuclear Disarmament (CND) mass rally in Glasgow in February 1961. At this rally participants included the SNC Chairman, Wilkie, who carried the placard 'Polaris is evil', and Muirhead, who in his 92nd year gallantly walked the first half mile of the procession.[47] The SNC even held its own Peace Conference in 1961 where it formed a working Committee which liaised with other anti-Polaris organisations, including the CND.[48] But these activities took so much time and energy out of the SNC that its nationalist campaign suffered. Some SNC members also appeared to be more concerned with the anti-war campaign than they were with the nationalist cause, so that when anti-war groups like the CND began to take off in the 1960s, they diverted their energies to these organisations instead. The SNC's fixation with the anti-war movement took away from its nationalist activities and left it in the weakened position of half fighting two causes.

By the 1960s, the SNC was also seriously weakened by the level of internal conflict within its organisation. Congress had always suffered a high degree of infighting because of the rebellious type of characters it tended to attract (see Chapter 3 for more details), but by the 1960s this had eaten away at Congress's numbers reducing its small Group network from just five to three. The biggest loss came in 1958, when Greenock Group resigned en masse, angered by the Executive's decision to shift the balance of power in favour of Glasgow Group. This shift in power had been instituted on a temporary basis until the next Annual General Meeting of the SNC was held and was justified by Glasgow Group on practical grounds because of a lack of time spent on Executive matters by members of other Groups.[49] But Sam Shields, Chairman of the Greenock Group, cried foul and publicly resigned taking with him the membership roll and formed his own independent Greenock Scottish Nationalists Group instead. Two years later, Aberdeen Group, which had been riddled with internal dispute, dropped off the SNC's group list too. Aberdeen Group had been at war with itself for many years with issues ranging from accusations of financial mismanagement and maladministration, to incorrect use of procedures.[50] Aberdeen also faced the added difficulty of not only competing with the main nationalist organisations like the SNP and the Covenant Association, but a small, independent, Aberdeen Nationalists Group, also existed which catered for a fringe membership similar to its own. By 1960, the SNC was left with just Glasgow, Edinburgh and Dundee Groups operating. Later in the year its youth branch then ceased operating due to a lack of support.[51] The SNC had gone into meltdown.

The SNC's fate was finally sealed in August 1964 when Muirhead died. The death of Muirhead effectively meant the death of the SNC as there was no one in the organisation who could replace him and provide the level of assistance, particularly financial, which he had provided over the years to keep the organisation going. Muirhead had also been something of a pacifying figure within the SNC whose mild manner had helped smooth tensions among its warring members. When he died, the SNC no longer had his calming influence to pacify and unite its quarrelsome membership. Also, some within the SNC, like Oliver Brown, had only been members of it out of respect to Muirhead, so when Muirhead died there was no longer a reason for them to continue their membership.[52] With his passing, the SNC was out of money, ideas and inspiration. It ceased to undertake any other pursuits and many of its members moved to alternative organisations like the SNP and the CND where the action was now taking place. It did not formally wind up like the Covenant Association, but by 1964, to all intents and purposes the SNC was dead.

Muirhead's death also spelled the end for another nationalist organisation, Scottish Secretariat. Scottish Secretariat, which acted as a propagandist nationalist machine and a hub for various nationalist organisations to meet and publish their ideas, was run by husband and wife team Tom and Agnes Spence on behalf of Muirhead. It had been kept financially afloat by Muirhead throughout its 40-year existence but it was left in turmoil following his death without his financial backing to keep it running. Its premises at 28 Elmbank Crescent in Glasgow, which it shared with the SNC, were also personally owned by Muirhead and were quickly sold off by the executors of his estate to Glasgow Corporation. Tom and Agnes Spence managed to keep it operating for another couple of years by renting the premises from Glasgow Corporation and by generating income from the sale of Muirhead's archive to the National Library of Scotland, which amounted to £480, and from sums raised from the sale of Scottish Secretariat's publishing stock.[53] Some money was also donated to Secretariat by sympathisers like Douglas Young, but eventually the Spences failed to meet overheads, and by the mid-1960s, Scottish Secretariat also dropped off the list of operating Scottish nationalist organisations.

Other small nationalist organisations also went the same way. Scottish Patriots, run by Wendy Wood, embarked on non-electoral activities, but like the Covenant Association and the SNC, these failed and it fell further into obscurity in the 1960s. The Patriots' main policy tactic was its attempt to recall the Three Estates which had been adjourned in 1707. It argued that as the last Estates sitting on 25 March 1707 ended with adjournment rather than dissolution, it was within Scotland's constitutional power to recall the Estates and resume her Parliament. The Patriots also argued that, as the General Council of the Estates was not referred to in the Treaty of Union, it was unaffected by it and could convene itself again and act as Scotland's parliament or government.[54] Wood took the Scottish Patriots' case to the Church of

Scotland's General Assembly in 1960 where she presented a petition to recall the Estates.[55] But like the SNC's Assembly idea, it was a policy which side-stepped the Scottish electorate and was rejected by the Church of Scotland and nationalists at large. Once this policy had failed, the Scottish Patriots' level of activity declined and it disappeared from public view for the rest of the decade. The Nationalist Party of Scotland (NPS) also declined around the same period. The NPS's extreme anti-English views had banished it from mainstream nationalism since its inauguration in 1955 and the initial level of support which it had drawn on then had dissipated by the late 1950s. With a lack of members and support for the views it held, the NPS undertook few policy activities of its own and became largely involved with other nationalist organisations' pursuits, like the SNC's Assembly scheme. On entering the 1960s, its operations had dried up and many of its members had become completely enmeshed within the SNC. United Scotland also ceased operations by the 1960s. United Scotland had been run as a one-woman band by Mary Ramsay since the early 1940s and concentrated on the dissemination of nationalist propaganda, but with only Ramsay running the show, little activity was carried out and Ramsay herself became increasingly involved in SNC activities. By the 1960s, United Scotland had stopped functioning altogether.

The collapse of these nationalist organisations, however, was not symptomatic of a deteriorating national movement or of weakened nationalist support during the early sixties. On the contrary, their demise showed a consolidated shift occurring within the movement which worked to the SNP's benefit. One obvious benefit for the SNP was that it was left as the sole party in the national movement and nationalists were forced to turn to it if they desired a political outlet for their expressions. The Scottish Covenant Association, the largest of the ailing nationalist organisations, provided the SNP with the greatest number of new members when it eventually collapsed. Some Covenant Association members, like Angus Gunn, went on to join the Plebiscite Society, where they launched a National Plebiscite Fund on St Andrew's Day 1961. But most gave up the ghost and flocked to the SNP instead. For those who did join the Plebiscite Society, some later turned to the SNP anyway when the St Andrew's Day Plebiscite Fund attracted little support. The decline of other Scottish nationalist organisations also led to an influx of nationalists joining the SNP. Members of the Nationalist Party of Scotland and Scottish Patriots initially resorted to the SNC when their organisations collapsed, but when the SNC collapsed too, they turned to the SNP and were absorbed into the Party. Some leaders like Wendy Wood and Mary Ramsay opted to stay outside the SNP, but for most others, the SNP was an acceptable alternative in which to continue the self-government fight. Some even switched to the SNP before their organisations' demise when support for the SNP began to rise and it appeared the most likely vehicle through which to deliver a Scottish parliament. New members of the national movement also automatically joined the SNP where in the past they could choose from several nationalist organisations which operated. This flock of new members to the SNP brought added resources to the Party and a wider nationalist network on which to call upon. The SNP's policy was not diluted either by the large influx of former nationalist members of other organisations into its midst. Efforts in fact became squarely focused on the SNP's electoral strategy as pressure group tactics were clearly shown to have failed. The results of repeated polls and surveys had also revealed that Scottish voters were more in tune with the Covenant Association's devolutionary plans than the SNP's aim of independence. However, an increasing number of Scots supported the SNP, which demonstrated that success was more about electoral tactics than constitutional aim, and as a result there was a renewed vigour within the SNP towards its electoral strategy. Some nationalists, such as Oliver Brown and James Glendinning, were also refused entry to the SNP to prevent its policy and leadership from being challenged. Brown had disagreed with the SNP's electoral policy in the forties and had joined the Covenant Association before becoming a member of the SNC, while James Glendinning had left the SNP in the fifties to form the NPS. But it was not just the SNP which gained from having a monopoly of the national movement. With Scottish nationalists all under the one roof, the national movement appeared united for the first time in decades and their consolidated efforts were able to push the cause much further than their divided attempts had achieved in the past. In the years and decades that followed, a few splinter organisations did surface but never again did the national movement suffer from the same level of division and diversity which existed prior to this modal shift towards the SNP.

The 1964 General Election

The General Election of 1964 offered the SNP the opportunity to turn its growing support into additional votes. It was the first General Election which Arthur Donaldson had presided over as Party leader since taking the Chair in 1960 and his style of leadership was very much focused on the parliamentary arena. Almost immediately he announced the Party's intention to stand 15 candidates, a figure which was unsurpassed in the history of the Party and triple that of the previous General Election. The candidates consisted of one journalist, three doctors, five teachers, and six business personnel.[56] Donaldson, who had a similar style to McIntyre's leadership, though perhaps slightly less dogged, also recognised the importance of the Party's policy content at the Election and backed Billy Wolfe's efforts to compile an undated policy statement and manifesto which became the main plank of the Party's campaign.

SNP and You, the title given to this document, was completed by Wolfe and published by the Party on 23 September in the run up to the Election as a 26-page booklet. It outlined many of the SNP's well-established policies on issues such as greater control of land ownership by the State, increased quality and quantity of housing as a priority and the nationalisation of certain key industries if deemed in the country's best interests but not as a matter of principle. It updated these policies but also listed new policy areas not mentioned in its previous policy documents, like Polaris. On this issue, the Party stated its opposition to the missile scheme being based in Scotland because, it argued, it put Scotland at greater risk as a target than the rest of the UK. It also argued that the cost was too heavy on Scottish taxpayers' pockets whereas an independent Scotland would have no truck with a nuclear defence policy in any event. Other areas also became more heavily featured in the SNP's new policy manifesto, such as rail transport and New Towns. The protection of Scotland's railway system and its improved integration with other modes of transport was outlined as a vital component to achieve a successful Scottish economy by the SNP. The Party's new-found interest in this area came in the wake of Beeching's rail closures announcement. A better approach to New Towns, geared towards smaller and more disperse communities along with the annual rate of housebuilding increasing to a minimum of 50,000, was also mooted as overcrowding continued. As always, the constitutional issue of self-government remained at the core of the SNP's policy statement around which its other policy areas were centred.[57]

SNP and You was an invaluable policy document not only because it updated the Party's policy position for the 1964 General Election, but also because it used facts and figures to back up some of the Party's main points. It quoted statistical information to dispel the notion that Scotland was subsidised by the Union and show, instead, that Scotland subsidised the Union. In its section on defence policy, for example, the SNP claimed that Scotland's share of the defence bill was £190 million for 1964, but the figure for Scotland's total defence costs should not have exceeded £75 million. It also claimed that only a quarter of Scotland's £190 million defence bill was actually spent in Scotland, meaning an annual subsidy of £142.5 million to England for defence alone. On taxation, it declared that Scotland had paid out £1,000 million in direct taxation over the last 10 years, none of which was spent in Scotland or for the benefit of Scotland. This type of statistical information was used as shock tactics to pack a punch with voters. Hard figures were also used as a carrot tactic when it came to policies like social welfare, showing Scottish voters what they might expect under an SNP government. Pensions, for instance, would be increased to at least £6 per week and unemployment and sickness benefit would be set at £5 for the first four weeks, then £7 thereafter. These figures were based on 1964 prices and linked to the cost of living.[58] With a greater commitment to social justice and opposition to Polaris, this policy statement also signalled a further shift left for the SNP on the political continuum.

Along with the drafting of its new policy statement, the SNP also explored an electoral pact with the Scottish Liberal Party in preparation for its campaign. Unofficial pacts between the SNP and the Liberals had long been a feature of elections with some local areas agreeing to stand aside and allow the other party's candidate to go forward to avoid splitting the third-party vote. Such local pacts involved deals under the table by local officials and were not endorsed by the SNP's National Council who looked upon them as a sell-out to the Liberals. Arthur Donaldson and Tom Gibson were two of the National Council's most ardent opponents of a pact who viewed the type of Home Rule the Liberals pedalled as too limited in scope for the SNP to be associated with. But this view was not shared by everyone within the National Council and Wolfe in particular pressed the issue for a Lib-SNP pact. Wolfe had been a vocal supporter of a pact since assuming his office-bearer roles in 1962 and pursued the issue aggressively following the SNP's poor 1963 Kinross and West Perthshire by-election result where the Liberals had also stood. He put a motion to the National Council for an invitation to be made to the Liberals for formal talks on the issue. Four points were mooted for discussion. First, both parties should agree not to contest the same seats. Second, when both parties collectively held a majority of Scottish seats they should convene a special meeting made up of all Scottish MPs and call on the UK Government to agree the formation of a Scottish government which would take the shape of a federal structure for the first couple of years. Third, branches or constituency associations of both parties should decide which party should contest the seat in their areas. Finally, there should be no 'bi-party label' for candidates and both parties' candidates and policies should remain independent of each other. But this motion failed to be backed by the National Council by 20 votes to 11 with ardent opponents of a pact such as Donaldson and Gibson talking down any such action.[59] A few months later, however, the SNP's National Council passed a revised motion by Wolfe to approach the Scottish Liberal Party in time for the next General Election. It was a far more limited motion which was simplified to just two main areas:

> 1) Will the Scottish Liberal Party put Self-Government at the head of its Electoral Programme and make it a requirement that all its candidates pledge themselves to give priority to it in their campaigns?
> 2) Will the Scottish Liberal Party and all its candidates pledge themselves jointly and severally to demand Scottish Self-Government if and when a majority of Scottish seats are held by National Party or Liberal M.P.s, and to return to Scotland to set up a Scottish Parliament if the Westminster Government of the day, irrespective of the party of which it is composed, should, under such circumstances, refuse to pass the necessary legislation necessary to give the Scottish people full control of the economy and finances of Scotland?[60]

It was a clever motion which the National Council realised offered something for both SNP proponents and opponents of a Lib-SNP Pact. If the Scottish Liberal Party accepted, it would put self-government at the top of its agenda and would raise the

Home Rule profile generally. If the Liberal Party declined, it could be accused of not taking Home Rule seriously and could be exposed to accusations of exploiting the issue. The Liberals' rising support at a number of by-elections in the 1960s and better performance in comparison to the SNP also led some National Council members to rethink the SNP's position and conclude that a pact was now prudent to avoid the Liberals standing in the same seats as SNP candidates and outperforming them. The Liberals responded, however, by declining the invitation of an alliance, which was music to the ears of Donaldson, Gibson and other SNP pact opponents. The Liberals had outpolled the SNP in recent elections so had less need for a pact than the SNP and they were not prepared to begin talks on the SNP's terms. Home Rule was also only one policy within the Scottish Liberals' overall package of policies and it was not prepared to promote it independently of the British Liberal Party by forming alliances with the SNP. In a statement to the press, Chairman of the Scottish Liberal Party, John Bannerman, also expressed his Party's unwillingness to become associated in any way with the SNP's more radical form of Home Rule:

> Nowhere is there a place in Liberal policy for any separatism of the extreme character advocated by the Scottish Nationalists. For that reason there is no possibility of a pact with the Nationalists unless they agree to travel the Liberal road of federal Home Rule for the United Kingdom.[61]

Although disappointing for Wolfe, it was a coup for the SNP who used the Liberals' rebuff to portray it as insincere and opportunist towards its self-government commitment. It also led to a rush by branches and constituency associations of the SNP to adopt their candidates as soon as possible for the impending General Election in the hope that the Liberals would be less likely to contest in their areas if an SNP candidate was already nominated, even if there was no official agreement in place.

When the Election arrived, at first glance, the results seemed disappointing for the SNP. Of the 15 SNP candidates who stood, only three, in the constituencies of West Lothian, East Perthshire, and West Perth and Kinross, saved their deposits. Others did come close as Clackmannanshire and East Stirling, Dumfries, and West Dumbarton all polled over 12 per cent, and the constituencies of Kirkcaldy, Glasgow Springburn, and Stirling and Falkirk Burghs followed closely behind with an average result of 10 per cent. But the rest scored an average of just five per cent. In Perth and East Perthshire, the SNP's vote also decreased from its previous electoral performance of 23.1 per cent at the 1959 General Election to 17.4 per cent at this Election. Some of the constituencies which the SNP had contested at the 1959 General Election were also dropped by the Party this time around. Aberdeen North and Hamilton both failed to put up candidates despite the groundwork which had already been done in these constituencies and the absence of a Liberal candidate. Even in Glasgow Bridgeton, where Ian Macdonald had pulled in an impressive 18.7 per cent vote at the 1961 by-election, no SNP candidate stood in 1964 despite the groundwork and absence of a Liberal candidate here also. In the constituencies of Woodside, Aberdeenshire East, Fife East, and Roxburgh, Selkirk and Peebles, where the SNP went head to head with the Liberals, the SNP came off worst and performed its poorest.[62] The rise of the Scottish Liberal Party and the SNP's failure to broker an electoral deal with it was a critical factor in undermining the SNP's performance at the 1964 General Election. The SNP also failed to stand candidates in any Highland constituencies where it could have gained voters' support for its manifesto policy to oppose Beeching's rail closures. The Highlands, with its thinly spread population, was particularly badly affected by the closures, but with no candidates in place in any of the Highland areas, the SNP was unable to make political gain from the situation at the Election.

However, it was not as bad as it seemed. In fact there was a definite improvement in the SNP's results at this Election. The number of SNP candidates who stood compared to the previous General Election was a vast improvement, increasing three-fold from five to 15. This gave many SNP supporters the opportunity to vote for the SNP for the first time. The SNP also made further inroads into traditional Labour territory by standing in seats such as Glasgow Springburn, Clackmannan, and Dumbarton for the first time. Interestingly though, in these constituencies the Tory vote declined more steeply than Labour's, and in Glasgow Springburn, Labour's vote actually went up. However, this did not necessarily mean that Tory voters had actually switched allegiance to the SNP, rather it gave the impression that they had and this may have increased the SNP's desire to win over Labour voters. In some constituencies, the SNP's vote also increased from the previous election, particularly at West Lothian where the SNP vote rose from an already impressive 23.3 per cent at the 1962 by-election to a remarkable 30.4 per cent in 1964. In West Lothian, the local Constituency Association kicked into action and flooded the area with SNP propaganda and merchandise with a core team of around 40 helpers who flocked to the assistance of Wolfe's campaign.[63] Wolfe himself, who had drafted the Party's manifesto, was well versed on policy and topical issues and was able to rouse contentious debates. The SNP's vote in Kinross and West Perthshire also surged ahead from 7.3 per cent at the 1963 by-election to 14.1 per cent, despite the presence of Communist candidate and fellow nationalist, Chris Grieve. Stirling and Falkirk Burghs was less dramatic but progress was made nevertheless with a rise from 6.6 per cent in 1959 to 10 per cent in 1964.[64] The Party's performance was a good result overall where it increased both its presence and support. Its new policy document, *SNP and You*, and its adoption of a record number of candidates helped its standing at the Election, while events such as its internal reorganisation in 1963, the realignment within the national movement towards the SNP and the state of the economy also benefited its result. With the aid of these factors, the General Election of 1964 showcased the Party's rising support and progress on the Scottish political scene.

Conclusion

The early sixties ushered a new dawn for the SNP as it moved from a position of stagnation on entering the decade to a new lease of life soon afterwards. The dislocation in the world economy which negatively impacted upon Scotland's manufacturing and export industries, and the Government's failings on regional planning to balance its effect, benefited the SNP as it was an alternative party for Scots to lodge their displeasure with the Government over the state of the economy. The SNP's good by-election results at Bridgeton and West Lothian showed evidence of its mounting support and its campaigns at these elections were significant in bringing the fresh talents of Macdonald and Wolfe into the Party's fold. The SNP's results at the General Election of 1964 displayed even more evidence of Party growth and how far it had come in just a few years. The sharp increase in the number of candidates which the Party put forward and the progress it made in some constituencies also stood it in good stead for parliamentary contests in the future. The SNP's internal changes also aided its support and growth as reorganisation enhanced Party activity and efficiency, while Macdonald's new role as National Organiser led to tremendous growth at the grassroots level. The decline of other organisations within the national movement and the failure of their non-electoral strategies also brought significant gains to the SNP as displaced nationalists brought new members and resources to the SNP and led to a clear focus towards parliamentary politics. It was no coincidence that the shift within the national movement towards the SNP coincided with a marked improvement in the SNP's growth. However, not everything was positive for the SNP in this period. The revival of the Liberals, which took place at the same time as the rise of the SNP, diminished the SNP's growing support. More supporters and voters turned to the Scottish Liberal Party as an alternative party than they did to the SNP which meant that the Liberals outstripped the SNP's performance. Notwithstanding that, the SNP still achieved considerable progress in the electoral field and in terms of its organisation with its growth and support mounting year on year. The Party was at last emerging from its fringe party status, and by the middle of the decade, it was quickly becoming a formidable political force.

6

SNP Breakthrough – 1965-67

Decline of British Identity

Just as a strong sense of British identity worked against the SNP in the 1950s, a decline in British identity amongst Scots in the 1960s conversely worked to the SNP's advantage. In the forties and fifties, various rallying factors had unified Britain. War, with its conscription, rationing, bombing and sense of 'we are all in it together', had helped forge a strong sense of British identity amongst Scots. Integration of military personnel from Scotland and other parts of the UK also broke down barriers and stereotypes in this period amongst serving men and women of the UK.[1] In the fifties, major events such as the Festival of Britain and the Queen's Coronation deepened a feeling of British identity, while the welfare state and the corporate economy remained ever-present in Scots lives and reinforced a strong message of 'Britishness' amongst the Scottish people. But by the sixties and as the decade wore on, this message weakened. The Suez Crisis, the contraction of the British Empire, and the emerging force of the European Economic Community (EEC) were key factors which contributed to this decline.

The Suez Crisis marked the beginning of the decline. It arose when Britain's Prime Minister, Anthony Eden, entered into talks with the French and Israelis to invade Egypt in 1956. The move came in response to President Nasser's decision to nationalise the strategically important Suez Canal Company which was partly owned by British and French interests. Israel invaded first, followed by an Anglo-French force a few days later, but the response was met with international condemnation from both sides of the Iron Curtain. The Soviet Union threatened intervention while Britain's ally, the USA, resorted to diplomatic and economic coercion. Confronted with worldwide hostility, Britain, along with France and Israel, withdrew its troops with its tail between its legs.[2] The Suez episode undermined Britain's standing in the world and left many Scots feeling rather less patriotic to be British by the time the sixties came around.

The dislocation of the British Empire in the post-war period also loosened the connection Scots had with Britain. Britain's retreat from the Empire in the post-war period had begun when it conceded independence to countries such as India, Burma and Ceylon (now Sri Lanka) during 1947-49. This was accelerated in the fifties and sixties with Britain's withdrawal from various Asian, Caribbean and African countries including Malaya (1957), Jamaica (1962) Trinidad and Tobago (1962), Uganda

143

(1962), Northern Rhodesia (1964) and Nyasaland (1964).[3] This loss of territory by the mid-sixties deflated British self-esteem and underlined to Scots that Britain was a declining power on the world stage. The granting of independence to a succession of colonial countries was also used by the SNP as ammunition to push for Scotland's independence. It contended that if independence was good enough for colonial countries, it was good enough for Scotland and it touted the argument that Scotland only remained a part of the Union because she was too lucrative for England to lose - 'Nyasaland now has independence – what about Scotland – but of course Scotland is a profitable colony. So long as we are a nation of labourers in our own land we will remain England's last satellite.'[4] The SNP also pointed to Rhodesia and Nyasaland to challenge the argument often used by pro-unionists that Scottish independence was impractical on grounds of economic interdependence with England. The Party argued that Rhodesia and Nyasaland had both been part of the Central African Federation whose economies had been knitted tightly together, but this had not acted as an impediment to their independence.[5] Britain's retreat from Empire had a progressive impact on the British psyche in Scotland as Scots no longer regarded Great Britain as the great power it had once been.

Britain's influence in the world and the Scots notion of British identity also declined when Britain was turned down for EEC membership in 1963 and 1967. Britain had initially refused to become a member of the EEC when it was established in 1958 following the signing of the Treaty of Rome the year before. The Community provided free trade and free movement of capital and labour between its member states and they soon surged ahead in terms of Gross Domestic Product (GDP) and economic performance. Realising the limits of the Commonwealth and the economic benefits that could be gained from membership of the Community, Britain sought membership in 1963 but was rejected by France who used its veto to refuse Britain's application. The French President, Charles de Gaulle, insisted that Britain was unfit to become a full member of the Common Market and wanted a 'European Europe' which did not include Britain and its 'special relationship' with the USA.[6] Britain's growing economic links with the Community and its declining influence in the Commonwealth led it to try its luck again in 1967 with a second application, but it was met with the same stony reaction from de Gaulle who rejected it again. It was a humiliating defeat for Britain which had for years turned its nose up at the EEC, only now to be turned away from its door twice. It was a further blow to British self-esteem which did nothing either to instil a sense of British pride in the Scottish people.

As British pride waned, voting along class lines also declined amongst the Scottish people. In the 1940s and 1950s when British identity was strong in Scotland, voting according to social class was also strong. Manual workers from the working class were generally drawn to the Labour Party while non-manual workers from the mid-

144

dle class tended to support the Unionist Party. Many working class people in Glasgow regarded themselves as having more in common with fellow working class people in Liverpool or Newcastle than people of their own nationality in areas such as the Highlands or the Western Isles. But in the 1960s, voting along class lines began to decline in Scotland. Voting for a particular party because of social grouping became less prominent as other issues, like the economy, Britain's performance on the world stage and Polaris, increasingly came to influence Scottish voters. Class voting still remained strong in this period (Peter Pulzer famously remarked 'Class is the basis of British party politics; all else is embellishment and detail'),[7] but its power was loosening, and in some surveys carried out during the 1964 General Election, national consciousness was shown to be as important, or more important, in influencing Scottish voters as social class.[8] The number of upwardly mobile people in Scotland who climbed the social ladder also increased in the 1960s. This type of voter identified less with social class and more along national lines at the ballot box which benefited the SNP.

As a sense of Britishness declined, a feeling of Scottish identity correspondingly rose amongst Scots during the 1960s. Scots had already become more aware of Scotland as a national entity in the sixties due to the growing disparities between the Scottish and English economies with England's economy performing markedly better than Scotland's. Events like the Suez Crisis, the decline of the Empire and Britain's failed attempts to join the EEC only solidified this. The growth in responsibility at the Scottish Office also forged a stronger sense of Scottish identity during this period. Scotland had always had her own institutions. Her educational and legal systems and her established church, the Church of Scotland, had been safeguarded by the Treaty of Union. Their existence was important in underpinning Scotland as a nation, even at the height of the Empire and British unity. The reinstatement of the Scottish Secretary post and the formation of the Scottish Office in 1885 gave rise to another distinctive Scottish institution and its expansion in the post-war period only fed Scots' identification with Scotland as a separate national unit.[9] The Scottish Office was set up in the nineteenth century mainly as a response to the demands from Scottish MPs and the Home Rule rumblings of the time. It began with very few functions, but it steadily picked up powers over the years and its expansion in the postwar period saw it become responsible for most areas of Scottish domestic policy. In the immediate years that followed the Second World War, it acquired responsibilities for the National Health Service, town and country planning, civil defence, agriculture, forestry, childcare and a host of other areas. In the fifties and sixties, its sphere expanded further with the creation of the Development Department and the establishment of new Scottish government boards such as the Scottish Economic Planning Council in 1965 and the Highlands and Islands Development Board in 1966.[10] Its expansion of power was significant in underpinning Scotland as a separate entity distinct from the rest of the UK. It sharpened the lines between Scotland and England

and it made the case for Scottish self-government seem more compelling, as noted by Miller:

> ...it is impossible to overlook the fact that under successive governments a Scottish governmental machine has been constructed complete with prime minister, subordinate ministers, its own civil service, and unlimited responsibilities if not unlimited powers. At the very least it makes devolution or independence a more credible option for Scotland than for Yorkshire and it continually reinforces the significance of a line on the map dividing Scotland from England.[11]

Ironically, the growth in Scotland's separate arm of government diminished democratic accountability within Scotland at the same time because it overburdened the Scottish Secretary which resulted in more decisions being taken by civil servants and less by elected ministers. For example, the Scottish Secretary was charged with a number of areas of responsibility which several Whitehall departments were responsible for. The Scottish Office's geographical distance from Westminster, based at St Andrew's House in Edinburgh, also meant that the Scottish Secretary spent less time in Scotland overseeing Scottish administration.[12] These circumstances helped create a democratic gap within Scotland and strengthened the argument for Scottish self-government based on democratic principles. Although it was the 1980s before this argument really came to the fore when a policy shift at the Scottish Office based on Thatcherism was forced upon a reluctant Scottish electorate. Nevertheless, the existence of the Scottish Office and its steady expansion in the post-war period did give emphasis to Scotland as a separate unit and promoted a stronger feeling of Scottish identity which was becoming increasingly apparent as the 1960s progressed.

As well as political and economic factors, cultural elements also increased Scottish national identity during the sixties. The growth in media around this period affected the Scots' national consciousness as STV began to broadcast more Scottish items in the sixties and prompted the BBC to do likewise. More people also had access to these programmes as a record number of households now owned or rented televisions. Sporting events like the World Cup in 1966 also highlighted the distinctiveness between Scottish and English culture and that Britain was four nations and not one. Response to England's victory which was met with pride and cheer in England and a more muted and disappointed tone in Scotland only confirmed the distinctiveness between the British nations. The Scots' subsequent victory over the English a year later further fuelled the distinction and promoted Scottish pride and Scotland's own sense of identity. As virtually the only nationalist party left in the 1960s, the SNP was the natural recipient of Scotland's ideological shift.

Breakthrough in Broadcasting

The issue of broadcasting which had occupied a large degree of the SNP's attention in the 1950s finally bore fruit when the Party was awarded party political broadcasts for the first time in 1965. The decision to overturn the Postmaster-General's directive of 1955, which had prevented smaller parties from undertaking political broadcasts without the prior agreement of the major parties, came about after ten long years of campaigning by the SNP. A number of factors account for this volte-face in policy. One reason was the establishment of the Committee on Broadcasting in 1960 which was set up by the Government to look into the future of broadcasting in the UK. The Committee, chaired by Sir Harry Pilkington, recommended in its published Report of June 1962 that Scotland should be allowed its own party political broadcasts. It also recommended that the Scottish Broadcasting Council should exercise authority over the BBC television service in Scotland and should become more representative to the people of Scotland.[13] The Committee's proposals bolstered the campaign to overturn the PMG's directive and allow political broadcasts for smaller parties.

Another reason for the U-turn was the SNP's accelerated rate of growth in the 1960s which put greater pressure on the broadcasting authorities to rethink its policy. The SNP's membership had grown four-fold in just five years from less than 2,000 in 1959 to 8,000 in 1964 and showed no sign of abating. Its share of the vote had also tripled during the same period from almost 22,000 to just over 64,000. It was becoming increasingly difficult therefore to deny the SNP airtime in terms of size and support and granting it some broadcasting allowance could soon become necessary anyway in order to reflect its expansion. The SNP's vote was also catching up with that of the Liberal Party in Scotland, which had access to party broadcasting by virtue of the British Liberal Party.[14] Changes to party broadcasting policy would also minimise the disparity in broadcasting which existed between the SNP and the Scottish Liberal Party.

The SNP's decade-long broadcasting campaign also helped deliver change. The Party had been most active in demanding the repeal of the PMG's ruling in the second half of the fifties but it kept the crusade going in the sixties by continuing to lobby government departments and raising new grievances. In a letter to the PMG in 1963, the Party argued that it was unfair to extensively cover the British Liberal Party's Annual Conference in Scotland as it had less direct relevance to Scotland where a separate Scottish Liberal Party existed. The SNP's Party Conference on the other hand, it complained, was afforded no coverage at all.[15] The SNP also maintained close links with other small parties to keep up the pressure. As a practical means of getting round broadcasting policy, leaders of the SNP and Plaid Cymru entered into discussions on the desirability of a Scots-Welsh alliance or confederation.

Such an alliance would require both parties to fight under a common name at general elections in order to obtain broadcasting facilities and gain a spot in general news bulletins. It would also highlight the plight of the other party in each country and might have a greater impact on policy-making than either party would be capable of affecting alone.[16] The idea was initiated by Plaid's President, Gwynfor Evans, at the beginning of 1965 and Arthur Donaldson was keen to develop it, but the lifting of the PMG's veto, which was to take effect from 31 May 1965, meant that both parties now had a reasonable chance at obtaining broadcasting time individually. The idea consequently came to nothing but their various united efforts had helped to deliver a fairer deal when it came to broadcasting time for smaller parties.

The exploits of Radio Free Scotland in the 1960s also helped bring about change. Radio Free Scotland had first taken to the airwaves in 1956, but its pirate broadcasts had failed to convince the PMG to overturn his ruling and it had all but petered out by the late fifties. In 1960, the Station was brought back to life under the new direction of Gordon Wilson as Director of Programmes. Under Wilson's leadership, Radio Free Scotland was modernised and took on a more professional appearance. It aired its first revamped show in April 1960 and began broadcasting on regular slots on Thursday nights. It also transmitted its shows at the same time each week which gave its broadcasts a level of stability which they had never had before, allowing listeners to tune in regularly.[17] The broadcasts largely featured nationalist propaganda and advertising, but they also covered some non-nationalist elements to appeal to a larger audience base. 'Pirate Pops', for example, was a programme dedicated to pop music to help pull in the younger listener who were treated to the likes of Bobby Darin, Fats Domino and Johnny and the Hurricanes.[18] Magazine-type programmes were also presented which were packed with news, interviews and examinations of current political, social and economic issues. Marketing tactics which included audience surveys and advertising were also deployed. In an audience survey conducted in Edinburgh, over 900 people were interviewed about Radio Free Scotland's broadcasts. Of the sample, 69 per cent said they had heard of Radio Free Scotland while 13 per cent said they had listened to its programmes. A further 80 per cent of those who had not yet listened to the Station stated their intention to do so.[19] Radio Free Scotland also began actively advertising its programmes and the line up of guest speakers who would appear on them. The downside to this was that the authorities were able to jam its transmissions more easily, which they invariably did to some of Radio Free Scotland's more publicised shows, such as special festival editions. Radio Free Scotland also became more responsive to audience views and even switched broadcasting nights to meet audience requests. It moved transmission to a Monday then to a Saturday by popular demand in order that its listeners could avoid unpopular repeats of BBC science programmes which were shown before its broadcasts.[20] Improvements to Radio Free Scotland's transmission network were also made. In the Autumn of 1961, more powerful transmitters were brought into operation which provided an improved reception and increased coverage in central Scotland. As a result, weekly coverage to Glasgow and West Dunbartonshire, Edinburgh and Fife, and monthly coverage to West Lothian was delivered.[21] The Station also took on a more legitimate appearance despite the illegality of its broadcasts and the occasional jamming by the authorities. It set up an office within the SNP's own Edinburgh office at 16 North St. Andrew Street and even printed its own company headed paper complete with logo, directors' names and company address in the face of its underground activities. Radio Free Scotland remained independent of the SNP, but given that it was now located within the SNP's premises and most of its leaders were SNP members, like Gordon Wilson who would soon become the SNP's National Secretary, it was to all intents and purposes controlled by the SNP.

The new and improved Radio Free Scotland in the sixties contributed to the change in broadcasting policy by drawing attention to the issue and its effect on smaller parties. The media picked up on Radio Free Scotland's rekindled broadcasts and raised its profile by reporting on it. Granada Television dedicated a whole programme to the issue of piracy and party political broadcasting, aptly named 'Compass – Pirates of the Air', in which the operators of Radio Free Scotland and their Welsh counterparts were given the opportunity to put forward their cases for party political broadcasts for smaller parties.[22] Radio Free Scotland also captured the imagination of other minority groups within the UK. The Welsh Nationalists and CND set up their own pirate radio stations which also turned up the ratchet for political broadcasting change. Despite Radio Free Scotland's growing profile, the authorities refrained from prosecuting its directors. A possible explanation for this is that they did not want to attract any more attention to the Station which prosecution of its operators would almost certainly bring. The authorities might also have had to defend current broadcasting policy in an open court which, given mounting criticism from the likes of Pilkington, was undesirable. For the operators of Radio Free Scotland, it seemed like free rein had been given to continue their activities:

> …it is interesting to consider that, at the present moment, R.F.S. is operating with a poise that has emerged from the knowledge that the Government authorities are both unwilling and unable to take action against the independent Scottish Radio.
>
> They are unwilling to take action because, aware that they are morally in the wrong over the banning of Scottish political broadcasts, they know that a prosecution would produce good publicity for the patriotic camp and inflame public feeling against them. Politically-wise, any attempt by the Government to impose its formal legal authority over R.F.S. would be a silly move and accordingly, it and its minions must thole this successful attack on its authority with the best grace it may.[23]

The dilemma for the authorities of prosecuting Radio Free Scotland and giving it more publicity and its day in court, or allowing it to continue with its underground activities, which were receiving mounting publicity and becoming wider known, only added to the need for broadcasting reform.[24]

The changes made to broadcasting policy in 1965 enabled the Broadcasting Councils of Scotland and Wales to grant party political broadcasts in their respective countries and allowed an allocation to be awarded to a party even if it had not obtained representation in Parliament. For the SNP, this amounted to an allocation of five minutes of television and five minutes of radio each year.[25] Utilising its quota, the SNP delivered its first televised party broadcast to the nation on 29 September 1965. It was delivered by Wolfe, the Party's most successful candidate in attracting votes. Wolfe reverted to the old SNP chestnuts of emigration and Scotland's subsidy to England and used figures to hammer home his points. In terms of emigration, he declared that 400,000 Scots had left Scotland to seek employment over the past fifteen years, while on subsidy, he claimed that £140 million would be lost from Scotland to England in the current tax year which amounted to £100 a year for every man working in Scotland. The remedy, he advised, was Scotland's own government with full control over her economic policy.[26] The effects of having its own party broadcast transmitted under the new arrangements were enormous for the SNP. The Party reached an estimated audience base of one and a quarter million and a large volume of enquiries instantly flooded its HQ. Within the first 24 hours of its broadcast alone, the SNP received upward of 500 letters from interested members of the public. Both Glasgow and Edinburgh offices were inundated and for the Party's National Secretary, Gordon Wilson, it was 'the most exciting week' of his life.[27] The SNP also received press coverage following its broadcast which only added to its exposure. The *Glasgow Herald* and the *Times*, for example, wrote articles about it in which they reiterated various parts of Wolfe's message as did other national and local newspapers.[28] The longer-term effects of being granted party broadcasts were also impressive. The SNP now had the opportunity to put its point across on television and radio without debate unlike on discussion programmes. The SNP also increased its profile amongst the general population and picked up more members and support along the way. With its enhanced profile and growing number of members and support, the Party was also invited on to more television and radio programmes than ever before as broadcasting companies became more inclined to follow what the SNP was doing. For example, the BBC screened half an hour of coverage of its 1966 Annual Conference.[29] The SNP even resorted to hiring an STV studio for the purposes of teaching its representatives television techniques.[30] Some non-SNP nationalists also found themselves appearing on air, like Wendy Wood, who was repeatedly invited onto programmes which also enhanced the profile of nationalism. On STV she took part in broadcasts such as 'Here and Now' and 'Today is Wednesday' and on the BBC she made several appearances on the children's programme 'Jackanory' in which she narrated Scottish stories with a nationalist slant.[31]

But despite this, the SNP was still disgruntled after receiving its party broadcast allowance. In fact, it actually stepped up its crusade for more broadcast exposure after receiving its award. The Party's main gripe under the new arrangements was that its time quota for television and radio was a paltry amount for the Party's size and compared unfavourably with the amount of broadcasting coverage the three major parties received. The SNP illustrated this point by stressing that on the same day its first party transmission went out, the Labour Party received thirty minutes of coverage on the BBC and STV collectively which swamped its annual party broadcast allowance six times over.[32] The Party also protested against party broadcasts being transmitted at different times of the day. Its party broadcast in 1966, for example, was shown in the early evening at a time when audience ratings and age levels were lower, meaning the Party failed to reach its target audience and gained access to fewer potential voter and supporter numbers whereas other parties had later screenings.[33] The Party also complained that it received inadequate news coverage and that it was not invited to take part in political programmes often enough. Despite increasing its broadcast appearances since receiving its allocation, the SNP argued that the main political parties had 'seized a monopoly' of political discussion programmes in Scotland like 'The Commons Touch' and 'Lobby Talk'. These programmes were parliamentary in nature so they did not tend to feature the SNP which had no MPs to represent it. The SNP was, however, still subjected to criticism on them by its political opponents yet, it complained, by not being represented it had no recourse to refute the attacks.[34] The SNP also pointed out that it was at a disadvantage because the broadcasting establishment in Scotland did not produce Scottish equivalents of political and topical programmes like 'Panorama', 'Dateline', '24 Hours' and 'Gallery' due to financial and production constraints. These productions were screened UK-wide and represented UK-wide parties, which meant that the SNP received an even smaller ratio of time compared to the main parties.[35] The Party also protested against the introduction of BBC 2 in the South of England while some areas of Scotland were still unable to receive BBC 1, like the Shetland Islands and some parts of Dumfries and Galloway.[36] The SNP protested louder on this issue after being allocated its broadcasting time. It was certainly in its best interest to get its message out to as many people as possible, including Shetland and Dumfries and Galloway, whereas the South of England was not in its audience range.

To rectify what the SNP believed was unfair broadcasting rules and to enhance its own position, the SNP made three principal recommendations to the broadcasting authorities. First and foremost it called for more broadcasting time to be allocated to itself to reflect its growing size. It acknowledged the symbolic gesture of being given party broadcasting time in the first place, but it called for this to be increased to fifteen minutes of television time rather than five, which it was happy to accept in

151

the form of three five-minute programmes or one ten-minute and one five-minute programme. On radio, it requested that its airtime be doubled to two five-minute programmes. For the SNP, this increase was necessary in order to compensate it for its under-representation on informal programmes as well as to reflect its growing size, which, the Party pointed out, under a proportional representation system of government would have resulted in SNP MPs being elected.[37] Second, the Party urged that its party political broadcasts be screened UK-wide rather than just in Scotland. Its justification for this was that as important decisions affecting Scotland were taken by the UK Government on the mandate of the people of the UK, it was only right that the whole population should be informed of the position of Scotland. It also argued that as many Scots lived in England, the interest in its party broadcasts would be high there as well.[38] Finally, the SNP recommended that it be granted representation on the Committee of Party Political Broadcasting, which was the body responsible for deciding allocation times. The SNP argued that, as it had become a participant in party broadcasting, it should be represented on the Committee to offer its views and to be kept up-to-date with developments. It pointed out that it had contacted the broadcasting authorities several times for information about new developments in the past whereas its representation on the Committee would have avoided this chasing of information and saved time for all concerned. Representation on the Committee would also solve the mystery for the SNP of how broadcasting time was actually calculated. The Party emphasised that it did not expect voter status on the Committee and it would be happy to conform to the same level of confidentiality exercised by other members.[39] The Government and broadcasting authorities were unwilling, however, to act upon the SNP's demands for further change. They had bowed to pressure once and were not prepared to give way to further demands especially given the SNP's lack of parliamentary representation. With no luck through officialdom, the SNP continued to use the tool of Radio Free Scotland as its unofficial means of getting on the air. The pirate station would eventually become redundant once television programming opened up more fully to the SNP in the seventies. But in the interim, it kept up its operations because of what it viewed was the unfair broadcasting time allocated to the SNP and its services continued to offer the SNP unofficial and undiluted access on the airwaves.

The Boom Years

The SNP had undergone an impressive rate of growth in the early 1960s but it paled into insignificance compared to the growth spurt it underwent in the second half of the decade. The Party's rapid rate of growth took off in Autumn 1965 when the SNP launched a recruitment drive on 29 September to coincide with its first party political broadcast. It ran for two months until the eve of St. Andrew's Day on 29 November and proved to be a runaway success by pulling in 5,000 new members, bringing the Party's membership figure to a total of 21,000.[40] Enthused by the result, the SNP launched another recruitment drive around the same time the following year and achieved even better results. In October and November 1966, it gained an astonishing 12,000 new members which brought its membership number to an impressive 42,000, double that of the previous year. Prizes were awarded to branches which had recruited the most members. Forres Branch took top prize with 271 new members, followed by Blantyre with 207, and then Keith which was given third prize for having a percentage increase of almost 200 per cent.[41] As the recruitment drive came to a close, 2,000 membership cards were being sold every week and the SNP won the accolade of being the fastest growing political Party in the UK.[42]

But it was not just the Party's rapid rise in numbers that was notable, it also picked up members in areas where it had had little presence before. By the summer of 1966, the SNP had made something of a breakthrough in the Highlands with the formation of 12 new branches.[43] Some areas along the West Coast of Scotland also saw the SNP begin to emerge. In Campbeltown, a branch was established in September 1966 and 101 members joined straight away.[44] In the south-east of the country, more branches also began to emerge including many in and around Edinburgh. Mischievously, the SNP even set about forming a branch in the English – and former Scottish - Border town of Berwick-upon-Tweed and classified it as a Scottish branch. By the spring of 1967, the SNP had some kind of formal organisation in place in most constituencies in Scotland and it even produced branch 'starter kit' booklets to meet some of the demands placed on its organisation resulting from its dramatic surge in branch formation.[45] Only two constituencies presented the Party with serious organisational problems, Orkney and Shetland, and West Aberdeenshire.[46] The number of constituency associations also rose dramatically. In August 1966, 14 had existed, scattered mainly across the central belt.[47] By December 1967, this figure had more than trebled to 44 with more waiting in the wings to receive official recognition.[18] This was a superb increase for the SNP which needed constituency associations in order to fight effective election campaigns. They played a vital role when it came to co-ordinating branches operating within the same constituency area and by pooling their resources to stand candidates and lead their campaigns. New members joining the Party also came from a broad spectrum. The SNP's radical policy of independence and its support for the aims of groups like the CND helped attract a large number of young people into the Party. The upwardly socially mobile who were less attracted to class politics were also drawn to the Party. Even more mature people convinced by the SNP's propaganda of a richer independent Scotland now flocked to the SNP. This type of member was particularly important to the Party because their views tended to be less fickle than younger members and they were more likely to be a member for life.[49] The SNP even attracted the odd aristocrat or two. The Duke of Montrose and the Earl of Home's grandson, Robin Douglas-Home, both took an interest in the Party. The Duke of Montrose expressed his support from his home in Rhodesia.[50] He had a family history of Scottish nationalism; his father had been President of the Scottish Party back in the early thirties. His support for Iain Smith's Unilateral Declaration of Independence (UDI) of Rhodesia, which sought to uphold white governance in the country following Britain's policy of No Independence Before Majority African Rule (NIBMAR), may have also spurred him to support the SNP as a means of protest against the British State. The Earl of Home's first grandson also supported the Party. He became a fully paid-up member and even volunteered his services to stand as a parliamentary candidate.[51]

To maintain the momentum of its growth, the SNP came up with ever increasingly novel ways to publicise itself. In the spirit of the times, it launched its own 'Miss SNP' contest in 1967 in which participating branches ran local competitions and put forward their nominations to compete at the Party's National Final contest. Minor celebrities were invited to act as judges at the Final where the winner was awarded a cash prize and a 'Miss SNP' gold sash. Although such a contest would be ruled out by today's standards, it was popular at the time and proved to be a roaring success in terms of generating publicity for the Party. The BBC and STV both provided coverage of the finale in their news bulletins, and branches that took part up and down the land also produced local publicity, which brought in new members.[52] It was such a success that the event became an annual feature in the SNP's calendar. The SNP also deployed a mobile information van and set up a stand at the Royal Highland Show to publicise itself. These ventures were undertaken by George Philp who received donations from the Party to fund them. They had some success. In the case of the Royal Highland Show, membership subscriptions for 52 adults and two minors were received, 110 Business Reply Cards were returned to the Party and over £80 was made from the sale of literature.[53] Moreover, many people within the farming community attended the event which meant that the Party was able to deliver its message to a scattered section of the electorate from the convenience of Ingliston, near Edinburgh. The publicity generated from these projects though was not as successful as the 'Miss SNP' contest and their operation costs made them prohibitive in later years.

The SNP's new Public Relations Department based in Edinburgh also kept up the Party's exposure. The Department, which began life at the beginning of 1965, produced press statements on a weekly basis and many gained the attention of the national press.[54] Alasdair Macdonald took over the role of PR Officer from Rosemary Hall in 1966 and he stepped up the Party's PR campaign. His appointment coincided with the 1966 General Election and during that period no fewer than 15 written press statements were issued, five more were delivered by phone, and seven press conferences were held at the Party's HQ in Glasgow. A large volume of telephone calls were also received from reporters interested in the Party's activities.[55] Due to the efforts of Hall, Macdonald and others involved with the PR Department, the public became more conscious of the SNP. Similarly, the Party's new position of Vice-Chairman for Publicity and Development following reorganisation in 1964 also helped Party publicity. The creation of this post made the office-bearer directly responsible for publicity which encouraged work in this particular area. Wolfe was the first office-holder of the post and he focused his efforts on getting the Party's PR Department up and running while his successor, James Braid, concentrated on the importance of targeting the press and encouraged more interaction with branch PR officers up and down the country. Their efforts increased public awareness of the SNP and, accordingly, aided Party growth.

The Party's financial position also became healthier during the boom years of the sixties. The Party's financial state of affairs had begun to improve in the early sixties as membership climbed, but Party finances still remained precarious by the beginning of 1965. In February of that year, the SNP was in the red by over £3,000 despite only having an overdraft of £2,500 and an appeal for funds was launched by Douglas Drysdale as Finance Convener to alleviate the situation.[56] But by 1967 this situation had completely reversed as the Party generated an income of almost £23,500, more than three and a half times its 1965 level.[57] The large rise in the number of new members joining the SNP naturally brought more money into the Party in the form of affiliation fees, donations, fundraising, the sale of SNP goods and other items, but this was only part of the story. The launch of a new initiative scheme, Alba Pools, also accounted for the Party's dramatic financial turnaround.

Alba Pools was a weekly sweep ticket system which was founded and run by SNP activist Angus McGillveray. It operated at the branch level and involved branch members selling tickets in their local areas. Half of all money collected was retained by the branches and the other half was divided between SNP HQ and the agent to cover prize money, printing and distribution costs. The scheme was largely devised to generate funds for branches but before long it would serve HQ well too. To encourage participation, a levy charge of £10 was imposed on branches that did not take part as their share towards Party upkeep.[58] The scheme began on 4 January 1965 and it collected the sum of £49 in its first week. Of this figure, branches retained £24 and HQ gained £9. In its fourth week its collection had trebled to £155 and then doubled again to £309 by week ten. By week twelve, £340 was collected from the scheme of which £170 was retained by the branches and £76 was earmarked for HQ. The incremental effect for branches and HQ over this first twelve-week period was £1,252 and £438 respectively, a handsome sum and that was just the beginning.[59]

As more people took part in the scheme, the prize figure increased and more people in turn became attracted to it. Before long the scheme went national as branches up and down the country participated in it and both SNP and non-SNP members purchased tickets. In the town of Penicuik, 600 tickets were sold to a population of

6,000.[60] By the end of its first year, £21,867 was collected in ticket sales, £10,933 went to branches and £4,009 went to HQ.[61] By the end of 1966, the numbers were more astonishing with £47,804 generated in ticket sales, £23,902 of which went to branches and £4,490 went to HQ.[62] By the end of 1967, HQ's income from Alba Pools sales had almost doubled to £8,125, which enabled the Party's balance sheet to remain in the black by a surplus figure of £4,764. Alba Pools was so successful in fact it was the largest single item of income generated by the Party in 1967. Branch dues and the sale of membership cards came a poor second with just £6,601.[63] But the size of Alba Pools also brought problems. There were concerns that a parallel scheme might have to be introduced because it was becoming so large that it could be deemed an illegal lottery. Angus McGillveray, who oversaw the scheme, also had difficulty getting return figures from agents which was a legal requirement under the terms of the Betting and Lottery Act. With such large amounts of money involved, a small proportion of agents also absconded with money, although they were too few in number to be deemed a serious concern.[64] These problems did not halt the success of the scheme, however, and just one year after its launch, Alba Pools had become the 'financial backbone' of the Party.

But it was not just Alba Pools; a branch lending scheme was also introduced to swell the Party's coffers. This scheme involved branches depositing any surplus monies they had with HQ at a five per cent rate of interest which would be redeemable on demand. HQ introduced the scheme in 1965 when its overdraft passed the £3,000 mark and it made more sense for surplus funds sitting in branch current accounts to be used to reduce it rather than HQ paying large overdraft charges to the bank which would only be passed onto branches anyway in charges of some shape or form. When Alba Pools took off, there was even more logic for continuing the scheme. The success of Alba Pools meant that there were more funds floating around individual branch current accounts which paid lower interest rates, whereas investing the funds centrally at HQ meant that the Party could command better investment opportunities. To encourage branches to lend to HQ, it reminded them that their money would not only achieve a five per cent rate of return, but that they could be confident that it would be used for the benefit of the SNP whereas commercial concerns like savings banks would not use their money for this purpose and it would probably end up in London hands.[65] The scheme was not the runaway success that Alba Pools had been as branches generally preferred to keep a hold of their own purse strings and retain the flexibility of calling upon their money whenever they needed it rather than being at the mercy of HQ being able to deliver its assurance and release on demand. However, some branches were lured with the five per cent rate of interest and the 'good cause' appeal of giving to SNP HQ rather than financial institutions. As such they invested a collective figure of £964 in the first year alone.[66]

The SNP's financial improvement during 1965-67 enabled the Party to inject much needed funds into many areas such as expanding its workforce. In 1965, the SNP's waged staff consisted of just a National Organiser, an office secretary, a typist and a newly-appointed Public Relations Secretary. In 1966, the Party added more posts to its payroll when it took on a national organising secretary, a shorthand typist and an office junior. This was followed by another shorthand typist and a bookkeeper in 1967.[67] As well as increasing staff numbers, the SNP was also able to increase the levels of pay it gave to its employees. The Party's pay rates had historically been lower than the going-rate for comparative positions in other organisations. The cash-strapped SNP tended to get by on the loyalty it received from its staff members who were dedicated to the cause and invariably overlooked their poor rate of pay. But as the Party's finances improved, pay rises correspondingly climbed and became broadly in line with other organisations by the end of 1966. One exception was the National Organiser whose pay level still fell behind the industry standard, but it was subsequently hiked in 1967 to a starting salary of £1,000 accompanied by two half-yearly increments of £125.[68] The SNP was also able to invest in new equipment and technology to improve its efficiency and modernise its operations. Between 1965 and 1966 it purchased new typewriters, dictating equipment, office furniture, a Roneo addressing machine and filing accommodation.[69] With its burgeoning funds, the SNP also invested more heavily in shares. The Party had already purchased shares in Scotia Securities in 1964 and bought new shareholdings in the Edinburgh trust company, Investors Mortgage Security Co., in December 1965 worth £500.[70] In the next financial year it bought a further £500 of shares in Associated Portland Cement Co. to add to its portfolio.[71] More significantly, having substantial amounts of funds in its accounts enabled the Party to fight more and better electoral campaigns. One of the significant benefits of Alba Pools in particular was that branches were also prospering and were more readily able to financially support candidates. HQ's share of the proceeds also meant that candidates could expect more financial backing from HQ for their campaigns. This benefit of Alba Pools significantly assisted the SNP's ability to put up a record number of candidates at the 1966 General Election.

As the SNP became more financially sound and businesslike, a business itself became attracted to the Party. Rowen Engineering Co. Ltd took great interest in the SNP when its financial assets began to swell and approached it to seek help to finance a new factory it hoped to build in Scotland. Rowen Engineering was a small social enterprise run by left-wing Labour councillor, Tom McAlpine. The company was based on the ethos of serving the community and co-operative ownership and had been set up as something of an economic experiment to show that small community-based industries could exist, could be competitive and could be a socially responsible alternative to large-scale shareholder or monopoly organisations, a view which sat well with the SNP's economic policy. Rowen was named after social reformer and philanthropist, Robert Owen, because of its co-operatively owned and community

157

spirited policy. It had two factories in operation, one in Glasgow employing 25 people and another more recent establishment in South Wales employing just six. Both factories were involved in the manufacture of electric storage heaters and McAlpine sought to start up a third in Scotland and establish 'Rowen Industries' which would act on behalf of the factories.[72] He met with the SNP's Executive Committee in 1967 to seek its help in raising capital funds for the third factory and was backed by the Party who agreed to appeal to its members to invest in the scheme.[73] The Party was attracted by its small community-based philosophy and also by the possible influence it may have over the shape and siting of the new factory though it stopped short of investing money directly in the company. Rowen failed in the long-run to bring about a new economic order but its approach to the SNP was significant in highlighting the increasing importance of the SNP in growth and financial terms. The SNP also subsequently recruited Tom McAlpine into its ranks and he proved to be a valuable Party activist and office-bearer in later years.

The Party's unprecedented growth and support during 1965-67 typically brought with it a series of new problems. One obvious difficulty was the additional work burden it created for the Party which put severe strain on both the Glasgow and Edinburgh offices. Despite the Party opening a new Edinburgh office in 1965 and taking on additional staff members, its office administration failed to keep pace with growth and showed immediate signs of buckling under the strain. In Glasgow, where a daily average of 40 letters were issued, around 30 phone calls were made or received and between one and two dozen callers were dealt with in person, agency staff had to be drafted in to deal with routine matters.[74] In Edinburgh, PR Secretary, Rosemary Hall, also had to rely on outside help from students of the Edinburgh University Nationalist Club to clear backlogs of press clippings.[75] Party officials like Billy Wolfe and Ian Macdonald, who worked closely with the offices, also felt the strain. They worked extremely long hours, sometimes up to 80 hours per week, and travelled extensively around the country, which became gruelling over a period of time. Such was the strain, Wolfe contemplated resigning from his position as Vice-Chairman of Publicity and Development but was persuaded to stay on by Arthur Donaldson who advised him to cut down on some of his travel engagements to ease the load.[76] Macdonald made no murmurings of resignation but Douglas Drysdale believed that he needed to take time out of his National Organiser role. Despite viewing Macdonald as indispensable to the SNP, Drysdale believed that it would be more beneficial in the long run if Macdonald joined the civil service and then came back refreshed and renewed to the Party with new government administration skills that would stand him in good stead as a cabinet minister when, or if, the SNP came to power.[77] The Party's Executive system, which had only been reorganised in 1964, also suffered as a result of the SNP's growth. The new structure showed cracks after just 18 months as the newly constituted roles of Vice-Chairmen for Publicity and Development and Organisation proved wholly inadequate to meet the rising levels of work facing the Party's office-bearers. National Council meetings also faced serious logistical problems as a multiplying membership led to a sharp increase in National Council attendance. At the time of reorganisation, National Council attendance had been in the region of 80 individuals made up of office-bearers, branch and constituency association delegates and observers, but by 1967 this number had grown to around 200. Although good for Party democracy, it resulted in National Council meetings taking on the appearance of mini-conferences and they became more disorderly. In some circumstances, individuals who were due to propose resolutions or speak disappeared in the crowd or vanished altogether which disrupted the flow of the meetings and the agendas. Conditions also became uncomfortable as hundreds of attendees crammed into the Golden Lion Hotel in Stirling where National Council meetings were held. The hotel had played host to the meetings for years but it was now too small to comfortably accommodate the Party and an alternative venue had to be found. With a dramatic rise in paperwork and discussion, the length of meetings also became a problem. In the case of the Executive Committee which filtered discussion before it reached the National Council stage, meetings sometimes went on until the early hours of the morning.[78] This was a major bone of contention for those present, particularly for those who had already put in a full day's work before attending.

To cope with these problems, the Party made more changes to its structure and procedures. The biggest change came with the appointment of two additional Vice-Chairmen in 1967 with responsibilities for finance and policy. Douglas Drysdale became the new Vice-Chairman for Finance and John Gair became the new Vice-Chairman for Policy. James Lees took on Drysdale's old role as Vice-Chairman for Organisation and James Braid replaced Billy Wolfe as Vice-Chairman for Publicity.[79] Wolfe moved to the more senior role of Senior Vice-Chairman and became second in command of the Party. Adding two additional Vice-Chairmen with specific responsibilities to the Party's structure not only created additional office-bearers to spread the load, it also acknowledged the greater importance of finance and policy within the Party. A new Research and Information Committee was also established whose remit involved undertaking research into areas likely to become the focus of policy making in the future, investigating the economic situation of Scotland, looking into the political and economic position of other countries for ideas and comparisons and keeping tabs on other political parties' policies. Wolfe, who had been left without portfolio as the new Senior Vice-Chairman, agreed to become the Chairman of this new Committee.[80] To tackle the burgeoning administration at the Party's Glasgow and Edinburgh offices, functions were also transferred between offices to improve their operations. The Edinburgh office, which had operated as the Party's public relations office, was given a much larger role and became responsible for external organisation under the direction of Rosemary Hall, who became the new Organising Secretary. Glasgow took over the role of public relations and became responsible for dealing with the National Secretary's vast array of correspondence, which fell to the management of Alasdair Macdonald as Public Relations Officer. These transfers helped divide the workload more evenly between offices. It also raised the status of Edinburgh's office from a PR Department to an HQ office, which reflected the Party's growing desire to have its HQ in the Capital.[81] New tactics were also deployed to improve the efficiency of National Council and Executive Committee meetings. Written resolutions and reports were made use of and circulated before meetings to cut down on discussion time and observers were separated from delegates at meetings to make them more orderly. In the short term, all of these changes helped the Party cope to some extent with the demands its mushrooming membership placed upon it, but it would not be long before the SNP would find itself reviewing Party structure again as its growth ran ahead of expectations.[82]

The 1966 General Election

The General Election of 1966 also saw significant progress for the SNP in the electoral field. In 1964, the SNP had put forward a record number of 15 candidates, but in 1966, it increased this figure to 23. It also retained 13 of its 23 deposits which was a significant advance given that it had lost 12 of its 15 deposits in 1964. West Lothian achieved the highest vote again where Wolfe gained 35 per cent. Wolfe not only increased his share of the vote by five per cent from the previous election, he also kept the Tory candidate in third place who failed to save his deposit with just 11 per cent. Stirlingshire West came second highest where McIntyre won 26 per cent, which was extremely impressive given that the Party had not fought the constituency before and he also knocked the Tory candidate into third place, albeit by a whisker of one per cent. Kinross and West Perthshire and Clackmannan and East Stirlingshire were the next highest scoring seats for the SNP where the candidates both gained 20 per cent. For Kinross and West Perthshire where Donaldson fought, this was an increase of six per cent from the previous election and it pushed the Labour Party into third place. For Clackmannan and East Stirlingshire where Drysdale stood, an increase of eight per cent was gained though it was not quite enough for the Party to achieve second place. The SNP's remaining seats which had retained their deposits obtained an average of 14 and a half per cent. A third of these had never been contested by the Party before and the remaining two-thirds all saw an increase in their share of the vote. Of the 10 which failed to secure their deposits, half of the SNP candidates were new to the constituencies and the other half still achieved an increase in their vote from the previous contest. The exception was Perth and East Perthshire which was the only seat fought by the Party to see a reduction in its vote, contracting from 17 to 15 per cent. In total, the SNP achieved a voting tally of 128,474, which was double its 1964 figure and almost six times its 1959 vote.[83]

160

Unlike the Scottish Liberals, however, the SNP did not have the knack of translating its votes into MPs and it gained nothing from its increased share of the vote because of the UK's first-past-the-post electoral system. It also failed to generate marginal seats even in its highest polling constituency of West Lothian where Labour's Tam Dalyell led by 17 per cent. The Liberals, by contrast, had established marginal constituencies which benefited them enormously in terms of parliamentary seats. The Scottish Liberal Party only gained 1.8 per cent more votes than the SNP but returned five candidates as MPs. Its vote had also declined at the Election by almost one per cent but the number of seats it secured actually rose by one. Despite the SNP's lack of parliamentary seats, however, it did still show an upward trend with each general election contest. Its ability to contest 23 seats just 18 months after the last General Election, and the record number of votes it polled, also gave the SNP high hopes that it would be able to contest all of Scotland's 71 constituencies at the next General Election in four or five years time.[84] Its poll was also closing ground on the Liberals and, if voting trends continued, it would only be a matter of time before it overtook the Liberal Party in Scotland altogether. This vindicated the views of Arthur Donaldson, Tom Gibson and others who had opposed moves for a Lib-SNP pact in 1964, and the Party's ambition to stand 71 candidates at the next election left such a pact redundant now in any case. Operating in a more receptive nationalist environment combined with the SNP's vastly improved organisational and financial position naturally contributed to the Party's electoral rise, but its own campaigning efforts also boosted its electoral return.

The SNP's election campaign and its new manifesto, *Putting Scotland First*, helped attract some voters. *Putting Scotland First* became the theme of the Party's 1966 election campaign and it showed considerable developments since the Party's *SNP and You* policy programme. One important development was the appearance of a new EEC policy which was an issue of growing interest following renewed government plans for UK membership. The SNP set out its position as sympathetic to Scotland joining the EEC as an independent nation but was vehemently opposed to Scotland's membership as part of the UK which, it stressed, would diminish Scotland's influence and voting power in Europe. It also opposed Scotland's incorporation with the UK because it would mean negotiations being carried out on a UK basis, which, it argued, would result in Scottish conditions and requirements being sidelined for the greater British interest. On the other hand, it claimed that Scotland's separate entry would be beneficial to England as well as to Scotland because it would yield a higher voting bloc for the British Isles overall:

> The SNP is completely opposed to Scotland being taken into the Common Market so long as she is incorporated with England. An independent voice and vote in Common Market affairs would not only ensure maximum benefit for Scotland, but would also be to the ad-

vantage of our main trading partner, England. The voting power and influence of the British bloc would be increased by separate independent Scottish membership of the Common Market, additional to the membership of England and Ireland.[85]

Major developments in existing policies also appeared in the Party's new manifesto. On transport policy, the SNP supported the creation of an independent Scottish Transport Board that would be accountable to the Secretary of State for Scotland rather than the Minister for Transport, and would become responsible for key transport areas including British Railways in Scotland and internal air services. On education, it proposed a new Minister of Education for Scotland with jurisdiction over schools and universities. The effect of this would be to remove Scottish universities from the control of the UK-wide University Grants Committee and bring them purely into Scottish hands. On housing, which remained a policy priority for the Party, it called for the appointment of a Scottish Housing Minister to oversee slum clearance and for the establishment of a Housing Research Laboratory to update building techniques, along with more training establishments for additional workers to enter the trade. Employment policy did not undergo any major developments but it was moved up the agenda to second place, second only to the SNP's master plan for an independent Scotland. To tackle Scotland's higher unemployment rate, the Party proposed tax breaks on fuel to stimulate the economy, more research and development projects, retraining in areas of industrial decline and, in the case of shipbuilding, government backing to a proposed consortium scheme to build a state of the art shipyard on the Clyde in order to compete successfully with foreign rivals like Japan.[86] A series of policy election broadcast sheets were also issued by the Party to complement its manifesto. Several sheets were published by the Party in the run-up to the election on single policy issues covering a diverse range of subjects like the NHS, shipbuilding, and agriculture and forestry.[87] These supplements were developed from the Party's main policy statement, *SNP and You*, and called for more powers to be directed towards Scotland in some form or another. They and the Party's main manifesto helped swell the SNP's vote because they played on the concerns of the Scottish electorate on important issues like Europe, unemployment, and health, while offering greater devolutionary powers as an immediate solution which many voters supported. Although most voters remained unsupportive of the SNP's full independence line, a great many of them did support devolution and some simply voted for the SNP on the premise that it would send out a clear signal to the incoming government to give more attention to Scotland.

As well as offering a persuasive set of policies, the SNP's propaganda campaign also bolstered its result. The Party's unprecedented number of candidates and their election agents and canvassers took the SNP's message to more doorsteps than at any election campaign in the past. The dramatic rise in the number of activists, which had risen alongside membership, gave candidates more manpower per constituency to get their campaign messages across. Changes made to broadcasting policy in 1965 also brought the Party into more households than ever before. The SNP's first party political broadcast in 1965 publicised the Party and its policies on an unprecedented scale and its subsequent increase in appearance on political and current affairs programmes also familiarised Scottish voters with the Party making it seem a more attractive proposition at the polls. Candidates like Wolfe, Donaldson, and McIntyre, who generally represented the SNP on television and radio programmes, also polled the highest. Wolfe, who was dubbed 'Mr SNP' because of his various broadcast appearances, gained the highest vote. The SNP's newly established PR Department also presented the Party to a wider audience through its press releases and publications. The Department released a dozen or so statements and held several more conferences during the election month of March, which were picked up and reported on by various press agencies. It was also the driving force behind the circulation of 80,000 copies of a General Election special edition of the *Scots Independent*, a figure that was substantially more than the Party's membership total at the time.[88] The department also became involved in branding the Party which made the SNP more memorable and wider-known by election time. A Saltire and thistle style logo that was initially used in Wolfe's 1964 election campaign, was rolled out by other candidates in the 1966 campaign. The Party had taken its inspiration from groups like the CND whose logo was instantly recognisable by a large swathe of the population, and, hoping to achieve similar results, the SNP produced badges, pendants and other merchandise bearing its own symbol. Its Saltire and thistle logo proved popular amongst supporters during the election and would become the Party's trademark in later years. The department also explored the desirability of party colours as another visual aid and a survey revealed that blue and white were the branches' top colours of choice (perhaps not surprisingly given that they are the colours of the Saltire).[89] These colours were not made mandatory, however, and black and gold eventually became the SNP's distinctive party motif. The combination of black against a gold background had first been used by Halliday during his 1955 election campaign. Halliday had intended to use blue and gold to represent the flag colours of Scotland, blue for the colour of the Saltire and gold for the Lion Rampant, but during production the colour blue came out black.[90] Black and gold, however, worked well together and was visually more noticeable than the main parties' colours. Black and gold, therefore, came to be the colours of the Party and were particularly effective during election campaigns when party placards were hung and the SNP's stood out among the rest.

The SNP also increased its vote at the 1966 General Election by acting on the lessons it had learned from its 1964 campaign. After the 1964 result, Gordon Wilson carried out an analysis to ascertain improvements that could be made to future campaigns to increase the Party's vote. One suggestion was for candidates to hold fewer public meetings and target their audience in larger locations. This would give the impression to the public and press of well attended meetings. It would also free up time for other campaigning duties and reduce incidental expenses such as room hire, transport and advertising costs. Another suggestion was for candidates and their helpers to flood the constituencies with posters. This would send out the message that candidates were fighting a strong campaign and it was a simple task which any willing volunteer could undertake. Another proposal was for candidates to send more letters to the editors of newspapers. This would not only get their names better known but it would also give out the appearance of a strong campaign and it entailed no monetary expenditure other than the price of a stamp. A further proposal was for candidates to spend a larger proportion of money at the beginning of their campaigns when floating voters' minds were more susceptible to propaganda and ideas than at the later stages when their minds were more likely to be made up. Also touted was the ferrying of known supporters to polling stations to cast their vote. This was done on a limited scale in the 1964 campaign and it was proposed that it should be rolled out at future elections. It only involved one day of work on polling day when campaigning had been concluded.[91] These suggestions were incorporated into the campaigns of Party candidates to varying degrees in 1966 and helped to some extent in strengthening their votes. Other ideas were also implemented to boost their campaigns. A parliamentary handbook was produced by the Party as a reference guide for candidates to help them in their campaigns. It was a standardised guidebook which provided useful hints and tips and it was also a time-saving device for the Party's organisational staff as candidates could refer to the handbook for information rather than overwhelming the Party's staff at their busiest time.[92] Campaign literature was also better prepared and better presented which benefited the SNP's result. More visuals and improved layouts were used to break up key policy areas. Wolfe's brochure, which was brightened up with colours and illustrations, particularly shone above the rest and was a stark contrast from his text-heavy and somewhat dull brochure of 1964. These small tactical changes deployed by the Party all helped in their own small way to improve the SNP's election campaign and achieve its record result.

Pollok By-Election and Local Elections

After the SNP's relative success in the 1966 General Election, the Party showed considerably more progress the following March when a by-election at Pollok came along. Pollok was the first parliamentary contest in Scotland since the General Election and the SNP grasped the opportunity to contest it. It promptly announced George Leslie as its candidate and he was soon joined by a horde of activists from around Glasgow to aid his campaign. Right from the beginning there was a buzz of activity as Leslie and his helpers canvassed households in the constituency, produced and distributed a stream of glossy leaflets, organised motorcades and undertook an extensive poster campaign to the extent that Leslie's Election Agent, Leslie Anderson, was threatened with action by Glasgow Corporation because of excessive posting.[93] On polling day, the Party's flurry of activity paid off as Leslie picked up 28 per cent of the ballot, which translated into 10,884 votes, just 1,185 behind Labour and 3,386 behind the Conservatives. It was an extraordinary result for the SNP for several reasons. First, the seat had never been contested by the Party before and, unlike McIntyre who had fought Stirlingshire West for the first time at the General Election and gained 26 per cent, Leslie was not a high profile candidate and did not receive votes automatically because of public recognition. Second, the contest had been a five-party race with the Liberals and Communists also standing candidates which gave electors more choice and opportunity to spread the third party vote. The Liberals gained only 735 votes despite having previously contested the constituency and the Communists came last with just 694,[94] which seemed to suggest that the SNP had overtaken the Liberal Party as the third party in Scotland. Third, and more importantly, Labour's vote decreased by more than 20 per cent at the Election while the Tories declined by just nine per cent. Pollok had also been a Labour seat but was lost to the Conservatives due to the SNP's performance. The SNP's increase in electoral support at the expense of Labour did not stop at Pollok either.

In the local elections that followed in May, Labour lost more ground to the SNP. In Glasgow, the SNP contested all 37 local election wards and gained 60,034 votes out of a total cast of 260,439. Labour's vote on the other hand fell by more than 7,000 to 81,040 votes. In Edinburgh it was a similar picture where the SNP contested seven electoral wards which was almost a third of the seats in the Capital and polled 10,415 out of 43,939 votes in the areas where it stood. By contrast, Labour's vote declined by more than 6,500 to just 34,053 votes. Moreover, in Stirling the SNP gained three additional seats bringing its total number to nine. This resulted in the SNP becoming the largest party within Stirling Town Council and McIntyre was subsequently elected Provost.[95] By the summer of 1967, it seemed that Labour was losing ground to the SNP faster than any other political party. Given this scenario, the question is why were some Labour voters now turning to the SNP?

One reason was the Labour Government's performance on the economy since its re-election in 1966. When Labour came to power in 1964 on Wilson's pledge to tackle the economy with the 'White Heat of Technological Revolution', a flurry of activity in Scotland ensued under the new Scottish Secretary, Willie Ross. Planning and industrial development became the prime focus of attention, as agencies such as the Scottish Development Department, the Highland and Islands Development Board and the Scottish Economic Planning Council, were set up to direct and enhance Scotland's economic activity. The whole of Scotland except Edinburgh was designated with development status under Labour's National Plan which brought aid to Scotland channelled through the new Development Department. Fairfield's

165

shipyard on the Clyde was also saved from closure with the aid of a government rescue package which maintained the shipyard as a going concern.[96] Major reforms in education and social work were also instituted and public spending in key areas like housing and transport rose. When the 1966 General Election arrived, Labour was duly rewarded for its energetic term of government with three additional parliamentary seats in Scotland, bringing its total number to 46. But with such a vigorous first term, it was a tall order to follow and almost from the word go things began to go wrong for Labour's new administration. Labour's huge spending programme in its previous term had resulted in budget deficit problems and a Selective Employment Tax was introduced to help balance the books. But this only made matters worse and a seamen's strike ensued which badly affected Scotland's island communities and sparked a sterling crisis. Deflationary policies promptly followed which led to higher interest rates, wage freezes and higher unemployment.[97] The electorate's high hopes for Labour were dashed. Many disgruntled Labour voters in Scotland switched to the SNP as a mark of protest to punish Labour at the polls. For those that did, some never returned to the Labour Party again.

The SNP also showed greater left-wing credentials in the sixties which made it the obvious choice for disaffected Labour supporters. The SNP's support for industries like shale oil and coal, its policy commitment to social justice and its opposition to Polaris showed evidence of its left-wing leanings. Localised SNP opposition to the war in Vietnam also demonstrated its left-wing tendencies. The SNP's Executive kept a low profile on the issue but individual constituency associations publicly opposed the war, like West Lothian, which issued its own press statement:

> West Lothian Association of the Scottish National Party have come out emphatically against interference in the affairs of Vietnam by any power, great or lesser. Scotland knows only too well what interference in her own affairs means, and should not support it in the case of other nations.[98]

Wilson's support for America in Vietnam on the other hand was resented in some Labour quarters, as was his support for nuclear armament and EEC membership, all of which the SNP opposed.

The SNP also targeted Labour audiences during the sixties by setting up its own trade union association and by encouraging its members to infiltrate co-operative societies. The Association of Scottish Nationalist Trade Unionists (ASNTU) was set up by the SNP in 1965 as an advisory body to the Party to encourage SNP activity in trade union affairs and to disseminate SNP policy amongst trade unionists in the hope of recruiting new union members. The Association was run by Bill Johnston, Alec Bissett and Unity Millar, and its remit naturally included campaigning for im-

166

proved pay and working conditions for workers in Scotland. [99] Only a year or so after its establishment, some trade union representatives began to take notice of the SNP. Several in fact approached it in relation to Kelvin Electronics company in Glasgow and the shipbuilding industry on the Clyde.[100] The SNP also encouraged its membership to become involved in co-operative societies by attending local co-op business meetings.[101] By doing so, the SNP hoped that it could muscle in on Labour territory and get its message across to traditional Labour supporters. The SNP also took the workers' and unions' side over the contentious issue of pay awards for Scottish members of the National Association of Local Government Officers (NALGO). The SNP leapt to the support of NALGO members when their pay awards were frozen in Scotland but not in England. Press releases were published by the Party on the matter and George Leslie sent a telegram to the Secretary of State for Scotland bitterly complaining about the situation in the run-up to the Pollok by-election which did his campaign no harm at all.[102] The SNP's championing of the Scottish worker and its stronger association with trade unionism made the Party seem a more attractive alternative for disheartened Labour supporters and made their transition from the Labour Party to the SNP an easier one.

Conversely, as mentioned earlier, the SNP also benefited from a general decline in class voting during this era as more working class voters than ever before moved up the social stratum to occupy the middle class group. Despite the SNP's obvious left-wing leanings, it was also perceived as having something of a 'classless image' and upwardly social mobile voters were attracted to it as an alternative to Labour. The SNP's emphasis of the national interest rather than sectional interests helped formulate this image and the SNP was particularly happy to project it in areas with more Unionist and Liberal support. In Labour strongholds dominated by the working class, it was keen to show off its left-wing policy elements. The SNP's ability to capture socially mobile Labour voters and sway the more traditional Labour voter showed its versatility during the 1960s.

On the issue of self-government itself, Labour also lost supporters to the SNP. Labour in times past had supported a Scottish parliament within the structure of the UK but had failed to deliver it when it came to power in 1945 and, to the contrary, introduced a series of centralised policies based around a planned economy concentrated in London. By the mid-fifties, Labour had turned its back on the issue altogether when Party leader, Hugh Gaitskell, denounced Scottish Home Rule at the Party's 1956 Conference of the Scottish Council.[103] Despite the efforts of individuals like John P. Mackintosh to keep the issue alive in the Labour Party, by the late fifties, Labour's official support for Home Rule was over.[104] Scottish Labour figures like Willie Ross and Tam Dalyell were particularly hostile to a Scottish parliament and vehemently rejected it in public and in the press. Ross and Dalyell both believed that devolution would result in the 'slippery slope' towards independence and opposed any demands for it. Dalyell later raised the West Lothian Question as mentioned previously and also supported the *Labour Vote No* campaign when a referendum took place on the issue on 1 March 1979.[105] Similarly, Ross spurned nationalism north of the border and mockingly referred to the meaning of the Royal Commission on the Constitution (otherwise known as the Kilbrandon Commission) as 'Kill-devolution' - he later converted to devolution in the mid-seventies but even then it was purely on expedient grounds.[106] But rejection of devolution by the Labour Party and strong opposition shown in public by some Labour figures was not well received by grass-roots supporters, a great many of whom still supported the premise of a Scottish parliament which had been supported by the Labour Party since the days of Keir Hardie. The SNP's support for a Scottish parliament was on the other hand unequivocal and some Labour supporters would not have failed to realise that switching their support to the SNP would likely result in support for devolution returning to the Labour Party's policy agenda.

But Labour was not the only Party losing ground to the SNP; the Tories and Liberals were also losing support to it, albeit to a lesser extent. The Tory Party in Scotland had long played the Scottish card by wrapping itself in symbols of Scotland to gain votes, but its Scottish image declined in the 1960s and it became more associated with Britain's disintegrating Empire, economic decline and failed EEC entry. It underwent a name change from the Scottish Unionist Association to the Conservative and Unionist Party in 1965 and was referred to as the Scottish Conservative Party to reduce its unionist connotations and make it more appealing to the electorate. But this failed to stem its shrinking support and by 1966 it had less than half the number of seats held by Labour in Scotland. At Pollok in 1967, its support continued to decline, reducing by almost 11 per cent from 47.6 per cent at the 1966 General Election to 36.9 per cent at the by-election. Instead of gaining protest votes from Labour supporters as the main rival party, a sizeable proportion of its voters had simply abandoned it for the SNP. Besides its poorer image in the sixties, a decline in religious voting may also explain its lost support to the SNP. Protestantism and unionism had historic connections which had resulted in Protestants, even working class Protestants, steering towards the Unionist Party.[107] But society in the sixties had become increasingly secular and working class Protestants no longer automatically identified with unionism.[108] This benefited Labour as well as the SNP.

The Liberal Party in Scotland also lost support to the SNP despite its surge in support in the first half of the decade. The Liberals and the SNP were both competing for the third-party vote and it initially seemed that the Liberals were winning the battle when they raced ahead at the 1959 and 1964 General Elections after a decade of contraction in the fifties. By the General Election of 1966, however, support for the Liberals was on the wane while support for the SNP was on the increase and a year later at Pollok, would-be Liberal supporters chose the SNP over the Liberal

Party. One explanation for this shift in support was the growing view amongst sections of the electorate that the SNP was a radical alternative to the Liberals and that a vote for the SNP would send out a more powerful signal to the main parties, particularly on the issue of Home Rule, than a vote for the Liberals. Even though the Liberal Party had long supported a policy of devolution and in 1966 the Liberal MP for Invernessshire, Russell Johnston, had introduced a Bill on Scottish self-government (which was rejected by the House of Commons), more and more voters chose the SNP over the Liberals as the most effective means of receiving a better deal for Scotland. The SNP had also benefited from a new breed of talented individuals who joined its ranks around the sixties, such as Wolfe and Macdonald, whereas the Liberals had lost some valuable members during the same period, like Ludovic Kennedy.[109]

Hamilton By-Election

The bandwagon continued to roll for the SNP in 1967 when the breakthrough it had been waiting for finally came along with a by-election at Hamilton. The Hamilton by-election had been a long time coming. It was expected to take place in 1966 when sitting Labour MP, Tom Fraser, was appointed Chair of the South of Scotland Electricity Board in 1966. But Fraser turned down the position and was appointed Chair of the North of Scotland Hydro Electric Board a year later instead, resulting in the by-election in November 1967. Hamilton was one of the safest Labour seats in the land – Labour's poll had been above 70 per cent at the 1964 and 1966 General Elections - and everyone assumed a Labour victory, including the SNP. Hoping to come a strong second, the SNP put forward the young energetic Winnie Ewing as its candidate. Ewing was not particularly well-known prior to her candidacy and had to be persuaded to put herself forward in the first place, but once selected she put her heart and soul into the role. She began touring SNP branches, delivering speeches and generally raising her profile in anticipation of a by-election being called in 1966 after Fraser's first Electricity Board appointment. So when it eventually came at the end of 1967, a considerable amount of groundwork had already been done. During the campaign period itself, a tremendous display of strength was put on by the SNP. Hundreds of canvassers from all over the country descended upon the constituency and even some Plaid Cymru members made the journey north to help out in the campaign.[110] Motorcades were held, SNP propaganda was distributed and a slide show on a lorry was even deployed. The top brass, including Arthur Donaldson, Robert McIntyre and Gordon Wilson, also mucked in and James Bond star, Sean Connery, even lent his support to the campaign.[111] Ewing was also more photogenic than most SNP candidates who had gone before her and she appeared in more press pictures and television interviews than any of her predecessors. By contrast, her Labour opponent, Alex Wilson, seemed rather awkward and unnatural in front of the camera. On the day of the election, Ewing swept the rug from under Labour's feet by overturning its huge majority and gaining 18,397 votes, which equated to 46 per cent of the vote. It was a truly superb result for the SNP which had contested the seat only once before in 1959 when it received just six per cent of the vote. Labour with its lacklustre campaign that had taken Hamilton voters for granted and assumed re-election from the outset, managed less than 42 per cent or 16,598 votes (a reduction of almost 30 per cent from the previous year's election).[112] The date of the election on 2 November, which coincided with a sterling crisis where the pound had devalued just days before, did nothing either to help Labour's vote.

For the SNP, the result gave an immediate euphoric morale boost to members all over the country, some of whom had been campaigning for a generation to have the Party elected again after McIntyre's short lived victory in 1945. Seizing on the jubilation, Rosemary Hall chartered a train to take Ewing and triumphant Party members to London. The 'Tartan Express', as it was dubbed, was packed full of excited members who accompanied Ewing on her maiden voyage to take her seat in the House of Commons. Victory at Hamilton also propelled the Party into the limelight more than it had ever experienced before. Ewing had already received a significant amount of press and television coverage prior to the result. After her victory, she was inundated with offers of television and press interviews. She was even given her own column in the Labour-leaning tabloid, the *Daily Record*, and received regular features in others like the *Scottish Daily Express* and the *News of the World*. She was also invited to take part in parliamentary broadcasts from which the SNP had been excluded in the past owing to its lack of parliamentary representation. Ewing's photogenic appeal, her charisma in front on the camera and her skills of debate earned her so much coverage in fact that the Party's National Executive requested she reduce her television appearances for fear of 'over exposure'.[113] It was ironic given the ongoing battle the SNP had fought for over two decades to gain fairer broadcasting treatment only for it now to fear the over exposure of its only MP. The Party's membership numbers also soared in the wake of the by-election. In the days and weeks that followed, SNP branches were flooded with people wishing to join and official membership figures according to the sale of SNP membership cards rocketed to 80,000. By March the following year, it would reach the 100,000 mark.[114] Although these figures are likely to be an overestimation as, Gordon Wilson notes, figures were based on membership cards sold which did not always translate into new members joining.[115] The Party's level of support at the polls correspondingly increased when it won a staggering 30.1 per cent of the vote at the local elections in May 1968. In Glasgow, its vote shot to 35.9 per cent and in Edinburgh it reached 35.1 per cent. It gained 107 local councillors across Scotland and it took control of Cumbernauld Town Council for the first time (the New Town which the SNP had objected to being built back in the fifties).[116] Research privileges were also gained following Hamilton as Ewing as an MP was afforded her own research assistant and was able to raise questions and seek answers to issues of importance to the SNP. The clear focus on the parliamentary arena by the end of 1967 did cause some within the Party to indulge in romanticism by joining the newly formed 1320 Club, named so after the year of the Declaration of Arbroath. But its secretive membership and a fear of nationalists like Wendy Wood, Hugh MacDiarmid and Douglas Young being brought together and linked to the SNP led to the Party outlawing its membership in 1968.[117] The explosion in SNP morale, membership and media coverage in the wake of Hamilton thrust the SNP from its fringe status in Scottish politics into the mainstream where it has remained, with varying degrees of support, ever since.

The result at Hamilton also had wider implications on Scottish politics as it sent shockwaves across the political establishment and signalled a policy shift towards some form of Home Rule amongst the major parties. For Labour and the Conservatives, Ewing's victory came as a bolt out of the blue despite the SNP's growing support at the polls and a nationalist victory by Plaid Cymru's Gwynfor Evans at Carmathen the previous year. For both major parties, Hamilton served as an overdue wake-up call to the nationalist surge that was going on and each responded to the unleashed 'nationalist beast' with their own taming devices. The Conservative leader, Ted Heath, declared his support for legislative devolution at the Party's 1968 Scottish Conference in Perth. His so-called Declaration of Perth, as it became known, claimed that:

> The Conservative Party is determined to effect a real improvement in the machinery of government in Scotland. And is pledged to give the people of Scotland genuine participation in the making of decisions that affect them – all within the historic entity of the United Kingdom.[118]

Accordingly, he proposed that an elected Assembly in Scotland should be set up with the power to legislate in conjunction with Westminster. It was a vague ideal and a constitutional committee was formed to draw up the details under the direction of Alec Douglas-Home. It reported in 1970 and its main recommendation called for an elected Scottish Assembly to be established with limited powers to deal with certain areas of Scottish legislation.[119] It was a weak form of legislative devolution and was adopted by the Conservative Party as a ploy to stave off the nationalist threat, although it did come up against staunch criticism from a significant minority within the Conservative Party who had joined the Party for its unionist policies rather than its devolutionary ones. Labour was slower off the mark to respond to the nationalist surge. Willie Ross's instinctive reaction following Hamilton was to ride out the nationalist storm in the hope that it would subside and simply go away. Rather than concede to the 'Tartan Tory' nationalists as he referred to the SNP (somewhat ironically given that much of its support now came from Labour), Ross called for the SNP to be fought head-on and used its surge to wring more resources from Westminster. But with no sign of the nationalist threat abating, others within the Labour Party moved towards a more conciliatory approach to the Scottish Question and a select committee on Scottish affairs was set up in 1968, followed by a Royal Commission on the Constitution in 1969, which was just the job to push the devolution issue to one side for a number of years.[120] Presided by Lord Kilbrandon, the Royal Commission eventually reported in October 1973 and a majority of commissioners recommended 'a scheme of legislative devolution for Scotland... [and] for Wales' in which 'responsibility for legislating on specifically defined matters would be transferred to a Scottish or Welsh legislature consisting of the sovereign and a directly elected assembly.'[121] Labour was sceptical at first but threw its weight behind devolution when the SNP made a splash at the polls a few months later in February 1974 as it took seven seats at the General Election and created a number of marginals in Labour-held constituencies. Not wanting to miss out, the Liberal Party also took the opportunity to reaffirm its pledge for devolved government by demanding the establishment of a Scottish parliament within a federal system of government at its Annual Conference in May 1968.[122] Unlike Labour and the Tories, it was not a policy shift but the issue did climb up the Liberal Party's agenda following Hamilton. Home Rule would remain on the political agenda for years to come after Ewing's victory. Only after 1979 when the SNP's level of electoral support declined did it falter.

Conclusion

The second half of the 1960s saw the SNP break through to become a major political force in Scottish politics. External forces outside the SNP's control had already made the ground fertile for SNP success as important issues like the decline of the Empire and the UK's failure to join Europe undermined a feeling of British identity amongst Scots, while slumps in the economy and a burgeoning sense of Scottish identity continued to feed nationalism. But the SNP's own endeavours were also pivotal to its breakthrough. Its long-fought campaign for a change in broadcasting policy helped to gain it party political broadcasts for the first time and improvements made to its own publicity machine, like the establishment of its Public Relations Department in Edinburgh and its branding, made it more familiar to the electorate than ever before. The SNP's growing level of financial astuteness also transformed it from a fringe party to a major political contender with its launch of Alba Pools and other financial schemes in this period. These factors enabled it to expand and fight more election contests than it had ever fought before. By 1967, external forces and internal dynamics had coupled together to make conditions conducive for Party success and when Hamilton came along at the end of the year, there was a degree of optimism already in the air. Parliamentary success had just been a matter of time and neither the SNP nor Scottish politics would ever be the same again.

Conclusion

From 1945 to 1967, the Scottish National Party transformed from a small marginal organisation into a major political party. Its advancement from an unimportant outfit with a small rump of members in 1945 to a serious political player by 1967 is a watershed period in the Party's history.

The SNP in the post-war period developed into a different type of political animal to the Party of its pre-war days. Back then, it had no decisive political objective, it had no socio-economic policy in place and it had no clear strategy on how to achieve its aim. But in the post-war period, the SNP rallied round a coherent political ideal, it implemented a socio-economic policy and it committed itself to a clear-cut political strategy. Introducing and maintaining these core ideological principles helped bind the Party together as a more cohesive force in the post-war period.

One of the most significant characteristics of the SNP during 1945-67 was its commitment to an unambiguous political aim of full independence for Scotland. The SNP had only just assembled behind this political ideal in 1942 but in the years ahead its commitment to this principle became resolute. Before the Second World War and the arrival of the SNP's splinter organisation, the Scottish Convention, the desire for different shades of Home Rule was prevalent amongst SNP members. 'Moderates' favoured a limited form of Home Rule whereby domestic affairs would be devolved to a Scottish parliament and Scotland would remain a firm part of the United Kingdom, while 'radicals' opted for a far wider-reaching version where Scotland would attain complete independence. But after the departure of John MacCormick and other moderates from the SNP in 1942, who formed the Scottish Convention, radicals made up the prevailing membership of the SNP and they gelled the Party together around the central issue of full independence. In 1948, this position strengthened when the SNP tackled the long-standing issue of dual membership. Scrapping this policy which had allowed SNP members to be members of other political parties removed those from the Party who had split loyalties to other organisations, like the Convention or the Liberal Party, which supported weaker forms of Home Rule. By removing those members who were in favour of devolution rather than independence, remaining SNP members increasingly identified with the Party's full independence strategy and a stronger ideological bond was forged. The SNP was also behaving more like a conventional political party by not allowing members of other political persuasions to direct or influence it.

The SNP's adoption of a left-of-centre policy broadened the Party's sense of political identity. The SNP adopted an official policy statement for the first time in 1946 and took a tremendous leap forward in doing so by operating more like a political party rather than a single-issue interest group. The SNP's decision to draft a policy framework was a brave step because it had the potential to expose the Party to count-less disputes and arguments amongst its members as it was the constitutional issue rather than the socio-economic one that unified it. Its new policy statement did not plunge the Party into chaos, however, but augmented its political identity and re-vealed to the electorate its left-of-centre liberalist leanings where the individual and community would be favoured over big business and state socialism. It put the SNP distinctly left of the Unionists, but right of Labour, providing the electorate in Scot-land with an alternative to the leading British parties of the day. This was accentu-ated in the fifties when the SNP developed further its distinctive policy by highlighting predominately Scottish issues like the fishing industry and the Party's support for communities rather than business or the state - the things that set it apart from Labour and the Unionists. This altered somewhat in the sixties when the SNP's support for nuclear disarmament, its stronger commitment to social justice and its connections to trade unions and co-ops shifted it further left along the political scale, which meant that it became a bigger challenger to the Labour vote.

In order to achieve its aim and policy, the SNP pursued an electoral strategy and practised a firm disciplined approach throughout 1945-67. Under the chairman-ship of Watson, McIntyre, Halliday and Donaldson, the Party became uncompro-misingly committed to a strategy of electoral mandate, and despite the pressures and temptations from various quarters to disregard this instrument, the SNP's leader-ship remained steadfast in its commitment to it. The SNP's refusal to become drawn into the pursuits of other nationalist organisations, particularly the Scottish Conven-tion, underscored this. The Scottish Convention, which became the Scottish Covenant Association, had captured the imagination of the country and initially seemed to show that pressure group tactics were the route to success. It also showed clear evidence through its National Assemblies, plebiscites and petitions that devo-lution rather than independence was what Scots actually wanted and its all-party no-party approach seemed to indicate that a non-parliamentary route was the way to achieve it. But the failure of politicians to act upon the Covenant Association's re-peated demands, and its lack of an electoral policy to enforce them, spelled its end. It also exonerated the leadership of the SNP who had argued correctly all along that an electoral strategy and electoral support were vital in the fight for Home Rule and that the Party would have to be prepared for the long haul in order to achieve suc-cess.

The establishment of Muirhead's Scottish National Congress also emphasised the Party's disciplined approach on electoral policy because it was the SNP's refusal to succumb to Muirhead's repeated requests for a change in tactical policy that led him to set up the SNC in 1950. Muirhead and others who formed the SNC believed that non-co-operative tactics were the most effective means to achieve a Scottish parlia-ment whereas the SNP's electoral strategy would fail to deliver it alone, or at least fail to deliver it anytime soon. Muirhead had chipped away at this point for a number of years within the SNP but was unable to alter the Party's firm approach despite his high-ranking position and the financial backing he gave to the Party. The establishment of the dissident 55 Group within the SNP similarly displayed a strong unwavering SNP leadership that was unwilling to buckle and remained focused on its methodology. The 55 Group had been born out of frustrations over the SNP's tactical approach and style of leadership which were viewed as dictatorial and ineffective by members of the new Group. They sought to overthrow the 'old' leadership of McIntyre and others and replace it with younger leaders who would be less rigid in their approach. But it was precisely the dogmatic style exercised by McIntyre and other SNP leaders and their ability to 'stay the course' in the face of adversity which saw the Party through its most difficult times. The refusal of McIntyre and other leaders within the SNP to give way to a change in leadership approach and deviate from an electoral strategy by going down the extra-parliamentary route only highlighted their strong uncompromising style of leadership which set them apart from their pre-war predecessors. The failure of splinter groups and other nationalist organisations in the fifties and sixties vindicated the SNP's unyielding approach and eventually led to nationalists of all colours uniting behind the SNP and backing the aim, policy and strategy long pursued by its leadership.

The SNP's distinctive political aim, its socio-economic policy, its single-party membership rule and its electoral strategy enforced by firm leadership, were immensely important for the Party because they provided it with a strong sense of political identity and cohesion in the post-war period which helped unite and sustain it, and also gave it the necessary devices to become a conventional political party. These forces, which had never been maintained in the SNP's pre-war days, became the cornerstone structures of the Party in the post-war period and still remain the foundations on which the Party stands today.

In the forties and fifties, the focus for the SNP had been on developing and maintaining policy, strategy and party discipline, but in the sixties another focal point emerged for the Party in the form of organisation. Organisation had long been a problem for the Party as it had had no organisational strategy or organiser in place throughout most of its existence and it suffered from having a poor party structure. Branches had been overburdened with the tasks of promoting the Party, bringing in new members and generating finance with little support from Headquarters with the result that many failed to maintain momentum or survive. Ian Macdonald's arrival in the early sixties as the Party's National Organiser, however, changed this. Macdonald's talent and hard work in the field helped turn the Party's organisational failures around by hugely expanding its branch network and membership roll over a relatively short period of time. Macdonald's and the SNP's emphasis on bringing new members into the Party also led to many young members in particular joining who had become attracted to it by its more radical distinction from the main political parties. Having so many young members in the Party also gave the SNP a youthful feel in the sixties and their energetic nature contributed to it becoming a major political force during this decade. The SNP's executive and committee restructuring programmes in the sixties and its increase in office staff numbers also helped facilitate growth, even if they did lag somewhat behind the Party's fast pace of membership growth. These improvements to organisation played a critical role in the SNP's breakthrough in the sixties and its historic by-election victory at Hamilton in 1967.

By 1967, the SNP had arrived in its modern day form. It had its aim, policy and strategy firmly in place, it was now a mainstream political party with parliamentary representation, and many of the people who had joined it in the sixties or just before like Billy Wolfe, Gordon Wilson and Winnie Ewing, would come to dominate it in the years ahead and take it to new heights in the seventies. The arrival of the SNP as a major political party in the sixties marked a new chapter in the Party's history and its efforts in subsequent years played a crucial role in bringing into being its goal of a Scottish Parliament in 1999. But now that a Scottish Parliament has been established, the job of the SNP remains far from complete. On the contrary, the devolved political structure now in place at Holyrood falls far short of what the SNP has long campaigned for and its fight for independence goes on.

The SNP's landmark victory at the polls in May 2007 brought its goal of independence a step closer when it became the leading party in Scotland for the first time and formed a minority government in the Scottish Parliament with Alex Salmond as First Minister at the helm. The Party's momentous re-election in 2011 in which it won an outright majority, taking 69 of the 129 MSP seats, has also meant that the question of constitutional change has never been so relevant. The SNP's historic win (which was even more remarkable given that the Scottish Parliament was not designed to produce outright party majorities) now gives the Party the opportunity to advance its independence goal like never before, and Scotland's constitution could be set to evolve again when the SNP takes forward its commitment to a referendum on Scottish independence in 2014. Its governmental phase also ushers in a new episode in the SNPs history and brings with it a new set of challenges for the Party while at the same time raising the profile of its past – perhaps making this research of greater consequence now than when it was first begun. The SNP has come closer than ever to achieving its long-standing goal of an independent sovereign Scotland, yet, with the majority of Scots still in favour of the Union, it also has a long way to go. It faces the enormous task of persuading a majority of voters in Scotland to end over 300 years of Union tradition, but its often difficult and sluggish years during 1945-67 at least stands the SNP in good stead to stay the course.

Introduction - Endnote

1)   See Richard J. Finlay, *A Partnership for Good? Scottish Politics and the Union Since 1880*, (Edinburgh, John Donald Publishers Ltd, 1997), pp.4-5.

Chapter 1 - Endnotes

1)   SNP Memo, undated, NLS McIntyre Mss. Acc. 10090, File 6.
2)   *Scots Independent*, March 1945.
3)   See article 'Dr McIntyre Hits Out' in *The Wishaw Press and Advertiser*, 23 March 1945.
4)   See article by Arnold Kemp 'Who asked Hitler to set up a Scots Republic?' in *The Observer*, 3 June 2001.
5)   Dick Douglas, *At the Helm: The Life and Times of Dr. Robert D McIntyre*, (Banffshire, NPFI Publications, 1995), p30.
6)   Letter from Muirhead to the Secretary of State for Scotland, 7 May 1941, NLS Muirhead Mss. Acc. 3721, Box 3, File 59.
7)   Evidence of Douglas Cuthbert Colquhoun Young before the Sheriff Substitute of Lanarkshire, 23 April 1942, and; Verbatim Report of the Trial of Douglas Young at the High Court of Justiciary, before Lords Cooper, McKay and Stevenson, 6 October 1944, Acc. 10090, File 15.
8)   Letter from the SNP to the Secretary of State for Scotland, undated, Acc. 10090, File 11.
9)   Although the SNP performed better at the polls during this period, its better performance was largely as a result of the wartime electoral truce which existed between the main parties.
10)   *The Wishaw Press and Advertiser*, 27 July 1945.
11)   For biography of McIntyre, see Dick Douglas, *At the Helm: The Life and Times of Dr. Robert D McIntyre*.
12)   Article by Alex Anderson, *The Edinburgh Clarion*, May 1945.
13)   *The Wishaw Press and Advertiser*, 20 April 1945.
14)   SNP Pamphlet for Motherwell & Wishaw By-election, Acc.10090, File 17.
15)   Ibid.
16)   SNP pamphlet McIntyre Motherwell & Wishaw By-Election, Acc. 10090, File 17, and; Statement by the SNP 'For Girls Sent to England', undated, Acc. 10090, File 11.
17)   *The Wishaw Press and Advertiser*, 20 April 1945.
18)   *Motherwell Times*, 13 July 1945.
19)   *The Scotsman*, 11 February 1950.
20)   *The Wishaw Press and Advertiser*, 20 April 1945.

21) *Hansard,* House of Commons, Fifth Series, Volume 410 (London, HMSO, 1945), 17 April 1945, pp.39-44.

22) Ibid p222, and; *The Wishaw Press and Advertiser*, 20 April 1945.

23) *The Wishaw Press and Advertiser*, 20 April 1945.

24) *Motherwell Times*, 13 July 1945.

25) Results listed in *The Wishaw Press and Advertiser*, 27 July 1945.

26) *Hansard,* House of Commons, Fifth Series, Volume 410, p2455 & p2449.

27) Letter from Arthur Henry to Muirhead, 27 April 1945, Acc. 3721, Box 3, File 49.

28) Colin Rallings and Michael Thrasher (Compiled and Edited by), *British Electoral Facts 1832-2006*, (Aldershot, Ashgate Publishing Ltd, 2007), p33.

29) *The Wishaw Press and Advertiser*, 27 July 1945.

30) Quoted in Ibid.

31) Alexander Anderson's Labour Party Parliamentary By-Election Brochure for the Motherwell and Wishaw By-Election, Acc. 10090, File 23.

32) Perth and East Perthshire was the exception where the Unionist candidate won the vote with 63.1 per cent.

33) *Scots Independent*, September 1945.

34) Letter from Muirhead to Sinclair Dunnett, 29 August 1945, Acc. 3721, Box 24, File 648.

35) Minutes of the Executive Committee of the SNP, 11 August 1945, NLS Scottish National Party Mss. Acc. 7295, Folder 16.

36) Richard Parry, *Scottish Political Facts*, (Edinburgh, T&T Clark, 1988), p50.

37) *The Newsletter of the Scottish National Party*, May/June 1948, Acc. 3721, Box 65, File 467.

38) Ibid.

39) Minutes of the Four Year National Programme Committee, 31 August 1946, Acc. 10090, File 14.

40) *The Newsletter of the Scottish National Party*, May/June 1948.

41) Ibid.

42) Letter from Muirhead to Andrew Dewar Gibb, 3 January 1947, Acc. 3721, Box 77, File 748.

43) Letter from Arthur Donaldson to Muirhead, 8 December 1946, Acc. 3721, Box 2, File 30.

44) Letter from Douglas Young to Muirhead, 6 January 1947, NLS Young Mss. Acc. 6419, Box 42, File 3.

45) *The Scotsman*, 7 December 1946.

46) Parry, *Scottish Political Facts*, p68.

47) Letter from Alexander Aitken to Muirhead, 12 November 1947, Acc. 3721, Box 96, File 104.

48) Memo by Young to the Committee of the SNP Kirkcaldy Branch, 8 February 1948, Acc. 10090, File 15.

49) Letter from Young to Muirhead, 12 March 1949, Acc. 3721, Box 89, File 27.

50) Peter Lynch, SNP, *The History of the Scottish National Party*, (Cardiff, Welsh Academic Press, 2002), p75.

51) Letter from Deputy Secretary of the BMA to McIntyre, 10 February 1950, Acc. 10090, File 26 (I).

52) *The Newsletter of the Scottish National Party*, April 1947, Acc. 10090, File 180.

53) SNP Memo, undated, Acc. 10090, File 6.

54) Ibid, and; *The Newsletter of the Scottish National Party*, April 1947.

55) Letter from Young to Gibson, 23 September 1946, Acc. 6419, Box 42, File 2.

56) Iain G. C. Hutchison, *Scottish Politics in the Twentieth Century*, (Basingstoke, Palgrave, 2001), pp.72-4.

57) *Scots Independent*, July 1946.

58) Minutes of the Executive Committee of the SNP, 17 November 1946, Acc. 10090, File 7, and; Report by the National Treasurer to the 1946 Annual Conference of the SNP, Acc. 10090, File 4.

59) Report by the National Treasurer to the 1947 Annual Conference of the SNP, Acc. 10090, File 4.

60) Resolutions passed at the 1948 Annual Conference of the SNP are contained within *Scots Independent*, July 1948.

61) Letter from the SNP National Secretary to branch secretaries, 27 April 1949, Acc. 10090, File 16.

62) See various letters from SNP branches in Acc. 10090, File 32.

63) Letter from Young to Jock, 30 March 1948, Acc. 10090, File 15.

64) Report by SNP National Treasurer, 1950, Acc. 3721, Box 70, File 582A.

65) Report by the National Treasurer to the 1948 Annual Conference of the SNP, Acc. 10090, File 5, and; Letter from David Crawford and Stenhouse Solicitors and Notaries to Muirhead, 24 November 1949, Acc. 3721, Box 74, File 658.

66) Letter from David Crawford and Stenhouse Solicitors and Notaries, to Muirhead, 22 September 1950, Acc. 3721, Box 74, File 658.

67) Report by the National Treasurer to the 1948 Annual Conference of the SNP, Acc. 10090, File 5, and; SNP Balance Sheet as at 31 March 1949, NLS McIntyre Mss. Acc. 12509, File 17.

68) Minutes of the Executive Committee of the SNP, 27 February 1950, Acc. 3721, Box 70, File 582C.

69) Letter from Donaldson to Muirhead, 8 December 1946, Acc. 3721, Box 2, File 30.

70) *The Newsletter of the Scottish National Party*, October/November, 1948, Acc. 10090, File 180.

71) Ibid.

72) Lynch, SNP, *The History of the Scottish National Party*, p60

73) Letter from Young to Dr Gray, 7 December 1949, Acc. 6419, Box 43, File 2.

74) Letter from Young to McIntyre, 11 December 1947, Acc. 6419, Box 42, File 3.

75) Letter from Young to the National Council of the SNP, 29 March 1947, Acc. 3721, Box 89, File 27.

76) Letter from Young to Tom Gibson, 2 January 1947, Acc. 6419, Box 42, File 3.

77) Letter from R Mackay (Secretary of the SSP) to the Secretary of the SNP, 25 January 1949, McIntyre Acc. 10090, File 32.

78) See John Young's article 'What is the Policy of the Scottish National Party' in *Scots Independent*, July 1946.

79) Sir Alexander M. MacEwen, John MacCormick & T. H. Gibson, *Scottish Reconstruction*, (Glasgow, SNP, undated), and; Report on SNP Published Policies by David Murison, 30 November 1944, NLS Mss. Acc. 7498, (Acc. 7498 is untitled and unnumbered).

80) Robert D. McIntyre, *Some Principles for Scottish Reconstruction*, (Glasgow, SNP, 1944).

81) Letter from F. Cameron Yeaman to National Council Members of the SNP, 21 September 1946, Acc. 10090, File 4.

82) Ibid.

83) The SNP's policy statement is published in full in the *Scots Independent*, January 1947.

84) See Young's article in *Scots Independent*, July 1946.

85) H. J. Hanham, *Scottish Nationalism*, (London, Faber and Faber, 1969), pp.179-180.

86) Letter from Young to Tom Gibson, 2 January 1947, Acc. 6419, Box 42, File 3.

87) Richard Finlay, *Independent and Free, Scottish Politics and the Origins of the Scottish National Party, 1918-1945*, (Edinburgh, John Donald Publishers Ltd, 1994), p182.

88) *Constitution and Rules of the Scottish National Party*, (Glasgow, Scottish National Party, 28 and 29 May 1949).

89) Letter from Muirhead to Young, 5 July 1948, Acc. 3721, Box 89, File 27.

90) *The Newsletter of the Scottish National Party*, November/December, 1948, Acc. 10090, File 180.

91) Minutes of the National Council of the SNP, 3 July 1948, Acc. 12509, File 10.

92) Letter from Young to Editor of Scots Independent, 6 December 1948, Acc. 6419, Box 64, File 1.

93) Walter Murray, *Home Rule for Scotland: The case in 90 points / With a foreword by James Barr*, (Glasgow, Scottish Home Rule Association, 1922), p120, and; Letter from Young to the Editor of the *Fife Free Press*, August 1951, NLS Young Mss. Acc. 7085, Box 4, File 4.

94) See letter by Young 'Liberals and Nationalism' published in *The Scotsman*, 17 December 1949.

95) Letter from Young to the Editor of *The Scotsman*, 20 December 1949, Acc.

6419, Box 63, File 1.

96) Letter from Young to Editor of the *Scots Independent*, 12 November 1951, Acc. 6419, Box 63, (No file number).

97) Letter from Young to Charlie Auld, 22 March 1959, Acc. 6419, Box 43, File 3.

98) For some of Young's post-1948 activities, see letter from Muirhead to Young, 8 November 1948, Acc. 7085, Box 2, File 3, and; Article by Young to *Forward*, 26 June 1950, Acc. 6419, Box 64, File 4.

99) Letter from Muirhead to Young, 8 November 1948, Acc. 7085, Box 2, File 3.

100) Letter from Arthur Henry to Muirhead, 16 November 1948, Acc. 3721, Box 3, File 49.

101) Letter from Muirhead to Lamont, 31 May 1949, Acc. 3721, Box 10, File 189A.

102) Minutes of the Executive Committee of the SNP, 17 November 1946, Acc. 10090, File 7.

103) *The Glasgow Herald* and *Evening Citizen*, both 1 December 1947.

104) Minutes of the National Council of the SNP, 10 January 1948, Acc. 10090, File 8.

105) Letter from Young to Jock, 4 April 1948, Acc. 10090, File 15.

106) Letter from Young to McIntyre, 11 December 1947, Acc. 10090, File 15.

107) Letter from Young to Jake Mackie, 16 April 1948, Acc. 10090, File 15.

108) Archie Lamont, *Scotland a Wealth Country, A Scientist's Survey of Scots Resources*, (Glasgow, Scottish Secretariat, 1945).

109) Quoted in the *Daily Herald*, 24 May 1948.

110) *Scottish Daily Mail*, 24 May 1948.

111) Ibid.

112) For example, *Scottish Daily Mail*, *Daily Herald*, *The Scotsman*, *Edinburgh Evening Dispatch*, *Manchester Guardian* and *News Chronicle*, 24 May 1948.

113) Letter from Muirhead to Lamont, 7 June 1948, Acc. 3721, Box 10, File 189A.

114) See Minutes of the National Council of the SNP, 8 September 1946, Acc. 10090, File 7.

115) Minutes of the National Council of the SNP, 22 November 1947, Acc. 10090, File 8.

116) Letter from McIntyre to Miss Scott, 20 May 1948, Acc. 10090, File 5.

117) Minutes of the National Council of the SNP, 23 June 1945, NLS Grieve Mss. Acc. 7361, File 16.

118) Ibid.

119) Ibid.

120) Ibid.

121) F.W.S. Craig (Compiled and Edited by), *British Parliamentary Election Results 1918-1949*, Third Edition, (Chichester, Parliamentary Research Services, 1983), p592 and p586.

122) Minutes of the National Council of the SNP, 28 July 1945, Acc. 10090, File 6.

123) Quote stated in article *'Nationalism in Britain'* by Paul Ferris, *The Observer,* 2 August 1959.

124) Letter from Wood to Muirhead, 14 July 1949, and; Letter from Wood to Muirhead, 8 July 1949, Acc. 3721, Box 14, File 273.

Chapter 2 - Endnotes

1) John MacCormick, *The Flag in the Wind: The Story of the National Movement in Scotland*, (London, Victor Gollancz Ltd, 1955), pp.103-104.

2) Letter from William Power and John MacCormick to Robert McIntyre, June 1942, NLS Muirhead Mss. Acc. 3721, Box 50, File 188.

3) Scottish Convention brochure *Questions We Are Asked*, NLS McIntyre Mss. Acc. 10090, File 30.

4) Ibid.

5) See pamphlet Scottish Convention, Non-Party and All-Party, undated, NLS James Porteous Mss. Acc 5978, Box 1, File 1.

6) Minutes of the National Committee of the Scottish Convention, 1 September 1945, NLS Scottish National Party Mss. Acc. 7295, Folder 4.

7) Minutes of the Fifth Annual General Meeting of the Scottish Convention, 22 June 1946, Acc. 7295, Folder 4.

8) Minutes of the National Committee of the Scottish Convention, 4 May 1946, Acc. 7295, Folder 4.

9) Minutes of the Fifth Annual General Meeting of the Scottish Convention, 22 June 1946.

10) Ibid.

11) See the Scottish Convention's policy brochure *The Policy of Scottish Convention, Into Battle*, January 1945, Acc. 5978, Box 1, File 1.

12) Ibid.

13) Circular letter from the Hon. Secretary of the Scottish Convention, December 1946, Acc. 5978, Box 1, File 1.

14) See the Scottish Convention Manifesto, January 1946, Acc. 5978, Box 1, File 1.

15) Minutes of the Fifth Annual General Meeting of the Scottish Convention, 22 June 1946.

16) *Declaration on Scottish Affairs*, 4 May 1944 (Kirkwood Printers, Glasgow).

17) Scottish National Assembly booklet *Some Principles for Scottish Reconstruction*, 22 March 1947, Acc. 10090, File 30.

18) Quoted in the *Edinburgh Evening Dispatch*, 22 March 1947.

19) Letter from SNP National Secretary to SNP members, 17 March 1947, Acc. 10090, File 29.

20) Ibid.

21) Scottish National Assembly booklet, *Report of Proceedings*, 22 March 1947, and; *The Scotsman*, 24 March 1947.

22) Scottish National Assembly booklet, *Report of Proceedings*, 22 March 1947.

23) See Richard Finlay, *Independent and Free, Scottish Politics and the Origins of the Scottish National Party 1918-1945*, (Edinburgh, John Donald Publishers, 1994), pp.229-230; James Mitchell, *Strategies for Self-Government: The Cam-*

paigns for a Scottish Parliament, (Edinburgh, Polygon, 1996), p195, and; H. J. Hanham, *Scottish Nationalism*, (London, Faber & Faber, 1969) p168.

24) For Young's views on self-government, see Scottish National Assembly booklet, *Report of Proceedings, 22 March 1947*, and; Letter from Young to *The National Weekly*, January 1950, NLS Young Mss. Acc. 7085, Box 2, File 4.

25) Scottish National Assembly booklet, *Report of Proceedings, 22 March 1947*.

26) Ibid.

27) Ibid.

28) For names of Committee members and the organisations they represented, see ibid.

29) Proposals for Scottish Self-Government made by the Committee of the Scottish National Assembly, September 1947, Acc. 10090, File 30, and; *Blue Print for Scotland, Practical Proposals: Scottish Self-Government*, (Glasgow, Scottish Covenant Association, undated).

30) Ibid.

31) MacCormick, *The Flag in the Wind*, p126.

32) Ibid. pp.126-127.

33) James Mitchell, '*Scotland in the Union, 1945-95: The Changing Nature of the Union State*', in T. M. Devine and R. J. Finlay (Edited by), *Scotland in the Twentieth Century*, (Edinburgh, Edinburgh University Press, 1996), p92.

34) Minutes of the Committee of the Scottish National Assembly, 10 October 1947, Acc. 5978, Box 1, File 3.

35) Report of Second Meeting of the Scottish National Assembly, 20 March 1948, NLS Scottish Covenant Association Mss. Dep. 242, file unnumbered.

36) *Scots Independent*, February 1949.

37) *Scots Independent*, March 1949.

38) MacCormick, *The Flag in the Wind*, p127.

39) Leaflet *Scottish Covenant*, Acc. 7295, Folder 6.

40) Statement by the National Party of Scotland 'Second Draft Covenant', 31 May 1930, Acc. 3721, Box 50, File 198.

41) Letter from Douglas Young to the Editor of *The Bulletin*, 12 December 1949, Acc. 7085, Box 2, File 4, and; Letter from Young to the Editor of the *Fife Free Press*, 17 September 1951, NLS Young Mss. Acc. 6419, Box 64, File 1.

42) MacCormick, *The Flag in the Wind*, p131 and p184, and; The Fourth Meeting of the Scottish National Assembly, 22 April 1950, NLS Dep. 242, (File unnumbered).

43) Scotland's electors amounted to 3,416,433 in 1951, see webpage http://www.politicsresources.net/area/uk/ge51/results.htm

44) See article by Paul Ferris 'Nationalism in Britain', *The Observer*, 2 August 1959.

45) For example, Hanham, *Scottish Nationalism*, p172; Christopher Harvie, *No Gods and Precious Few Heroes, Twentieth Century Scotland*, Third Edition, (Edinburgh, Edinburgh University Press, 1998), p107; William L. Miller, *The End*

of *British Politics: Scots and English Political Behaviour in the Seventies*, (Oxford, Clarendon Press, 1981), p20; and Andrew Marr, *The Battle for Scotland*, (London, Penguin Books, 1992), p97.

46) The Covenant's sponsors actually claimed to have gathered the signatures of well over two million people but the figure was rounded down to counteract the spurious signatures. See *Blue Print for Scotland, Practical Proposals: Scottish Self-Government*. However, a figure well exceeding two million people is questionable given that just over 2.7 million people in Scotland voted in the 1950 General Election.

47) Article by Young to Forward, 12 August 1950, Acc. 6419, Box 64, File 4.

48) MacCormick, *The Flag in the Wind*, p135.

49) Quoted in Ibid. p137.

50) Pamphlet *Covenant Qs*, Acc. 10090, File 30.

51) The results were 20,800 electors voted for a Scottish parliament, 4,200 voted against, see pamphlet *The Covenant Yesterday, Today and Tomorrow*, Acc. 7295, Folder 12 (i).

52) *Glasgow Herald*, 27 October 1950.

53) Minutes of Special Meeting of National Committee of the Scottish Convention to discuss the Education (Scotland) Bill, 3 March 1945, Acc. 7295, Folder 4.

54) Minutes of the National Committee of the Scottish Convention, 14 September 1946, Acc. 7295, Folder 4.

55) Minutes of the Executive Committee of the Scottish Convention, 5 February 1948, NLS Scottish Convention Mss. Acc. 6649, File 3.

56) Quoted in MacCormick, *The Flag in the Wind*, pp.120-121.

57) Ibid. p.123.

58) Ibid. p.122.

59) Minutes of the National Committee of the Scottish Convention, 1 May 1948, Acc. 7295, Folder 5.

60) The election result was: Douglas Johnston, 27,213; MacCormick, 20,668, see F. W. S. Craig (Compiled and Edited by), *British Parliamentary Election Results 1918-1949*, Third Edition, (Chichester, Parliamentary Research Services), p605.

61) Quoted in article 'U.S. Customs Delay Covenant', *Glasgow Evening News*, 22 June 1950.

62) See MacCormick, *The Flag in the Wind*, pp.151-154.

63) See article 'Mr MacCormick and Col. McCormick' in *Forward*, 1 July 1950.

64) Ibid.

65) MacCormick, *The Flag in the Wind*, p158.

66) Report by the National Secretary to the 1948 Annual Conference of the SNP, Acc. 10090, File 5.

67) Letter from Muirhead to the Rev. John M. MacMillan, 26 June 1950, Acc. 3721, Box 12, File 233, and; Letter from Young to the Editor of the *Fife Free*

Press, 17 September 1951, Acc. 6419, Box 64, File 1.

68) Letter from Muirhead to G. Morgan, 29 November 1949, Acc. 3721, Box 25, File 663.

69) Letter from Young to Muirhead, 19 March 1951, Acc. 3721, Box 89, File 27.

70) *The Observer*, 14 January 1951.

71) Article by Douglas Young 'Labour and Self-Government for Scotland' published in *The Patriot*, July-August 1967.

72) See Young's letter to the Editor of the *Fife Free Press*, April 1950, Acc. 6419, Box 64, File 1.

73) Letter from Morgan Phillips (British Labour Party Secretary) to the Hon. Secretary of the Scottish Covenant Association, published in the *Scottish Covenant Newsletter*, August-September 1956, Acc. 7295, Folder 12 (ii).

74) See article 'Grieve for Kelvingrove' in *The National Weekly*, 18 February 1950.

75) *Hansard*, House of Commons, Fifth Series, Volume 469, 16 November 1949, (London, HMSO, 1949), pp.2096-2097.

76) See David Torrance, *The Scottish Secretaries*, (Edinburgh, Birlinn Ltd, 2006), for biographies of Woodburn and McNeil including their views on Scottish nationalism.

Chapter 3 - Endnotes

1) Report by the National Treasurer to the 1950 Annual Conference of the SNP, NLS McIntyre Mss. Acc. 10090, File 39, and; Report by Neil Mathieson to the National Council, Organisation Committee, National Organiser, Area Organisers, Constituency Associations and Branches, 7 May 1950, Acc. 10090, File 39.

2) Pamphlet *What is the Scottish National Congress?*, Acc. 3721, Box 10, File 189 (Item 195B).

3) Letter from Muirhead to Sam Shields, 19 October 1959, Acc. 3721, Box 117.

4) SNC leaflet, 22 March 1950, Acc. 3721, Box 51, File 205.

5) Letter from Muirhead to Patrick Leonard, 9 June 1953, Acc. 3721, Box 30, Item 935.

6) Letter from Muirhead to Wendy Wood, 8 May 1950, Acc. 3721, Box 14, File 273.

7) Letter from Muirhead to Edward Canavan, 12 March 1951, Acc. 3721, Box 39, Item 1382.

8) Scottish National Congress Newssheet *Forward Scotland*, Edition No.2, October 1957, Acc. 3721, Box 10, File 189 (Item 195B).

9) See article in *Edinburgh Evening Dispatch*, 12 September 1952.

10) Letter from Muirhead to David Jamieson, 25 November 1954, Acc. 3721, Box 110, File J – 1951-1962.

11) Letter from Muirhead to Editor of *Forward*, 5 November 1951, Acc. 3721, Box 2, File 30.

12) See article 'Heckling Points' in *The National Weekly*, 13 October 1951.

13) Wendy Wood, *Yours Sincerely for Scotland, the Autobiography of a Patriot,* (London, Arthur Barker Limited, 1970), pp.79-80.

14) Scottish National Congress booklet *Scots Awake!! Say "No!" to Conscription,* Acc. 3721. Box 13, File 271A.

15) Letter from the Scottish National Congress to Michael Grieve, 27 September 1950, Acc. 3721, Box 3, File 42.

16) *Edinburgh Evening Dispatch*, 2 May 1957, and; Letter from Muirhead to Mary Ramsay, 28 September 1951, Acc. 3721, Box 13, File 271.

17) The Scottish Patriots was established by Wendy Wood in 1949 and is not the same organisation as the earlier nationalist organisation with the similar name, Scottish Patriots Association, which was founded in Glasgow in 1901 and headed by the Rev. David Macrae.

18) Letter from Muirhead to Mary Ramsay, 24 November 1950, Acc. 3721, Box 13, File 271.

19) Letter from Muirhead to Dr Russell, 3 November 1953, Acc. 3721, Box 22, File 621.

20)   Letter from Bank of Scotland to Muirhead, 8 March 1952, Acc. 3721, Box 1, File 11.

21)   See letter from Muirhead to Archie Lamont, 3 August 1950, Acc. 3721, Box 10, File 189A.

22)   Letters from Lamont to Muirhead, 26 January 1951, 21 March 1958, and 25 March 1958, Acc. 3721, Box 10, File 189; Letter from Mary Ramsay to Muirhead, 9 January 1954, Acc. 3721, Box 13, File 271A; Letter from Wood to Muirhead, 5 August 1957, Acc. 3721, Box 14, File 273; Letter from Sam Shields to Muirhead, 26 August 1958, and; Letter from Muirhead to Walter MacFarlane, 3 October 1958, Acc. 3721, Box 36, Item 1257.

23)   See letter from Muirhead to Oliver Brown, 25 June 1958, Acc. 3721, Box 7, File 109.

24)   Letter from Muirhead to Gordon Murray, 19 September 1952, Acc. 3721, Box 38, Item 1362.

25)   Letter from Mary Ramsay to Muirhead, 15 January 1957, Acc. 3721, Box 13, File 271A.

26)   For an indepth explanation of the retrieving of the Stone of Destiny and its movements, see Ian R. Hamilton, *No Stone Unturned: The Story of the Stone of Destiny,* (London, Victor Gollancz Ltd, 1952); Ian R. Hamilton, *A Touch of Treason,* (Glasgow, Neil Wilson Publishing, 1994) pp.49-66, and; John MacCormick, *The Flag in the Wind: The Story of the National Movement in Scotland,* (London, Victor Gollancz Ltd, 1955) pp.165-183.

27)   Minutes of the National Council of the SNP, 13 January 1951, Acc. 10090, File 40.

28)   See MacCormick, *The Flag in the Wind*, pp.165-183.

29)   *Scots Independent*, January 1951.

30)   Ibid, March 1951.

31)   *Report of the Church and Nation Committee to the General Assembly of the Church of Scotland*, (Edinburgh, Church of Scotland, May 1951), pp.340-341.

32)   Letter from W. D. Kerr to Hilton Brown, BBC, 18 February 1952, Acc. 3721, Box 3, File 60.

33)   Letter from Muirhead to McDonald, 16 June 1953, Acc 3721, Box 23, File 623.

34)   *Evening Express*, 16 April 1953, Acc. 3721, Box 38, Item 1362.

35)   *News Chronicle*, 2 October 1954, Acc. 3721, Box 57, File 296.

36)   The Articles of the Treaty of Union of 1707 can be found in Christopher A. Whatley, *Bought and Sold for English Gold, Explaining the Union of 1707,* (East Linton, Tuckwell Press, 2001), pp.101-117.

37)   MacCormick, *The Flag in the Wind*, p188-190.

38)   For Dicey's doctrines on constitutional law and his reference to the Act of Union being no more significant in constitutional terms than any other Act of Parliament, see A.V. Dicey, *Introduction to the Study of the Law of the Constitution*, Tenth Edition, (Basingstoke, Macmillan Education Ltd, 1959), pp.39-

85 and p145 respectively.

39) *The Scotsman*, 31 July 1953.

40) Opinion of Lord Russell in the Petition of MacCormick and Another [Ian Robertson Hamilton] against Her Majesty's Advocate, 30 July 1953, Acc. 3721, Box 44, File 56.

41) *The Scotsman*, 31 July 1953, and MacCormick, *The Flag in the Wind*, p195.

42) *Scots Independent*, March 1953.

43) *The Scotsman*, 14 February 1953.

44) *Daily Mail*, 28 February 1953.

45) *Daily Express* 13 April 1953.

46) Letter from Muirhead to Ramsay, 8 October 1953, Acc. 3721, Box 13, File 271A.

47) *Sunday Pictorial*, 14 October 1951.

48) *Daily Mail*, 28 February 1953.

49) *Scottish Sunday Express*, 16 February 1958.

50) *London Times*, 24 November 1953.

51) *New Statesman*, 5 December 1953.

52) See *Daily Record,* 26 November 1953, for details about Cullen in the immediate aftermath of the trial.

53) *The People*, 10 October 1954 & 17 October 1954.

54) Letter from Gordon Murray to Muirhead, 7 August 1954, Acc. 3721, Box 112, File M.

55) Robert Curran as SNP National Secretary received requests from Scots wishing to join the SRA, see article the *Picture Post*, 25 April 1953, Acc. 3721, Box 54, File 235.

56) *Edinburgh Evening Dispatch*, 17 December 1953.

57) Minutes of the Executive Committee of the SNP, 2 December 1953, Acc 10090, File 42, and; *Scots Independent*, January 1954.

58) *The Scotsman*, 16 December 1953.

59) *Scots Independent*, 20 March 1954, and; Letter from Mary Dott to McIntyre, 12 January 1954, Acc.10090, File 64.

60) Minutes of the Executive Committee of the SNP, 6 October 1954, Acc. 10090, File 43.

61) Minutes of Meeting of the Executive Committee of the SNP, 14 July 1954, Acc. 10090, File 43, and; *Edinburgh Evening News*, 27 July 1954.

62) Letter from Muirhead to Ramsay, 22 July 1953, Acc. 3721, Box 13, File 271A

63) See article 'The Pillar Box Commandos' in *Scottish Daily Mail*, 8 January 1953.

64) *Glasgow Herald*, 17 July 1954.

65) See circular letter from Muirhead as Chairman of the Nationalist Mutual Aid Committee, April 1948, Acc. 3721, Box 28, Item 891.

66) Letter from Muirhead to Raymond Palmer, 10 April 1956, Acc. 3721, Box 30, Item 935.

67) Scottish National Party Parliamentary Contests Statistics, Acc. 3721, Box 62, File 402.

68) For a detailed analysis of the 1951 General Election and the issues surrounding it, see David E. Butler, *The British General Election of 1951*, (London, Macmillan Press Ltd, 1999).

69) Report by Neil Mathieson to the National Council, Organisation Committee, National Organiser, Area Organisers, Constituency Associations and Branches, 7 May 1950, Acc. 10090, File 39.

70) Report by the Organisation Committee to the 1952 Annual Conference of the SNP, Acc. 10090, File 49.

71) Report 'The Filing "System" at Headquarters', 1951, Acc. 10090, File 40.

72) Ibid.

73) Letter from Muirhead to Ramsay, 30 October 1951, Acc. 3721, Box 13, File 271.

74) Report by the National Treasurer to the 1952 Annual Conference of the SNP, Acc. 10090, File 49.

75) Minutes of the National Council of the SNP, 21 April 1951, Acc. 10090, File 40.

76) Report by Editor of *Scots Independent* to the 1950 Annual Conference of the SNP, Acc. 10090, File 39, and; Report by the Editor of the *Scots Independent* to the 1952 Annual Conference of the SNP, Acc. 10090, File 49.

77) Report by the Overseas Secretary to the 1952 Annual Conference of the SNP, 11 April 1952, Acc. 10090, File 49.

78) Letter from Young to the Editor of the *Courier and Advertiser*, 27 August 1951, NLS Young Mss. Acc. 6419, Box 64, File 1.

79) *Scots Independent*, May 1953.

80) SNP Submission to Catto Committee on Anglo Scottish Financial Relations, 29 January 1951, NLS Donaldson Mss. Acc. 6038, Box 1, File 18.

81) *Report of the Committee on Scottish Financial and Trade Statistics*, Presented by the Secretary of State for Scotland to Parliament by Command of Her Majesty, July 1952, (Edinburgh, HMSO), Cmnd. 8609, p78.

82) Preliminary Statement from the SNP on the Catto Committee Report on Scotland's Financial and Trading position, 29 July 1952, Gibson Acc. 6058, Box 3, File 9.

83) *Scots Independent*, September 1952.

84) See article by James Porteous 'This New White Paper Leaves Us in the Dark', in *Scots Independent*, 6 February 1954.

85) Quoted in the *Stirling Journal and Advertiser*, 31 July 1952.

86) *Scotsman*, 25 July 1952.

87) *Royal Commission on Scottish Affairs 1952-1954*, Report presented to Parliament July 1954, (Edinburgh, HMSO), Cmnd. 9212, p7.

88)   MacCormick, *The Flag in the Wind*, pp.185-186.

89)   Memorandum submitted to the Royal Commission on Scottish Affairs by the SNP, 31 December 1952, published in the SNP's internal journal, *Scottish Newsletter*, December 1952 –January 1953, Acc. 3721, Box 77, File 765.

90)   65 per cent was something of an understatement as polls such as the Kirriemuir and Scotstoun plebiscites, the Scottish Covenant and the study undertaken by the University of Edinburgh's Psychology Department all displayed higher results (see chapter 2). However, 25 per cent was something of an overestimation as the SNP had never received this much support.

91)   Minutes of Evidence taken before the Royal Commission on Scottish Affairs, Third Day, 9 April 1953, Memorandum submitted by the SNP, Acc. 3721, Box 114, File R.

92)   Statement by the Scottish National Congress to the Royal Commission on Scottish Affairs, December 1952, Acc. 3721, Box 77, File 765.

93)   McCormick, *The Flag in the Wind*, pp.186-187.

94)   Memorandum of Evidence on behalf of the Scottish Covenant Association submitted to the Royal Commission on Scottish Affairs, undated, File reference: HH41/962, National Archives of Scotland.

95)   *Scottish Daily Mail*, 28 February 1953.

96)   *Edinburgh Evening Dispatch*, 1 October 1953.

97)   *Scots Independent*, June 1953.

98)   *Royal Commission on Scottish Affairs 1952-1954*, Cmnd. 9212.

99)   Letter from McIntyre to the Earl of Balfour, 3 August 1954, Acc. 6058, Box 1, File 6.

100)   *Scots Independent*, 31st July 1954.

101)   Statement by the Scottish National Congress, 5 February 1955, Acc. 3721, Box 40, Item 1442.

102)   *Scots Independent*, 28 August 1954.

103)   Letter from Muirhead to the Secretary to the Royal Commission, 2 December 1952, Acc. 3721, Box 77, File 765.

104)   *Scots Independent*, 2 October 1954.

105)   *Scots Independent*, 28 May 1955.

106)   Supplementary Statement on Policy as presented to the Special Conference of the SNP on Policy at Edinburgh, 29 November 1952, Acc. 6419, Box 43, File 4.

107)   *Scottish Newsletter*, March 1952, Acc. 10090, File 180.

108)   *Scottish Newsletter*, April 1953, Ibid.

109)   *Scottish Newsletter,* March 1952, Ibid.

110)   Pamphlet *SNP 10 X 10 Plan*, undated, NLS McIntyre Mss. Acc. 12917, Box 4 (File untitled and unnumbered).

111)   Letter from McIntyre to Rollo, 22 July 1954, Acc. 10090, File 64.

112) *Scots Independent*, July 1950.

113) *Scots Independent*, September 1950.

Chapter 4 - Endnotes

1)   F. W. S. Craig (Compiled and Edited by), *British Parliamentary Election Results 1950-1973*, Second Edition, (Chichester, Parliamentary Research Services, 1983), p626 & p662.

2)   See NLS McIntyre Mss. Acc. 10090, File 32.

3)   Minutes of the National Executive of the SNP, 3 August 1955, Acc. 10090 File 44.

4)   Report by the SNP 'State of Branches as at 9-4-55', Acc. 10090, File 44.

5)   According to James Halliday, the number of paid-up SNP members was in fact only in the region of 250 at this time. Interview with James Halliday, 13 March 2008.

6)   Letter from G. F. Black (solicitor) to the SNP Treasurer, 9 May 1955, Acc. 10090, File 65.

7)   Richard Parry, *Scottish Political Facts*, (Edinburgh, T & T Clark, 1988), pp.2-3.

8)   Royal Commission on Scottish Affairs 1952-54 Report, presented to Parliament July 1954, HMSO, Cmnd. 9212, p97.

9)   Quoted in James Mitchell, *Conservatives and the Union: A Study of Conservative Party Attitudes to Scotland*, (Edinburgh, Edinburgh University Press, 1990), p50. For more information on the Unionist Party playing the Scottish card, see pp.48-50 of this book.

10) The Conservative and Unionist Party's Policy, *United for Peace and Progress*, 1955.

11) The Labour Party's Election Manifesto, *Forward with Labour: Labour's Policy for the Consideration of the Nation*, 1955.

12) Richard Finlay, *A Partnership for Good*, p139.

13) Special Areas policy was introduced in the 1930s which identified areas in Britain where unemployment was high and targeted them with direct government help. These areas were: Tyneside, West Cumberland, South Wales and the whole of Scotland.

14) Statement by Sam Shields, James Glendinning, H. A. Barr, Donald Stewart and Violet Sinclair to the 1955 Annual Conference of the SNP, Acc. 10090, File 65.

15) Minutes of the Board of the *Scots Independent*, 11 May 1955, NLS Muirhead Mss. Acc. 3721, Box 69, File 575.

16) Minutes of the Board of the *Scots Independent*, 8 June 1955, ibid.

17) Wilkie was expelled again from the SNP at a National Council meeting on 7 April 1956 because of disparaging statements he made in a letter to the SNP's National Secretary, John Smart, and for distributing copies of it at a Glasgow meeting. See Minutes of the National Council of the SNP, 7 April 1956, Acc. 10090, File 45.

18) Newssheet of the 55 Group, 28 May 1955, Acc. 3721, Box 53, File 234.

19)   Newssheet of the 55 Group, 25 June 1955, ibid.

20)   Statement by W. Wallace 'The Rebel', 9 July 1955, Acc. 3721, Box 53, File 234.

21)   Ibid.

22)   Letter from H. A. Barr, 10 July 1955, Acc. 3721, Box 40, Item 1442.

23)   Newssheet of the 55 Group, 28 May 1955.

24)   Minutes of the National Council of the SNP, 24 September 1955, Acc. 10090, File 44.

25)   Minutes of the Executive Committee of the SNP, 5 October 1955, Acc. 10090, File 44.

26)   *Scottish Daily Express*, 26 October 1955.

27)   Ibid.

28)   Letter from SNP National Secretary to all branches and groups, 12 December 1955, NLS Scottish National Party Mss. Acc. 6038, Box 1, File 11.

29)   *Scottish Daily Express*, 31 October 1955.

30)   *Edinburgh News*, 17 November 1955.

31)   Ibid.

32)   Nationalist Party of Scotland pamphlet, *The English Are They Human?*, NLS George Dott Mss. Acc. 5927, Folder 3.

33)   *Advance*, June 1956, Volume I, No III, Acc. 3721, Box 64, File 433.

34)   Nationalist Party of Scotland Manifesto, September 1956. NLS Scottish National Party Mss. Acc. 7295, Folder 27 – (i).

35)   The Nationalist Party of Scotland President's New Year Message, 1 January 1956, Acc. 3721, Box 77, File 767.

36)   Nationalist Party of Scotland booklet, *The New Nation: The Voice of Fighting Scotland*, Volume 1, Number 2, undated, Acc. 3721, Box 77, File 767.

37)   Letter from Administration Director of the Nationalist Party of Scotland to Muirhead, 1 January 1956, Acc. 3721, Box 77, File 767.

38)   Advance, June 1956, Volume I, No III, Acc. 3721, Box 64, File 433.

39)   *Edinburgh Evening Dispatch*, 14 November 1955.

40)   See article 'Protest in Bills Against Limey Law' in *Evening Citizen*, 28 November 1955.

41)   Quoted in *Edinburgh Evening Dispatch*, 31 October 1955.

42)   See article, 'Nationalists Disclaim 'Race Hate' Faction' in *Daily Herald*, 7 November 1955.

43)   *Daily Record*, 31 October 1955.

44)   Letter from George Dott to McIntyre, 6 November 1955, Acc. 10090, File 65.

45)   Letter from John Smart to SNP branch secretaries, 18 October 1955, Acc. 6038, Box 1, File 11.

46)   Letter from John Smart to all SNP branches and groups, 12 December 1955, Acc. 6038, Box 1, File 11.

47) Letter from George Dott to McIntyre, 17 October 1955, Acc. 10090, File 65.

48) Memorandum by Tom Gibson on the Present Position of the SNP, 17 January 1956, Acc. 10090, File 56.

49) Letter from the Greenock Group of the Scottish National Congress, undated, NLS Gibson Mss. Acc. 6058, Box 2, File 1.

50) *The South African Scots Courier*, published by SNP Secretary D. M. Low, January 1957, Acc. 6058, Box 4, File 3.

51) Letter from Gibson to Andrew Stenhouse (solicitor), 25 September 1956, Acc. 6058, Box 1, File 6.

52) Letter from John Smart to all SNP branches and groups, 12 December 1955, Acc. 6038, Box 1, File 11.

53) Ibid.

54) Minutes of the Executive Committee of the SNP, 2 December 1955, Acc. 10090, File 44.

55) *The South African Scots Courier*, January 1957.

56) Statement 'The Free Scot', January 1955, Acc. 10090, File 185; For more information about the student and early political life of James Halliday, see James Halliday, *Yours for Scotland, A Memoir by James Halliday*, (Stirling, Scots Independent (Newspaper) Ltd, 2011), pp.19-50.

57) Interview with James Halliday, 13 March 2008.

58) *Scots Independent*, 25 May 1957.

59) *Scots Independent*, 29 December 1956.

60) *Scots Independent*, 22 December 1956.

61) *The Clyde Valley Regional Plan 1946*, by Sir Patrick Abercrombie and Robert H. Matthew, (Glasgow, The University Press, June 1946), p691.

62) SNP Statement by John Smart 'Glasgow's Overspill', 28 February 1957, Acc. 10090, File 56.

63) Ibid, and; Letter from John Smart to Harold Macmillan, Prime Minister, 3 March 1959, Acc. 10090, File 53.

64) Ibid.

65) SNP Statement by John Smart 'Choose Scotland Campaign', 1957, Acc. 10090, File 56.

66) SNP Executive Committee Report, 2 March 1957, Acc. 10090, File 56.

67) Minutes of the 250th Anniversary Committee, 16 February 1957, Acc. 3721, Box 71, File 588.

68) Circular letter from Tom Spence, 26 March 1957, Acc. 3721, Box 10, File 189, and; *Edinburgh Evening Dispatch*, 2 May 1957.

69) Article 'Blame Yourselves' published in the SNP's *The Scottish Newsletter*, March 1957, Acc. 10090, File 180.

70) Letter from George Dott to Muirhead, 7 January 1956, Acc. 3721, Box 15, File 326.

71) SNP Supplementary Statement on Policy, 29 November 1952, NLS Douglas

Young Mss. Acc. 6419, Box 43, File 4.

72) Plaid Cymru pamphlet *The Wicked Ban*, (Cardiff, Priory Press Ltd, undated), Acc. 10090, File 103.

73) The PMG's letter is published in the Report by the SNP's BBC Committee to the Annual Conference of the SNP, 18 and 19 May 1957, Acc. 10090, File 52.

74) Ibid.

75) *Glasgow Herald,* 28 July 1955.

76) SNP Memorandum on Scottish Political Broadcasting to the Postmaster General, 11 May 1956, Acc. 10090, File 58.

77) Report by the SNP's BBC Committee to the Annual Conference of the SNP, 18 and 19 May 1957.

78) *Scots Independent*, 25 October 1958.

79) For information on the origins of Common Wealth and its key features, see History seminar paper "Revivalist' Politics – The Character of the Common Wealth Movement', Angus Calder, 13 May, no year. NLS Calder Mss. Acc. 9851, File 1.

80) Press Statement 'Break the Radio Ban on the Smaller Parties', 21 March 1956, Acc. 10090, File 58.

81) Transcript of speeches of the Trafalgar Square Rally 'Break the Radio Ban on the Smaller Parties', 31 March 1956, Acc. 10090, File 58.

82) Ibid.

83) Minutes of the Five-Party Committee on Rights of Minority Parties, 29 January 1957, Acc. 10090, File 56.

84) Report by the SNP's BBC Committee Convener, D R Rollo, to the Annual Conference of the SNP, 17 and 18 May 1958, Acc. 10090, File 53.

85) Pamphlet *Radio Free Scotland, its Background and its Policy* (Undated), Acc. 6058, Box 4, File 2.

86) *Scots Independent*, 1 December 1956.

87) *Scots Independent*, 27 August 1960.

88) Minutes of the National Council of the SNP, 8 December 1956, Acc. 3721, Box 70, File 582B.

89) *Scots Independent*, 15 December 1956.

90) *Scots Independent*, 19 October 1957.

91) *Scots Independent*, 25 May 1957.

92) *Glasgow Evening Times*, 27 November 1956.

93) *Illustrated*, Volume XVIII, 9 February 1957, Acc 3721, Box 76, File 713, and; Interview with SNP activist, Hamish McQueen, 11 December 2007.

94) *Scots Independent*, 28 July 1956 and 10 November 1956.

95) *Scots Independent*, 11 October 1958.

96) *Scots Independent*, 19 September 1959.

97) Press Statement by the SNP, 8 November 1956, Acc. 10090, File 45.

98) Reported in the SNP's *The Scottish Newsletter*, March 1958, Acc. 10090, File 180.

99) Letter from SNC Chairman to the SNP National Secretary, 27 March 1958, Acc. 3721, Box 102, File 187.

100) Article by Robert Balir Wilkie 'Scottish National Congress and the Appeal to Russia' in *Greenock Telegraph*, 28 February 1958.

101) Minutes of the Executive Committee of the SNP, 15 January 1958, Acc. 10090, File 47.

102) Letter from David Rollo to SNP Executive Members, undated, Acc. 10090, File 56.

103) Letter from James Halliday to SNP Executive Members, 12 March 1958, Acc. 10090, File 56.

104) Letter from David Rollo to SNP Executive Members, undated, Acc. 10090, File 56.

105) Minutes of the Executive Committee of the SNP, 26 March 1958, Acc. 10090, File 56.

106) Letter from Tom Gibson to Macon Lee Howard, 18 November 1957, Acc. 6058, Box 1, File 6.

107) The change in ownership control of the *Scots Independent* from 1935 is set out in a letter from Muirhead to McIntyre, 13 March 1956, Acc. 10090, File 66.

108) Letter from SNP Chairman, 2 March 1956, Acc. 10090, File 71.

109) Letter from Muirhead to Lamont, 21 March 1956, Acc. 3721, Box 10, File 189, and; Letter from Muirhead to Barr, 19 March 1956, Acc. 3721, Box 40, Item 1442.

110) Report by the SNP National Secretary, 7 April 1956, Acc. 10090, File 45.

111) See letters from Lamont to Muirhead, 21 March 1958, 25 March 1958, and from Lamont to Carmichael (Printers), 24 March 1958, Acc. 3721, Box 10, File 189.

112) Tom Gibson notably made pleas for the SNP to oust Muirhead and others who rejected SNP policy even if it resulted in a split, see Gibson's Memorandum on the Present Position of the SNP, 17 January 1956, Acc. 10090, File 56.

113) Report by the SNP National Secretary to 1959 Annual Conference of the SNP, Acc. 6038, Box 1, File 15.

114) SNP National Election Plan 1959, 9 January 1959, Acc. 10090, File 48.

115) *This Can Be the New Scotland* is printed in full in the *Scots Independent*, 14 February 1959.

116) SNP Manifesto 1959, Acc. 6038, Box 1, File 15.

117) Report on the Scottish Economy by the SNP, undated, Acc. 10090, File 48.

118) Statement by John B. Smart 'Call for Dreadnought Programme, National Party Proposal', 30 April 1959, Acc. 10090, File 48.

119) Policy Booklet by the Labour Party, *Let Scotland Prosper, Labour Plans for Scot-*

120) Press Statement by the SNP, undated, Acc. 10090, File 56.

121) *Scottish Government*, Special Report of the Executive Committee to the Special Conference of the Scottish Council of the Labour Party, 13th and 14th February 1958, (Glasgow, Scottish Council of the Labour Party, 1958) pp.11-12.

122) Press Statement by the SNP, undated, Acc. 10090, File 56.

123) SNP Statement by John Smart, 'Scottish National Party Expansion', undated, Acc. 10090, File 56.

124) Press Release by the SNP 'S.N.P. Annual Conference', 5 May 1956, Acc. 10090, File 45

125) Report by the Publications Convener to the Annual Conference of the SNP, 18 and 19 April 1959, Acc. 10090, File 53.

126) SNP National Election Plan 1959, 9 January 1959, Acc. 10090, File 48.

127) Report by the National Secretary to the Annual Conference of the SNP, 18 and 19 April 1959, Acc. 10090, File 53.

128) Results listed in Parry, *Scottish Political Facts*.

129) *Scots Independent*, 16 May 1959.

Chapter 5 - Endnotes

1) Richard J. Finlay, *'Unionism and the Dependency Culture: Politics and State Intervention in Scotland, 1918-1997'* in Catriona M. Macdonald (Editor), *Unionist Scotland 1800-1997*, (Edinburgh, John Donald Publishers, 1998), p110.

2) T. M. Devine, *The Scottish Nation 1700-2000*, (London, Penguin Books, 1999), p570, and; Jack Brand, *The National Movement in Scotland*, (London, Routledge & Kegan Paul, 1978), p83.

3) Richard Weight, *Patriots, National Identity in Britain 1940-2000*, (London, Macmillan, 2002), p166.

4) Brand, *The National Movement in Scotland*, p84.

5) Devine, *The Scottish Nation 1700-2000*, p570.

6) See Peter L. Payne, *'The Decline of the Scottish Heavy Industries 1945-80'* in R. Saville (Edited by), *The Economic Development of Modern Scotland*, (Edinburgh, John Donald Publishers, 1985), p95.

7) *Inquiry into the Scottish Economy 1960-1961*, Report of a Committee appointed by the Scottish Council (Development and Industry) under the Chairmanship of J. N. Toothill, (Edinburgh, Scottish Council (Development and Industry), 1961), pp.21-22.

8) See James Kellas, *Modern Scotland, The Nation Since 1870*, (London, Pall Mall Press, 1968), pp146-147.

9) Devine, *The Scottish Nation 1700-2000*, p573.

10) Speech by Arthur Donaldson to the Annual Conference of the SNP, 26 May 1962, NLS Donaldson Mss. Acc. 11908, File title 'Arthur Donaldson Speeches, 1949-78'.

11) *Scots Independent*, 2 December 1961 and 30 June 1962.

12) Letter from John Smart to the Minister of Agriculture and Fisheries for England & Wales and the Secretary of State for Scotland, 14 May 1960, NLS McIntyre Mss. Acc. 10090, File 89, and; Minutes of National Executive Committee Meeting of the SNP, 20 December 1963, Acc. 10090, File 100.

13) Clydesdale and North of Scotland Bank Ltd, *Annual Survey of Economic Conditions in Scotland in 1958*, (Glasgow, March 1959), p7.

14) *Scots Independent*, 1 October 1960 and 11 August 1962.

15) Richard Parry, *Scottish Political Facts*, (Edinburgh, T & T Clark, 1988), p52.

16) Report by the National Secretary to the Annual Conference of the SNP, 26 and 27 May 1962, NLS Donaldson Mss. Acc. 6038, Box 1, File 18.

17) Billy Wolfe, *Scotland Lives, The Quest for Independence*, (Edinburgh, Reprographia, 1973), pp.26-27.

18) Ibid. p8.

19) Parry, *Scottish Political Facts*, p71.

20) The West Lothian Question highlighted the anomaly that if a Scottish Assembly was established within the UK framework, MPs in Scotland could

vote on purely English subject matters but not on purely Scottish subject matters at Westminster which would be devolved to the Scottish Assembly. MPs in England would also be unable to vote on purely Scottish matters. See Tam Dalyell, *Devolution, the End of Britain?* (London, Jonathan Cape, 1977), pp.245-251.

21) The SNP's track record of promoting and encouraging the shale oil industry in Scotland by attacking government taxation policy also helped Wolfe's campaign in this particular area.

22) See Wolfe, *Scotland Lives*, pp.10-25, for Wolfe's account of his 1962 West Lothian Campaign.

23) Minutes of the National Executive Committee of the SNP, 20 December 1963, Acc. 10090, File 100.

24) Results listed in Parry, *Scottish Political Facts*.

25) Wolfe, *Scotland Lives*, pp.37-38.

26) Letter from Tom Gibson to C. D. Drysdale, 4 March 1964, NLS Gibson Mss. Acc. 6058, Box 1, File 6.

27) Report by Gordon Wilson on Organisation to the National Executive Committee of the SNP, December 1963, Acc. 10090, File 100.

28) Report by William Wolfe to the National Council of the SNP, 6 October 1965, Acc. 10090, File 84.

29) Quoted in Report by Gordon Wilson on Organisation to the National Executive Committee of the SNP, December 1963.

30) Ibid.

31) Figures quoted in Memorandum by the SNP to European States, 31 May 1967, Acc. 10090, File 98.

32) *Scots Independent*, 17 April 1965.

33) SNP Branch List, November 1965, Acc. 10090, File 90.

34) Report by Alan Niven 'Review of Constituencies' to the National Council of the SNP, 28 November 1964, Acc. 10090, File 100.

35) *Scots Independent*, 22 September 1962.

36) SNP HQ Income and Expenditure Statement for Year ending 31 December 1964; SNP HQ Balance Sheets as at 31 December 1962 and 1964; Minutes of Special Meeting of the National Executive Committee of the SNP, 21 November 1964, Acc. 10090, File 89, and; SNP HQ Finance Statement for Year to 31 December 1962, Acc. 10090, File 116.

37) 18 per cent recorded their support for a fully independent parliament, 66 per cent desired a parliament dealing purely with Scottish affairs, and 13 per cent desired no parliament at all - results listed in *Scots Independent*, 13 June 1959.

38) *Glasgow Herald*, 15 June 1959.

39) Minutes of the National Committee of the Scottish Covenant Association, 25 November 1961, NLS Gibb Mss. Dep. 217, Box 1 (B), File 7.

40) Letter from Angus Gunn to Gibb, undated, Dep. 217, Box 1 (B), File 7.

41) Letter from the Scottish National Congress to Shadow Parliament invitees, April 1959, NLS Gunn Mss. Dep. 209, Box 15, Folder 3.

42) Minutes of the Constituent Assembly Preliminary Meeting, 1 October 1960, NLS Porteous Mss. Acc. 5978, Box 2, File 2.

43) The Commissioners were: Catherine Snodgrass, Hugh Anderson, Archie Macpherson, Oliver Brown, Roland Muirhead, John Nicolson, Matthew Somerville, David Murray, Sam Shields, J. Miller, Annie Wilson and Angus McIntosh.

44) Report of Proceedings of the 1st Plenary Session of the Provisional Assembly, 21 April 1962, Acc. 6038, Box 1, File 18.

45) Statement by the Office of the Commissioners, 1962, Acc. 6038, Box 1, File 18.

46) *A Constitution for Scotland* published by Scottish Secretariat, (Glasgow, 1964), Acc. 12917, Box 12, (File unnumbered and untitled).

47) *The Observer*, 19 February 1961.

48) Letter from Muirhead to Ramsay, 20 January 1961, Acc. 3721, Box 13, File 271A.

49) Letter from Muirhead to Walter Macfarlane, 10 June 1958, Acc. 3721, Box 113, File P.

50) Letter from George Watt to Muirhead, 11 June 1955, Acc. 3721, Box 120, File W.

51) Letter from George Beck to Tom Spence, 18 October 1960, Acc. 3721, Box 106, File B.

52) Letter from Oliver Brown to Muirhead, 23 November 1961, Acc. 3721, Box 106, File B.

53) Letters from Agnes Spence to Young, 8 February 1966 & 22 February 1966. NLS Young Mss. Acc. 6419, Box 43, File 5.

54) Scottish Patriots pamphlet *The Estates of Scotland*, Acc. 6419, Box 47, File 4.

55) *Scottish Daily Mail*, 31 May 1960.

56) *Scots Independent*, 22 August 1964.

57) *SNP & You*, published by the SNP, Autumn 1964.

58) Ibid.

59) Minutes of the National Council of the SNP, 7 December 1963, Acc. 10090, File 100.

60) Amendments to the Minutes of the National Council of the SNP, 7 March 1964 (Issued on 27 May), Acc. 10090, File 84.

61) Quoted in *Glasgow Herald*, 10 March 1964.

62) See Parry, *Scottish Political Facts*, and; SNP Election Committee Report on the 1964 General Election by McIntyre, 28 November 1964, Acc. 10090, File 94.

63) Report by Billy Wolfe to Gordon Wilson, 10 November 1964, Acc. 10090, File 94.

64)   For General Election results, see Parry, *Scottish Political Facts*.

Chapter 6 - Endnotes

1)   Richard J. Finlay, *Modern Scotland 1914-2000*, (London, Profile Books Ltd, 2004), p188.

2)   For more information on the Suez Crisis, see Peter Clarke, *Hope and Glory, Britain 1900-2000*, Second Edition, (London, Penguin Books, 2004), pp.255-263.

3)   See John Stewart, *The British Empire, An Encyclopaedia of the Crown's Holdings, 1493 through 1995*, (London, McFarland & Company Inc. Publishers, 1996) for a complete list.

4)   Billy Wolfe, *Scotland Lives, The Quest for Independence*, (Edinburgh, Reprographia, 1973), p53.

5)   *Scots Independent*, 2 May 1964.

6)   Desmond Dinan, *Ever Closer Union? An Introduction to the European Community*, (Hampshire, Macmillan Press Ltd, 1994), p49.

7)   Peter G. J. Pulzer, *Political Representation and Elections in Britain*, (London, George Allen and Unwin, 1967), p98.

8)   See Ian Budge and Derek W. Urwin, *Scottish Political Behaviour, A Case Study in British Homogeneity*, (London, Longmans Green & Co. Ltd, 1966), pp.112-129.

9)   The post of Scottish Secretary was created in 1660 when John Maitland first took up the position, but was repealed as a punitive measure following the defeat of the Jacobites at Culloden in 1746.

10)   For detailed information on the growth and development of the Scottish Office, see John S. Gibson, *The Thistle and the Crown, A History of the Scottish Office*, (Edinburgh, HMSO, 1985); James G. Kellas, *The Scottish Political System*, Fourth Edition, (Cambridge, Cambridge University Press, 1989), pp.27-61, and; H. J. Hanham, *Scottish Nationalism*, (London, Faber & Faber, 1969), pp.50-63.

11)   William L. Miller, *The End of British Politics: Scots and English Political Behaviour in the Seventies*, (Oxford, Clarendon Press, 1981), p10.

12)   Vernon Bogdanor, *Devolution in the United Kingdom*, (Oxford, Oxford University Press, 1999), p114.

13)   *Scots Independent*, 7 July 1962.

14)   Without the British Liberal Party, the Scottish Liberal Party would not have qualified for party broadcasting time because it failed to contest 50 seats in the 1960s at any one election.

15)   *Scots Independent*, 21 September 1963.

16)   Letter from Gwynfor Evans to Robert McIntyre, Arthur Donaldson and Gordon Wilson, 18 February 1965, NLS McIntyre Mss. Acc. 10090, File 111.

17)   *Scots Independent*, 9 April 1960.

18)   Ibid, 14 May 1960.

19)   Ibid, 13 August 1960.

20)   Ibid, 22 February 1964.

21)   Ibid, 15 July 1961 and 2 January 1963.

22)   Script for Granada Programme 'Compass – Pirates of the Air', Issued 12 January 1961, Acc. 10090, File 103.

23)   *Scots Independent*, 7 January 1961.

24)   For more information about Radio Free Scotland, see Gordon Wilson, *Pirates of the Air, The Story of Radio Free Scotland*, (Stirling, Scots Independent (Newspapers) Ltd. 2011)

25)   Memorandum by the SNP on Party Political Broadcasting, Winter 1965, Acc. 10090, File 103.

26)   SNP Press Statement 'Party Political Broadcast', 29 September 1965, Acc. 10090, File 102.

27)   *Scots Independent*, 9 October 1965.

28)   *Glasgow Herald*, 31 September 1965, and; *The Times,* 31 September 1965.

29)   Minutes of the National Executive Committee of the SNP, 13 May 1966, Acc. 10090, File 91.

30)   Minutes of the National Executive Committee of the SNP, 11 August 1967, Acc. 10090, File 92.

31)   Various letters from television producers and directors to Wendy Wood. NLS Wood, Mss. Acc. 8072, File 2.

32)   Memorandum by the SNP on Party Political Broadcasting, Winter 1965.

33)   Memorandum of Evidence by the SNP to Mr. Speaker's Conference on Electoral Law (Broadcasting) 1967, Acc. 10090, File 103.

34)   See *Scots Independent*, 4 February 1967, and; Memorandum by the SNP to the Committee on Party Political Broadcasting, 13 June 1966, Acc. 10090, File 103.

35)   Memorandum by the SNP on Party Political Broadcasting, Winter 1965.

36)   *Scots Independent*, 26 June 1965.

37)   Memorandum by the SNP to the Committee on Party Political Broadcasting, 13 June 1966, and; Memorandum by the SNP to Mr. Speaker's Conference on Electoral Law (Broadcasting) 1967.

38)   Draft letter from Douglas Drysdale to the Prime Minister, 1965, Acc. 10090, File 116.

39)   Memorandum by the SNP on Party Political Broadcasting, Winter 1965.

40)   Minutes of the National Council of the SNP, 4 December 1965, Acc. 10090, File 84.

41)   SNP Newsletter, December 1966, Acc. 10090, File 91.

42)   Minutes of the National Executive Committee of the SNP, 11 November 1966, Acc. 10090, File 91.

43)   Report by the National Organiser to the Annual Conference of the SNP, 4 & 5 June 1966, Acc. 10090, File 80.

44)   *Scots Independent*, 3 September 1966.

45)   Booklet 'SNP a Guide to Branch Organisation' undated, Acc. 10090, File 100.

46)   Minutes of Organisation Committee of the SNP, 23 April 1967, Acc. 10090, File 92.

47)   Report by the Executive Vice-Chairman (Organisation) to the National Executive of the SNP, 12 August 1966, Acc. 10090, File 91.

48)   Minutes of the National Council of the SNP, 2 December 1967, Acc. 10090, File 86.

49)   *Scots Independent*, 4 March 1967.

50)   Letter from the Duke of Montrose to Ian Macdonald, 29 July 1966, NLS SNP Mss. Acc. 11987, File untitled.

51)   Letter from Arthur Donaldson to Robin Douglas-Home, 4 April 1967, Acc. 10090, File 94.

52)   Minutes of Publicity Committee, 17 February 1967, Acc. 10090, File 92.

53)   Report by Dr George Philp to the Secretary of the SNP, July 1967, Acc. 10090, File 92.

54)   Report by Executive Vice-Chairman (Publicity & Development) to the National Council of the SNP, 5 June 1965, Acc. 10090, File 84.

55)   Report by the Public Relations Officer to the National Executive of the SNP, 14 April 1966, Acc. 10090, File 91.

56)   Statement by C. D. Drysdale 'Financial position – 1 May 1965', Acc. 10090, File 79.

57)   SNP Headquarters Income and Expenditure Statement for year ending 31 December 1965, Acc. 10090, File 91 and; SNP Consolidated Income and Expenditure Account for the year ending 31 December 1967, Acc. 10090, File 86.

58)   Minutes of Special Meeting of National Executive Committee of the SNP, 21 November 1964, Acc. 10090, File 89.

59)   Alba Pools Report 1965, by Angus McGillveray, 21 May 1965, Acc. 10090, File 79.

60)   Report by the Finance Convener to the Annual Conference of the SNP, 22 & 23 May 1965, Acc. 10090, File 79.

61)   Report by Angus McGillveray on Alba Pools to the National Council of the SNP, 3 September 1966, Acc. 10090, File 85.

62)   Alba Pools Income and Expenditure from 3 January to 26 December 1966, by Angus McGillveray, Acc. 10090, File 92.

63)   SNP Consolidated Balance Sheet as at 31 December 1967, with Consolidated Income and Expenditure Account for year ending 31 December 1967, Acc. 10090, File 86.

64)   Report by the Finance Convener to the Annual Conference of the SNP, 4 & 5 June 1966, Acc. 10090, File 80; Report by Angus McGillveray on Alba Pools to the National Council of the SNP, 3 September 1966, Acc. 10090, File 85, and; Minutes of the Finance Committee of the SNP, 23 March 1967, Acc. 10090, File 92.

65) Reports by the Finance Convener to the Annual Conferences of the SNP, 22 & 23 May 1965 and 2, 3 & 4 June 1967, Acc. 10090, Files 79 and 81 respectively.

66) SNP HQ Balance Sheet as at 31 December 1966, Acc. 10090, File 91.

67) Report by the National Secretary to the Annual Conference of the SNP, 4 & 5 June 1966, Acc. 10090, File 80, and; Report by the National Secretary to the Annual Conference of the SNP, 2, 3 & 4 of June 1967, Acc. 10090, File 81.

68) Minutes of the Finance Committee of the SNP, 27 December 1966, Acc. 10090, File 91.

69) Report by the National Treasurer to the Annual Conference of the SNP, 4 & 5 June 1966, Acc. 10090, File 80.

70) Report by the Finance Convener to the Annual Conference of the SNP, 4 & 5 June 1966, Acc. 10090, File 80.

71) Minutes of the National Executive Committee of the SNP, 13 January 1967, Acc. 10090, File 92.

72) Statement by Tom McAlpine to the SNP, 1967, Acc. 10090, File 92.

73) Report by the National Secretary to the Annual Conference of the SNP, 31 May, 1 & 2 June 1968, Acc. 10090, File 82.

74) Report by Ian Macdonald on SNP Office Organisation, 1 December 1965, Acc. 10090, File 116.

75) Report by the Executive Vice Chairman (Publicity and Development) to the National Council of the SNP, 4 September 1965, Acc. 10090, File 84.

76) Letter from Arthur Donaldson to Billy Wolfe, 27 October 1965, Acc. 10090, File 111.

77) Memorandum from Drysdale to McIntyre, Donaldson, Wolfe and Wilson, 14 December 1965, Acc. 10090, File 111; Gordon Wilson also refers to the long hours SNP officials regularly undertook in his book, *SNP: The Turbulent Years 1960-1990*, (Stirling, Scots Independent (Newspapers) Ltd, 2009), pp.27-29.

78) Memorandum by the Convener of the Organisation Committee to the National Executive Committee of the SNP, 22 January 1967, Acc. 10090, File 92.

79) Report by the National Secretary to the Annual Conference of the SNP, 2, 3 & 4 June 1967, Acc. 10090, File 81.

80) Minutes of the National Executive Committee of the SNP, 11 August 1967, Acc. 10090, File 92.

81) Report by the Executive Vice-Chairman (Organisation) to the National Council of the SNP, 5 March 1966, Acc. 10090, File 85, and; Report by Organising Secretary, 13 July 1967, Acc. 10090, File 100.

82) Another report into the SNP's Executive structure was compiled by Billy Wolfe, Gordon Wilson and Archie Young and submitted to the National Council in Spring 1968, see Acc. 10090, File 86.

83) Statistics compiled from Peter Lynch, *SNP: The History of the Scottish National Party*, (Cardiff, Welsh Academic Press, 2002).

84) The SNP contested 65 seats of its 71 target at the 1970 General Election.

85) Scottish National Party Manifesto, *Putting Scotland First*, March 1966.

86) Ibid.

87) For various Election Broadcast sheets by the SNP, see Acc. 10090, File 104.

88) Report by the Public Relations Officer to the National Executive of the SNP, 14 April 1966, Acc. 10090, File 91.

89) SNP Report on Party Colours by Provost James Braid to the National Council of the SNP, 2 December 1967, Acc. 11987, File title 'National Council Reports, 1967 to 1969'.

90) Interview with James Halliday, 14 March 2008.

91) Various letters and reports on suggestions for election campaign improvements in the wake of the 1964 General Election are contained within Acc. 10090, File 94.

92) SNP Parliamentary Handbook, Acc. 10090, File 94.

93) SNP Report on the Pollok By-Election, June 1967, Acc. 10090, File 92.

94) F. W. S. Craig (Compiled and Edited by), *British Parliamentary Election Results 1950-1973*, Second Edition, (Chichester, Parliamentary Research Services, 1983), p616.

95) Figures compiled from *Glasgow Herald*, 4 May 1966 and 3 May 1967.

96) Christopher Harvie, *Scotland and Nationalism, Scottish Society and Politics 1707 to the Present*, Fourth Edition, (London, Routledge, 2004), pp.128-129.

97) For further reading on the Labour Government's economic record in the 1960s, see Jim Tomlinson, *The Labour Governments 1964-1970, Economic Policy*, Volume 3, (Manchester, Manchester University Press, 2004), pp.49-64, Kenneth O. Morgan, *The People's Peace, British History Since 1945*, Second Edition, (Oxford, Oxford University Press, 1999), pp.239-316, and; Bob MacLean 'Labour in Scotland since 1945: Myth and Reality' in Gerry Hassan (Edited by), *The Scottish Labour Party: History, Institutions and Ideas,* (Edinburgh, Edinburgh University Press, 2004), pp.39-41.

98) Press Statement by the West Lothian Constituency Association of the SNP, 3 August 1965, Acc. 10090, File 116.

99) Report of Meeting between Sub-Committee of SNP Executive and delegation from A.S.N.T.U., 15 January 1967, Acc. 10090, File 92.

100) Minutes of the National Executive Committee of the SNP, 18 August 1967, Acc. 10090, File 92, and; Report by the National Secretary to the Annual Conference of the SNP, 2, 3 & 4 of June 1967.

101) Minutes of the National Executive Committee of the SNP, 10 September, 1965, Acc. 10090, File 90.

102) SNP Press Statement 'S.N.P. Candidate Acts over N.A.L.G.O. Telegram Sent to Secretary of State', 2 February 1967, Acc. 10090, File 102.

103) See MacLean, 'Labour in Scotland since 1945: Myth and Reality', p38.

104) Ibid.

105) Ibid, p42.

106) David Torrance, *The Scottish Secretaries*, (Edinburgh, Birlinn Ltd, 2006), p262.

107) David McCrone, *Understanding Scotland, The Sociology of a Stateless Nation*, (London, Routledge, 1992), pp.157-158.

108) For more information on declining Protestant and Unionist links, see T. M. Devine, 'The Challenge of Nationalism', in T. M. Devine (Edited by), *Scotland and the Union 1707-2007*, (Edinburgh, Edinburgh University Press, 2008), pp.151-152.

109) Kennedy supported Winnie Ewing at Hamilton in 1967 but stopped short of actually joining the SNP because of his leanings towards Liberalism, see Ludovic Kennedy, *On My Way to the Club, an Autobiography*, (London, Collins, 1989), p307.

110) Interview with Iain Hutchison, 6 February 2008.

111) Winnie Ewing, *Stop the World: The Autobiography of Winnie Ewing*, Edited by Michael Russell, (Edinburgh, Birlinn Ltd., 2004) pp.10-11.

112) F. W. S. Craig, *British Parliamentary Election Results 1950-1973*, p652.

113) Minutes of the National Executive Committee of the SNP, 12 January 1968, Acc. 10090, File 93.

114) Report by the National Organiser to the Annual National Conference of the SNP, 31 May, 1 & 2 June, 1968, Acc. 10090, File 82.

115) Gordon Wilson, *SNP: The Turbulent Years*, p40.

116) Figures compiled from *Glasgow Herald*, 8 May 1968, and; Lynch, *SNP, The History of the Scottish National Party*, p118.

117) Minutes of the National Council of the SNP, 2 March 1968, Acc. 10090, File 86.

118) Quoted in Scottish Conservative booklet 'Devolution Brief' (Edinburgh, Scottish Conservative Central Office, December 1975), NLS Scottish Conservative & Unionist Association Mss. Acc. 11368, File 80.

119) Ibid.

120) Christopher Harvie and Peter Jones, *The Road to Home Rule, Images of Scotland's Cause,* (Edinburgh, Polygon, 2000), pp89-90.

121) *Royal Commission on the Constitution 1969-1973*, Volume 1 Report, (London HMSO, 1973), pp.336-337. Those Commissioners favouring Scottish legislative devolution were: Lord Kilbrandon, Mr. Davies, Sir Mark Henig, Dr Longmuir, Professor Newark, Professor Street, Sir Ben Bowen Thomas and Mrs Trenaman. Professor Street and Mrs Trenamen did not support legislative devolution for Wales.

122) Scottish Liberal Party Agenda Booklet for Annual Conference, 11 May 1968, NLS Scottish Liberal Party & Scottish Liberal Democrats Mss. Acc. 11765, File 58.

Bibliography

Personal Manuscripts:

Acc. 7498 (Untitled), National Library of Scotland

Andrew Dewar Gibb, Dep. 217, National Library of Scotland

Angus Calder, Acc. 9851, National Library of Scotland

Arthur Donaldson, Acc. 6038, Acc. 7656 and Acc. 11908, National Library of Scotland

C. M. Grieve (Hugh MacDiarmid), Acc. 7361 and MS 260323, National Library of Scotland

Douglas C. C. Young, Acc. 6419 and Acc. 7085, National Library of Scotland

George Dott, Acc. 5927, National Library of Scotland

James A. A. Porteous, Acc. 5978 and Acc. 7882, National Library of Scotland

Neil M. Gunn, Dep. 209, National Library of Scotland

Robert D. McIntyre, Acc. 10090, Acc. 12509 and Acc 12817, National Library of Scotland

Roland E. Muirhead, Acc. 3721, National Library of Scotland

Tom Gibson, Acc. 6058, National Library of Scotland

Wendy Wood, Acc. 8072, National Library of Scotland

Party Manuscripts:

Scottish Conservative & Unionist Association, Acc. 11368, National Library of Scotland

Scottish Convention, Acc. 6649, National Library of Scotland

Scottish Covenant Association, Dep. 242, National Library of Scotland

Scottish Liberal Party & Scottish Liberal Democrats, Acc. 11765, National Library of Scotland

Scottish National Party, Acc. 6679, Acc. 7295 and Acc. 11987, National Library of Scotland

Important Nationalist Pamphlets and Publications:

Lamont, Archie, *Scotland a Wealthy Country, A Scientist's Survey of Scots Resources*, (Glasgow, Scottish Secretariat, 1945)

MacEwen, Alexander, MacCormick, John, M., & Gibson, T. H., *Scottish Reconstruction*, (Glasgow, SNP)

McIntyre, Robert, D. *Some Principles for Scottish Reconstruction*, (Glasgow, SNP, 1944)

Murray, Walter, *Home Rule for Scotland: The Case in 90 Points/ With a foreword by James Barr*, (Glasgow, Scottish Home Rule Association, 1922)

Nationalist Party of Scotland, *The English Are They Human?*

Nationalist Party of Scotland, *The New Nation: The Voice of Fighting Scotland*, Volume 1, Number 2

Plaid Cymru, *The Wicked Ban*, (Cardiff, Priory Press Ltd)

Radio Free Scotland, *Radio Free Scotland, its Background and its Policy*

Scottish Convention, *Covenant Qs*

Scottish Convention, *The Policy of Scottish Convention, Into Battle*

Scottish Convention, *Scottish Convention, Non-Party and All-Party*

Scottish Convention, *Questions We Are Asked*

Scottish Covenant Association, *Blue Print for Scotland, Practical Proposals: Scottish Self-Government*, (Glasgow)

Scottish Covenant Association, *The Covenant Yesterday, Today and Tomorrow*

Scottish Covenant Association, *Scottish Covenant Association*

Scottish National Assembly, *The Fourth Meeting of the Scottish National Assembly*, 22 April 1950

Scottish National Assembly, *Report of Proceedings of the Scottish National Assembly*, 22 March 1947

Scottish National Assembly, *Report of Second Meeting of the Scottish National Assembly*, 20 March 1948

Scottish National Congress, *Forward Scotland*, Scottish National Congress Newssheet

Scottish National Congress, *Say "NO!" to Conscription*,

Scottish National Congress, *What is the Scottish National Congress?*

Scottish National Party, *Constitution and Rules of the Scottish National Party*, (Glasgow, 28th and 29th May 1949)

Scottish National Party, *Scottish Newsletter*

Scottish National Party, *10 X 10 Plan*

Scottish National Party, *The Newsletter of the Scottish National Party*

Scottish Patriots, *The Estates of Scotland*,

55 Group, *Newssheet of the 55 Group*

A Constitution for Scotland, (Scottish Secretariat, 1964)

Advance

Declaration on Scottish Affairs, 4 May 1944, (Kirkwood Printers, Glasgow)

The South African Scots Courier

Manifestos:

Conservative and Unionist Party, *United for Peace and Progress*, 1955

Labour Party, *Forward with Labour: Labour's Policy for the Consideration of the Nation*, 1955

Nationalist Party of Scotland Manifesto, September 1956

Scottish Convention Manifesto, January 1946

Scottish National Party, *Putting Scotland First*, March 1966

Scottish National Party, *SNP & You*, Autumn 1964

Scottish National Party, *This Can be the New Scotland*, 1959

Official Papers and Files:

Balfour (Chairman), *Report of the Royal Commission on Scottish Affairs 1952-54*, (Edinburgh, HMSO, July 1954), Cmnd. 9212

Catto (Chairman), *Report of the Committee on Scottish Financial and Trade Statistics*, (Edinburgh, HMSO, July 1952), Cmnd. 8609

Hansard, House of Commons, (London, HMSO)

Kilbrandon (Chairman), *Royal Commission on the Constitution 1969-1973, Volume 1 Report*, (London, HMSO, 1973)

The Scottish Office - File Reference HH41/962, National Archives of Scotland

Newspapers & Journals:

The Bulletin

Daily Express

Daily Herald

Daily Mail

Daily Record

The Edinburgh Clarion

Edinburgh Evening Dispatch

Edinburgh Evening News

Edinburgh News

Evening Citizen

Evening Express

Fife Free Press

Forward

Glasgow Evening News

Glasgow Evening Times

Glasgow Herald

Greenock Telegraph

Manchester Guardian

Motherwell Times

The National Weekly

The New Statesman

News Chronicle

The Observer

The Patriot

The People

Picture Post

Scots Independent

Scotsman

Scottish Daily Express

Scottish Daily Mail

Scottish Sunday Express

Stirling Journal and Advertiser

Sunday Pictorial

The Times

The Wishaw Press and Advertiser

Biographies/Autobiographies:

Douglas, Dick, *At the Helm: The Life and Times of Dr. Robert D McIntyre*, (Banffshire, NPFI Publications, 1995).

Ewing, Winnie, *Stop the World: The Autobiography of Winnie Ewing*, Edited by Michael Russell, (Edinburgh, Birlinn Ltd, 2004)

Halliday, James *Yours for Scotland, A Memoir by James Halliday*, (Stirling, Scots Independent (Newspaper) Ltd, 2011)

MacCormick, John, *The Flag in the Wind: The Story of the National Movement in Scotland*, (London, Victor Gollancz Ltd, 1955)

Wolfe, Billy, *Scotland Lives, The Quest for Independence*, (Edinburgh, Reprographia, 1973)

Wood, Wendy, *Yours Sincerely for Scotland, the Autobiography of a Patriot*, (London, Arthur Barker Limited, 1970)

Other Primary Works:

Abercrombie, Sir Patrick, and Matthew, Robert H., *The Clyde Valley Regional Plan 1946*, (Glasgow, The University Press, June 1946)

Church of Scotland, *Report of the Church and Nation Committee to the General Assembly of the Church of Scotland*, (Edinburgh, Church of Scotland, May 1951),

Clydesdale and North of Scotland Bank Ltd, *Annual Survey of Economic Conditions in Scotland in 1958*, (Glasgow, March 1959)

The Labour Party, *Let Scotland Prosper, Labour Plans for Scotland's Progress*, (London, The Labour Party, 1958)

The Scottish Conservatives, *Devolution Brief*, (Edinburgh, Scottish Conservative Central Office, December 1975)

The Scottish Council of the Labour Party, *Scottish Government*, Special Report of the Executive Committee to the Special Conference of the Scottish Council of the Labour Party 13th and 14th February 1958, (Glasgow, Scottish Council of the Labour Party, 1958)

Inquiry into the Scottish Economy 1960-1961, Report of a Committee appointed by the Scottish Council (Development and Industry) under the Chairmanship of J. N. Toothill, (Edinburgh, Scottish Council (Development and Industry), 1961)

Secondary Sources:

Addison, Paul, *Now the War is Over, A Social History of Britain 1945-51*, (London, Jonathan Cape, 1985)

Bogdanor, Vernon, *Devolution in the United Kingdom*, (Oxford, Oxford University Press, 1999)

Brand, Jack, *The National Movement in Scotland*, (London, Routledge & Kegan Paul, 1978)

Brown, Alice, McCrone, David, and Paterson, Lindsay, *Politics and Society in Scotland*, (Hampshire, Macmillan Press Ltd, 1998)

Budge, Ian, and Urwin, Derek W., *Scottish Political Behaviour, A Case Study in British Homogeneity*, (London, Longmans Green & Co. Ltd, 1966)

Butler, David E., *The British General Election of 1951*, (London, Macmillan Press Ltd, 1999)

Clark, Peter, *Hope and Glory, Britain 1900-2000*, Second Edition, (London, Penguin Books, 2004)

Chick, Martin, *Industrial Policy in Britain 1945-51, Economic Planning, Nationalisation and the Labour Governments*, (Cambridge University Press, 1998)

Craig, F. W. S. (Compiled and Edited by), *British General Election Manifestos 1900-1974*, (London, Macmillan Press Ltd, 1975)

Craig, F. W. S. (Compiled and Edited by), *British Parliamentary Election Results 1918-1949, Third Edition*, (Chichester, Parliamentary Research Services, 1983)

Craig, F. W. S. (Compiled and Edited by), *British Parliamentary Election Results 1950-1973*, Second Edition, (Chichester, Parliamentary Research Services, 1983)

Dalyell, Tam, *Devolution: The End of Britain*, (London, Jonathan Cape, 1977)

Devine, T. M. (Edited by), *Scotland and the Union 1707-2007*, (Edinburgh, Edinburgh University Press, 2008)

Devine, T. M., *The Scottish Nation 1700-2000*, (London, Penguin Books, 1999)

Devine, T. M., and Finlay, R. J. (Edited by), *Scotland in the Twentieth Century*, (Edinburgh, Edinburgh University Press, 1996)

Dicey, A. V., *England's Case Against Home Rule*, Third Edition, (London, John Murray, 1887)

Dicey A. V., *Introduction to the Study of the Law of the Constitution, 1885*, Tenth Edition, (Basingstoke, Macmillan Education Ltd, 1959)

Dinan, Desmond, *Ever Closer Union? An Introduction to the European Community*, (Hampshire, Macmillan Press Ltd, 1994)

Finlay, Richard J., *A Partnership for Good? Scottish Politics and the Union Since 1880*, (Edinburgh, John Donald Publishers Ltd, 1997)

Finlay, Richard J., *Independent and Free, Scottish Politics and the Origins of the Scottish National Party, 1918-1945*, (Edinburgh, John Donald Publishers Ltd, 1994)

Finlay, Richard J., *Modern Scotland 1914-2000*, (London, Profile Books Ltd, 2004) *he Thistle and the Crown, A History of the Scottish Office*, (Edinburgh,

an R., *A Touch of Treason*, (Glasgow, Neil Wilson Publishing, 1994)

on, Ian R., *No Stone Unturned: The Story of the Stone of Destiny*, (London, Victor
Jllancz Ltd, 1952)

Hanham, J. H., *Scottish Nationalism*, (London, Faber & Faber, 1969)

Harvie, Christopher, *No Gods and Precious Few Heroes, Twentieth-Century Scotland*, Third
Edition, (Edinburgh, Edinburgh University Press, 1998)

Harvie, Christopher, *Scotland and Nationalism, Scottish Society and Politics 1707 to the
Present*, Fourth Edition, (London, Routledge, 2004)

Harvie, Christopher, and Jones, Peter, *The Road to Home Rule, Images of Scotland's
Cause*, (Edinburgh, Polygon, 2000)

Hassan, Gerry (Edited by), *The Scottish Labour Party: History, Institutions and Ideas*, (Edinburgh, Edinburgh University Press, 2004)

Hennessy, Peter, *Never Again, Britain 1945-51*, (London, Jonathan Cape, 1992)

Hutchison, I. G. C., *Scottish Politics in the Twentieth Century*, (Basingstoke, Palgrave,
2001)

Kellas, James G., *Modern Scotland, The Nation Since 1870*, (London, Pall Mall Press,
1968)

Kellas, James G., *The Scottish Political System*, Fourth Edition, (Cambridge, Cambridge
University Press, 1989)

Kemp, Arnold, *The Hollow Drum, Scotland Since the War*, (Edinburgh, Mainstream Publishing, 1993)

Kennedy, Ludovic, *On My Way to the Club, an Autobiography*, (London, Collins, 1989)

Lynch, Peter, *SNP, The History of the Scottish National Party*, (Cardiff, Welsh Academic
Press, 2002)

Macdonald, Catriona M. (Edited by), *Unionist Scotland 1800-1997*, (Edinburgh, John
Donald Publishers Ltd, 1998)

Marr, Andrew, *The Battle for Scotland*, (London, Penguin Books, 1992)

McCrone, David, *Understanding Scotland, The Sociology of a Stateless Nation*, (London,
Routledge, 1992)

Miller, William L., *The End of British Politics: Scots and English Political Behaviour in the
Seventies*, (Oxford, Clarendon Press, 1981)

Mitchell, James, *Conservatives and the Union: A Study of Conservative Party Attitudes to
Scotland*, (Edinburgh, Edinburgh University Press, 1990)

Mitchell, James, *Strategies for Self-Government: The Campaigns for a Scottish Parliament*,
(Edinburgh, Polygon, 1996)

Morgan, Kenneth O., *Labour in Power, 1945-1951*, (Oxford, Oxford University Pr. 1985)

Morgan, Kenneth O., *The People's Peace, British History Since 1945*, Second Edition, (Oxford, Oxford University Press, 1999)

Nairn, Tom, *The Break-Up of Britain, Crisis and Neo-nationalism*, Third Edition, (Edinburgh, Big Thinking, 2003)

Parry, Richard, *Scottish Political Facts*, (Edinburgh, T & T Clark, 1988)

Pelling, Henry, *The Labour Governments, 1945-51*, (London, Macmillan Press Ltd, 1984)

Pulzer, Peter G. J., *Political Representation and Elections in Britain*, (London, George Allen and Unwin, 1967)

Raillings, Colin and Thrasher, Michael, *British Electoral Facts 1832-2006*, (Aldershot, Ashgate Publishing Ltd, 2007)

Saville, R. (Edited by), *The Economic Development of Modern Scotland*, (Edinburgh, John Donald Publishers Ltd, 1985)

Stewart, John, *The British Empire, An Encyclopaedia of the Crown's Holdings, 1943 through 1995*, (London, McFarland & Company Inc. Publishers, 1996)

Tiratsoo, Nick (Edited by), *From Blitz to Blair: A New History of Britain Since 1939*, (London, Phoenix, 1998)

Tomlinson, Jim, *The Labour Governments 1964-1970 Economic Policy*, Volume 3, (Manchester, Manchester University Press, 2004)

Torrance, David, *The Scottish Secretaries*, (Edinburgh, Birlinn Ltd, 2006)

Warner, Gerald, *The Scottish Tory Party: A History*, (London, Weidenfeld and Nicolson, 1988)

Weight, Richard, *Patriots, National Identity in Britain 1940-2000*, (London, Macmillan, 2002)

Whatley, Christopher, A., *Bought and Sold for English Gold, Explaining the Union of 1707*, (East Linton, Tuckwell Press, 2001)

Wilson, Gordon, *Pirates of the Air, The Story of Radio Free Scotland*, (Stirling, Scots Independent (Newspapers) Ltd, 2011)

Wilson, Gordon, *SNP: The Turbulent Years 1960-1990*, (Stirling, Scots Independent (Newspapers) Ltd, 2009)

Website:

www.politicsresources.net